Book cover and lay-out by Thomas Monsen
thomasmonsen@me.com

©All rights reserved 2024
Miss Marple Universe Association

Shakespeare
- a dog with a broken brain

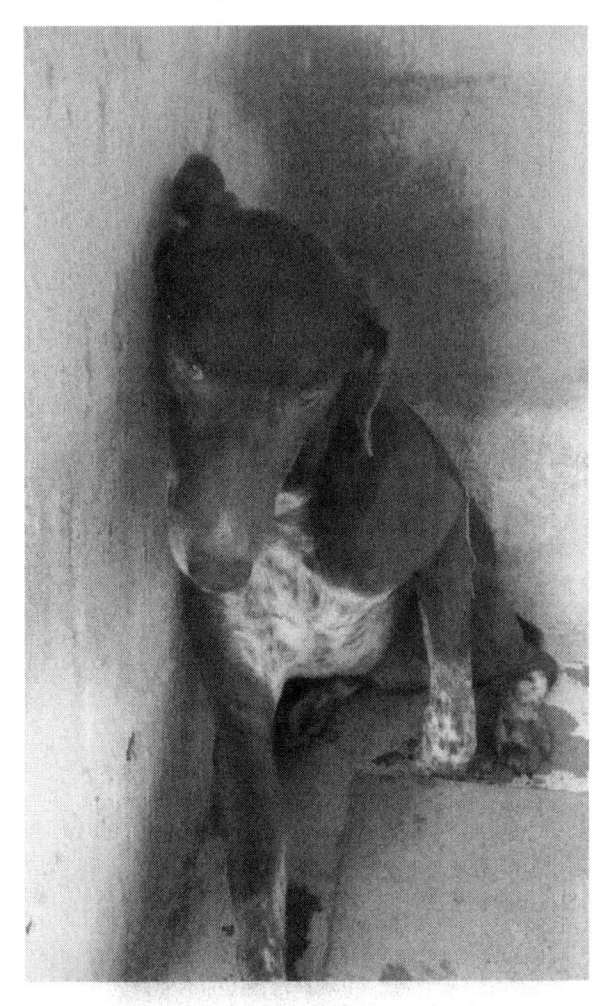

How a Norwegian woman living in France embarked on
a journey to rescue a broken dog from Cyprus
– and gave him his life back.

By

Borghild Strandenes

> We know what we are,
> but not **what we may be**.
> -William Shakespeare,
> *Hamlet*

PROLOGUE

21st February 2020

    The Paris temperature was only a couple of degrees above zero. The wind was freezing. I was leaning against the grey weather manoeuvring my oversized suitcase towards the revolving doors at Charles de Gaulle Airport, heading for the check-in counter of AEGEAN Airlines. The early flight had given me an additional night away from home at an airport hotel where I had slept uneasy. I had missed the familiar feeling of a purring blind cat sleeping on my back.

I had said goodbye to my seven rescue dogs, four rescue cats and my husband, to embark on a journey to bring three blind dogs from Cyprus to France, where my non-profit rescue association had already found homes for two. Lupin and Andy would be going home on the day of my return whilst the third, a Pocket Pointer pup I had named Sir Henry would stay with me and my pack until his family could be found.

When I had left Norway for France some nine years earlier, it had never been in my plans to start a non-profit association specialised in blind and traumatised dogs.

Nor had I planned to end up with a large pack of blind, deaf, and broken dogs and cats - but all-in-all, it was life's most generous gift to me.

Helping voiceless and often forgotten dogs made perfect sense to me and that, in combination with my natural gift of determination, kept bringing results.

In reality it had all started when I adopted my first French dog two days after we arrived in France. We had just moved into the ruin that was to become our home amongst the vines, when this huge bundle of insecurity and love arrived. We named him Captain Hastings. He was a forty-three kilo Cognac coloured mix, with white socks and chest. He simply looked like a large version of a wrongly coloured Golden Retriever.

I always suspected he was a mix between a St Bernard and some sort of a Setter, but whatever his genetic pool, he was the gentlest dog, with a constantly wagging tail, licking tongue and wise eyes that looked straight into your soul.

After Captain Hastings' arrival, the pack grew with one dog a year – and of course none of them were "straight forward" dogs. All were rescued from various less than desirable circumstances, and they all came with some sort of handicap or deep emotional scar – and for me, their imperfections made them perfect.

Over the years we had also added cats to the diversity of our home and pack.

Of the eleven animals I had at home in February 2020, two were born blind: Miss Marple my cat born without eyes, and Miss Kathryn Grey our Staffie-mix also born blind.

Also in the pack was the adorable born-deaf American Cocker Spaniel named Inspector James D. Japp and our sparkling white Countess Elena, a forty-five kilo Dogo Argentino that was diagnosed as deaf due to her white gene defect. Elena also had limited vision. I was also the proud mum of Hercule Poirot, a nervous chap who had been abandoned as a tiny pup. Isabel Duveen and Lady Eileen "Bundle" Brent were both Bruno de Jura hounds, with silky long ears and the best noses in the dog universe.

It was not difficult to have such a diverse pack. In theory, it should not work at all, but because Captain Hastings was the one showing and enforcing dog etiquette on any new pack member, or cat for that matter, who arrived at our home, it all went smoothly. I rarely interfered and the Captain was left to run the pack with a soft paw and whilst he rarely raised his voice, he sometimes did use his majestic power. If there was a problem, he would simply go physically in-between dogs involved in a tiff and with that, any potential argument fizzled out.

When Captain Hastings first arrived, I had the misguided idea that I saved him, but it would in time turn out he saved me, or rather we had simply saved each other - as so often is the case when a home is shared with a dog in need.

***

Captain Hastings looked at me with his chocolate brown eyes as I packed my suitcase. He knew what a suitcase meant and as I left with a lump in my throat, the pack sat in line, sad and subdued, whilst I dragged my heavy suitcase along the garden path.

My travel route was long – a fifty-minute drive to the train station, two hours train-ride to Paris, a hotel overnight and then the plane to Athens for a flight change to Cyprus, where I would be met at the airport by someone I had never met - Constantina. All to help three blind dogs.

I missed everyone at home before I had even pulled out of the driveway and questioned why I did this. I hated leaving them all and I always had a constant sense of unease when the pack and my husband were not around.

The week before my departure I had oddly commented to a close friend that in a very strange way it felt like this specific journey would somehow change my life. We had both laughed at the thought - I rescued blind dogs all the time – this was nothing exceptional. I could however not shake the feeling that something unexpected would happen – all whilst talking myself out of being ridiculous.

As I watched the Eiffel Tower disappear beneath us, I was thinking of Captain Hastings and the pack, hoping Hercule would not stop eating as he tended to do when I went away. In seven days, I would return with three blind dogs - Lupin, Sir Henry, and Andy – who would go on to live wonderful lives and I would return home to my own, settling back into my daily routine of rescue and loving my animals. Nothing would have changed apart from me having been away for a week – or at least that is what I thought.

As France fell behind me, I wondered how I would manage with three large dog flight crates by myself for the return journey. I did not have the answer, but I never worried about details like that. I have an embedded belief that there is always a solution.

> **Fate, show thy force**.
> Ourselves we do not owe:
> What is decreed must be;
> and be this so!
> -William Shakespeare,
> *Twelfth Night*

I opened my eyes with the anticipation of waking in a new place.

There was silence in the house and the warm body of a dog without eyes, Lupin, was curled up next to me. I lay still, stroking her. I could hear cars passing on the road outside. Sheer curtains revealed it was still too early for sunrise. Lupin did not move as I kept stroking her, feeling her silky soft charcoal black fur under my hand. She is medium sized, a cross between a small Pointer and another black dog of unknown origin. Her regular breathing gave away how completely relaxed she was.

    It was heart breaking to think how, just months earlier, she had been shot in the face, leaving her blind and in excruciating pain. With a head and face full of shotgun pellets, blind and alone, she had found her way to a derelict building to give birth to six pups. It was hard to imagine - even for me who knew blind dogs so well - how she had managed to survive, let alone take care of her pups. Hungry, exhausted, and petrified, she and her pups were rescued from amongst rubble and debris in the empty building where she had sought sanctuary. I had seen photos of her so often. I found it hard to believe she was actually curled up next to me, warm and sleeping peacefully.

After Lupin was rescued, she had undergone enucleation surgery.

Her badly injured and blind painful eyes had been removed and her eye sockets closed. The scars from the surgery were very visible, but soon the fur would fully cover where once the eyes had been, leaving her entire face furry black.

I had come to Cyprus because of Lupin. Through my nonprofit association I rescued and rehomed dogs. Blind and shut-down dogs were my "speciality." I was contacted by rescue colleagues from far and wide and asked to help blind dogs from all over Europe and further afield. Others would simply tag the Facebook page of my tiny non-profit association asking for help.

In the case of Lupin, someone had tagged me in a post, and I had contacted the Cypriote rescue association, SPDC (Saving Pound Dogs Cyprus), and offered to take her, landing me here in Cyprus.

I had prepared my journey for a couple of months, as travelling to Cyprus meant me putting other rescue work on hold whilst away and Lupin needed to decompress and recuperate before she travelled. The rescue journey also meant me leaving my own dogs, rescue cats and Are, my Norwegian husband - things that demanded planning.

Four out of Lupin's six pups had miraculously survived and they were all adopted by loving families in England and in seven days blind Lupin would be on a plane with me, going back to France. During the planning, two other blind dogs had been added to my return ticket - the pocket Pointer I had named Sir Henry and Andy, a Springer Spaniel.

Amanda and Tim were Lupin's new family together with two Spanish rescue dogs. Are and I had driven to their house some two hours away from us in France to meet them. Amanda had made the most scrumptious lunch and as we sat around the table, we had talked about life with a blind dog. My advice had been as it always is - do not overthink or overcomplicate things. The dog will figure things out and it will teach you.

Lupin had already shown me she was getting used to a life without eyes as she found her way around. She knew the stairs up to the bedroom where we had spent our first night, and the evening before, she had mapped out the bedroom without problems.

I lived with a dog born without eyes, my Miss Kathryn Grey, and a cat born without eyes, Miss Jane Marple. These two had given name to my association. Living with them both had made me truly and fully realize the astonishing capability of dogs - and cats - to function one sense or even two senses down.

I continued stroking Lupin, reflecting on how wrong all the sayings about eyes being the mirror of the soul, are. It is an untruth we grow up with, spread and claimed whilst being nothing but a total misunderstanding. Eyes are eyes - the soul is of course completely unrelated, and the saying is a deep injustice to both people and animals that do not have eyes.

It is the soul that mirrors the soul and all the blind animals I have dealt with, including my own, are constant affirmation of that!

I turned over and held Lupin closer as my voice softly told her about her new life and her new family that were waiting.

That we would go on a plane to fly home. How she would be safe and loved and have siblings, never to be alone ever again. She stretched lazily, waking slowly with her tail wagging under the duvet.

Then, as sharp pointed missiles to a dart board, the rescue dogs in the house went crazy. All twenty-six of them. Many were in the hallway just outside my door creating a hurricane of sound.

I had been warned the night before that the dogs would be noisy, but my body was unprepared for the force that broke the silence.

The bangarang showed no sign of subsiding, so it was official; my first day in Cyprus had begun.

As I dressed, Lupin moved to the edge of the bed, nose in the air. She was memorising me. She lowered her head, put her front paws on the floor and sleepily dragged her back half off the bed as she stretched. I had packets of dried duck dog treats in my suitcase and as I opened one, she launched straight for it. I laughed. As I stroked her, I handed her a treat. She increased the rotating movement of her tail, wagging in gratitude. I gave her more, and more until the packet was empty.

Come on beautiful. Time to meet the world and a new day. I stroked her again, tied my last shoe, gave her a kiss on the head before I touched the door handle. By this, she knew we were leaving the room.

Lupin followed me without hesitation as I opened the door just enough for, she and I to slide through the gap without giving way to twenty-six dogs!

There were dogs of all sizes, all colours.

All discarded, all dumped in one form or another. Some had gone through severe abuse, starvation, cruelty, and some had suffered sexual abuse by humans.

Some had been dumped for no apparent reason, some were under medical care before they could be adopted, and some were waiting for surgery. All with one thing in common.

They were safe in the house of Constantina, known as C, and her partner Andreas, and all under the wings of SPDC where C was one of the founders.

Some of the dogs were barking at me with noses in the air to filter scent information. Some were sniffing my clothing, one obsessing with the smell on my shoe, some had tails up, some tail down. One had his nose glued to my shoes deciphering what dogs I had interacted with before I arrived. Some had ears pointing straight up whilst others were flat along their skull, wary of my presence.

I moved through the crowd, relaxed and arms down by my sides, giving them a chance to know I was a friend. They curiously followed me from the landing, down the marble stairs, over the floor and into the kitchen where C was on the phone.

The kitchen was divided into two zones; the first where C had her desk. Placed along the wall was a huge medical storage space that would be the envy of any vet office. In reality this was a living room unit for books and ornaments with glass doors to the cabinet display, now solely used to hold the enormous amount of medication that C needed to treat all and any kind of injury and illness.

In the second zone of the kitchen, divided by a step up and a baby gate for division, was the kitchen itself, with sink, counters, and a dining table.

When you have twenty-six dogs in your home, a division like a baby gate is essential to ensure some degree of separation and comfort!

I waved at C and formed a silent good morning. She held her hand over the speaker and directed me to coffee. My first morning in Cyprus I had strong black coffee and a biscuit, surrounded by wagging tails and curious noses.

My Cypriote journey had officially begun.

> **Love comforted** like sunshine after rain.
> -William Shakespeare, *Venus and Adonis*

I would stay in Cyprus for seven days. The flights were on winter itinerary, with few flights to choose to and from the island. Last time I had been to this island in the Mediterranean Sea, north of Egypt, east of Greece, south of Türkiye and west of Lebanon, was many years prior when I worked as a manager in the travel industry.

I was hoping to make myself useful to SPDC whilst I was there, and I had offered to help at the sanctuary where the association always had around forty rescue dogs.

SPDC was founded and run by several women, and I had been in touch with them all at one stage or another during the time I was planning my trip. Thus far I had only met C. I had spoken on the phone to Suhair, who lived in Denmark, but still not met Elena and Katy.

In my conversation with Suhair, I had explained about my work with blind dogs and how I had worked with disconnected and shut down dogs. Immediately she told me about a dog they had in the sanctuary.

Shakespeare had been with them for almost five years. No one had ever seen him stand up, eat, or move around. He sat in the same corner day after day, year after year. He only ate at night when there were no humans present at the sanctuary and that was also the only time he would move.

They had tried everything possible to help him, but to no avail and when seeking advice from trainers and behaviourists they had been told there was nothing to be done for him. Shakespeare was a lost cause, but C and the others still refused to give up. As Suhair explained more about him my curiosity was awoken and I was looking forward to meeting this dog that no one seemed able to help.

Could I visit him whilst in Cyprus? Suhair had asked. Of course I could, and if there was anything I could do to help him, I would. He had been on my mind a lot since that conversation.

My coffee cup was empty, and I felt an urge to get the day started, to see the shelter and to meet Shakespeare. I was curious. Very curious. What would it be like to meet him?

Would he be another dog like my Lady Eileen Bundle Brent, who I adopted after she had been in a refuge for about two years without people being able to touch her? Lady had since her arrival with us gone from a "ghost-dog" only wanting distance, to becoming my dog-shaped shadow.

Coffee and phone conversation over, we left the house - heading for the shelter, a kennel some kilometres away from C's urban home. C drove the small red car as if danger were pursuing her. I was not a relaxed passenger at the best of times, so I thought: deep breaths and buckle up.

We left the asphalted street onto a dirt road to the right, climbing, at high speed, leaving any sign of city environment behind. I was sure our dust trail could be seen for miles.

The surroundings were truly beautiful and seemed remote after only a short climb.

Rolling hills and mountains in the distance, not Norwegian high, wild, and rugged mountains like I was used to from my native country, but still mountains. From a distance, C pointed to the sanctuary that looked like a compound set on a plateau.

Getting closer, I could see the track ending outside a large, industrial steel gate. Gates to keep people out and dogs in.

It was a bright, cold, windy morning, the sun hanging winter low. As I stepped out of the car the fragrance in the air was that of wild herbs and fauna unfamiliar to my sensory system. The beautiful landscape with those views made it seem unreal that behind the gates were forty dogs in need of new homes. C unlocked and opened the huge gate, and we stepped inside - into another world.

To the right was another metal gate, and we entered a small courtyard where a dog was loose, roaming free, having done the job as the kennels watchdog overnight. C explained that the watchdog job was circulated between the dogs as it was not only giving the dog a job to do, but it also gave the dogs freedom for the night. Overjoyed to see C, the dog came over to greet us. He was a large, stunningly beautiful pedigree German Shepherd, who had spent the first two years on this planet tied up on a microscopic balcony before his owners had signed him over. The dog had been a Christmas present and as all dogs do, had gone from a pup to an adult, leaving him less desirable. The story was all too familiar and one a rescuer in any country worldwide could tell you.

When will people learn I said as I stroked him.

No dog is supposed to live on a stamp-size balcony in baking sun and freezing winter nor is a dog supposed to live in a sanctuary without a family, but I knew all too well that for many of these dogs, the sanctuary was just that - a sanctuary, a haven after abuse and neglect. From my first step inside it was clear; this sanctuary was the cleanest and tidiest refuge I had ever visited. On a small fence by the feeding cabin to the right of the last gate, there were leads hanging neatly and readily available. The door to the small cabin was open and sparkling clean dog bowls were stacked on top of each other, ready for use. C explained that the sanctuary had no electricity but an aggregate at the back of the land. There was no public water system, but two huge, elevated water tanks collected rainwater to be used for drinking and cleaning.

The individual kennels were built in four rows. One to the left as you entered and one to the right had dogs facing each other and many of them had full view of who entered and who left. Back-to-back with the kennel block to the right was another row. These dogs had no view and looked straight into the back of the last kennel row that was facing the mountain road.

I walked by each kennel of the two first rows. Every door to every box had a poster with the name, gender and age of the dog that was looking at me through the wired mesh door.

Sad eyes, excited tails, front paws on their gate in the hope of being stroked, nervous energy, hopeful stretched legs. I stroked them all. I gave them all a treat from my pocket. One by one. The look of longing, the hope in their eyes of me opening the door to their individual kennel and whisking them away, made me tear up.

It felt odd, as despite the enormous amount of stressful energy, these dogs had hope. It was like they knew everyone was working so hard to get them out. Working to find them homes. They had daily human interaction. They were all fed, all well-cared for, all had medical treatment and good quality food.

Food is so important in environments like these. The stress levels of the dogs make them burn calories super-fast, often leaving them underweight despite being fed amounts more than adequate for a dog in a homely stress-free environment.

A glance at these dogs showed that this sanctuary was far-above-average, well run in every way possible, down to the last croquette of high-quality food.

I went back to the feeding cabin where C and Urage, the man who volunteered at the sanctuary, were discussing a medication dosage for one of the dogs.

Excuse me, but would you mind if I saw Shakespeare?

Of course not. Last row. Second kennel.

I locked myself through the metal gates dividing the different areas of the sanctuary. Everyone who knows the world of rescue knows that the more obstacles a dog faces if it escapes from its own kennel box, the higher the chances of the dog safely returning, preventing it from escaping into the outside world where it can hide, be lost forever, or killed by a passing car as it crossed a road in panic.

I turned the corner and stopped for a second, inhaling the fresh air and taking in the view.

The dogs were barking but were already calmer compared to when we arrived. Every dog knew we were on the premises, and they were all fully aware that one – me - was a stranger. Many had seen me, and for those who had not visually seen me they still knew I was there. Their noses were in the air, detecting me.

The first kennel box on the last row was the home of the German Shepherd I had stroked when I first arrived. He was back in his box and settled. The second box belonged to Shakespeare. I had read the information Suhair had sent me about this dog. There were old Facebook posts stating Shakespeare was a shutdown dog, and as I stood outside his box, I was not sure what to expect.

There was no sound from his box. I could see no one from where I was standing on the path that passed by all the boxes in the same row as Shakespeare.

From inside there was deathly silence.

I opened the gate, which had Shakespeare's name on, and closed it safely behind me as I entered the small courtyard. The walls were tiled with dusk pink tiles on the outside wall to the left and bright sunny yellow tiles on the wall to the right; the concrete floor was tiled in a dull beige colour reminding me of my childhood classroom walls.

The opening of the kennel box itself was of such a height that I could easily walk through the opening without having to bow my head.

I moved unhurriedly as not to scare anyone.

There was between three and four meters from the gate to the entrance of Shakespeare's kennel box. I was talking aloud to myself, making my presence and voice known as I did not want to startle the dog inside. I spoke in Norwegian as the meaning of words is of no interest or importance in a situation like that. All that matters is the tone of the voice.

In response to my voice, the dog to the right got up on his hind legs and put his front paws under the five-centimetre opening left between the pink tiled concrete wall and the fenced top. The enclosure was three meters high. He was a beautiful black Great Dane mix, a gentle giant. A glance at the gate to his box had told me his name was Billy. I stroked his paws in affection and handed him a beef treat from my pocket. He gratefully accepted. I later learnt that no one wanted Billy because of his size and the fact that he was leishmaniasis-positive. Leishmaniasis is a cruel illness given to dogs by the sand fly. If left untreated it has the most horrific consequences for the dog. There is no cure but there are medications to keep the dog symptom-free for life if the medications work properly, which is often the case. Billy looked like a poster-kid of good health. I gave him a second treat and moved with baby steps towards the entrance of what had been Shakespeare's home for almost five years.

I carried my large crossover bag in my hand. In the bag I had dried duck treats from France. I had brought four kilos worth, and I was hoping that I would be able to get Shakespeare to accept some of my offerings. My bag also held two water bottles, some chocolate, and the brick-thick Volume One of Agatha Christie's omnibus on Miss Marple.

I fished out some duck treats and left the bag outside on the floor before I stood in the entrance with my body turned sideways as to not fill the opening. I could see no dog straight ahead of me. My shadow hit part of the floor inside making me look tall and extremely thin. Inside the box the temperature was much lower than outside where the sun was warming the Cypriot winter air. The light inside was dull and dim between four concrete walls, and the room also functioned as a trap for humidity.

On the wall straight ahead, a feeding bowl and a separate water bowl were raised from the floor by a metal wall-mount.

In the corner to the left was a charcoal black plastic dog bed with a brick-red thin blanket bundled up inside. My eyes swept the concrete walls. They were cold and prison grey. I had a déjà-vu to my visit to Robin Island and Nelson Mandela's prison cell years earlier. Nelson Mandela had - had company in his cell. Here was none.

I was breathing as quietly as I could, but my heart was racing. I could feel his fear! It was tangible.

I did not turn my head but moved my eyes - to catch the image of a dogs squeezed in between a square slab of concrete on the floor, and the wall. He was slumped over, shaking, and the dead eyes were fixated straight ahead. The only sign of him acknowledging my presence were some tiny almost undetectable movements of his legs. The movements signalled for me to step back. His head was frozen, glued to the wall. He was in a fixed position like someone had placed him there, like a prop in a horror movie.

My heart sank. I had physical and emotional reaction that felt like a gunshot.

I caught myself as I whispered *Dear God.*

For some strange reason, I was talking to him in English.

What happened to you?

I was completely overwhelmed and for once at a loss. My eyes were fully adjusting to the grey, flat inside light, taking in what was in front of me. In the corner where two cold, grey, concrete walls met, a skeleton of a soul, in a beautiful body shaped for running, was a dog frozen in time and space. I would guess he was around twenty-two kilos. His shorthaired fur was dull brown. He had white knee socks with copper coloured Dalmatian spots. He had white, spotted paws, to match his socks and a white, spotted chest.

I knew he was thought to be a German Shorthaired Pointer mix. He was thin but by no means underweight.

He was a boy frozen in a concrete corner, in a concrete box, in a sanctuary, on a beautiful natural plateau in Cyprus. A dog without hope. I was shocked. I was swallowing several times so as not be sick. It was like all the energy was drained out of me.

Silent tears were running, and I had to concentrate so as not to gasp for air.

I had seen many sad and horrific cases, but I had never seen anything like this! His face had an expression of an animal in deep raw pain, not of the physical kind. His lips were drooping downwards with saliva dripping.

His velvet ears were mostly lifeless. His eyes told a story of unimaginable emotional pain. I could see each vertebra in his back as his body was crouched forward, in fear, like my presence was squeezing the last droplets of life out of him.

I knew all the duck treats in the world would be of no value. That dog would take nothing from anyone. It was the last piece of control he had over his life. The only thing he could still control was when and what to eat. He would deny himself a red steak to keep that control. His nostrils did not move, telling me his sensory system was shut down. He did not smell me like other dogs would. He heard me as I could see minute movement in his ear muscles, but he neither saw nor smelt me. I took one step back and leaned against the opposite wall. It was all in slow motion. It was as if my body had lost its internal scaffolding during those minutes of our first meeting.

I kept whispering – rambling, like one does when faced with something too overwhelming for the brain to process.

What happened to you? They tell me your name is Shakespeare. I have been looking forward to meeting you. I made sure as not to look at him.

I want you to know there still is a world out there. There is hope. There are huge fields. There are other dogs for you to play with. There is sunshine and there is wind. I kept rambling. *There is rain.*

I tried to be motionless – to mirror him so he would not perceive me as a threat. My tears trickled down and reached the corner of my mouth. I tasted salt. I did not dare to raise my hand to wipe my tears as I did not want to scare him more than my presence already did.

Out there, there is moonlight, there is sunrise and sunset. There is a whole world out there, beautiful, beautiful you.

I was afraid he would break and disintegrate in front of me. Turn to dust. He was now sliding towards the concrete floor as if my presence had made him give up.

I so wanted to catch him as he slides.

I had seen many scared dogs in my life. I had worked with many and even lived with some at home. But this? This was something else. Shakespeare was not an *ordinary* shut down dog. He was way, way beyond that and anything I had ever seen. Beyond any emotion, any link to a life, any link to this world. His true self had left, as he had not been able to take any more - leaving this shell of a body behind.

I wanted to hold him. But no! I knew that that would be the worst thing I could do. Absolutely the worst. If I did reach out to touch him, he would never trust me. He was moving his paws again in tiny almost undetectable movements telling me again to back off.

I hear you I whispered. *I will go but I will not leave.*

As if I were a ghost, I retracted into my own footsteps. Outside, I slid myself onto the tiled floor close to my bag, as if I were trying to hold on to something familiar. I sat leaned up against the wall in a position where I could see his paws. I could see that he had stopped moving. He felt safe again with me on the outside.

I could not see his eyes nor his body, only part of the white socks with the spotted pattern. I was trying to process what I had seen.

I was absolutely prepared for him being in a bad frame of mind, but this was something different. Shakespeare was a dog without any want for life. He had no hope. His soul had been broken into pieces and scattered around. His heart was beating but there was nothing else. No hope, just existence; nothing more and nothing less.

Dogs are creatures with rich emotional needs and none of them were met in that corner where he had stopped living, believing that nothing he did would make a difference. A shackled elephant can physically break free any time, but is taught from a tender age, often through beatings, that no matter what it does the result will be the same. Hence it stops trying to alter its existence in captivity. The shackles he is wearing around his ankles are nothing compared to the shackles in his mind. Shakespeare's mind was the same. He had come to believe that no matter what he did the outcome would be the same, making me think he had tried every way possible to escape during the early years of his captivity, to no avail. With the belief that he could change nothing, he had placed himself in the corner to let himself die.

I picked up my book. I tried hard to focus. I turned the first three pages and started to read aloud through tears. But that day in the winter sun, in the corner of Shakespeare's courtyard was one of those rare occasion not even the story of Miss Marple's detective adventures in St Mary Mead could calm my racing brain.

I took a deep breath and with that inhalation came the knowledge that my life had changed forever. Inside that box was an illustration of how I had felt in some of my darkest moments after the car accident.

He was a dog version of PTSD (please see page 331) me. Shakespeare was without question a dog with severe PTSD, a diagnosis only recognised in dogs for the last fifteen years.

But, in my opinion canine PTSD has been around for as long as dogs have been experiencing trauma. I had read stories about how service dogs during World War One had returned from the trenches as "completely changed and scared of their own shadow." Back then the word used for humans with PTSD were shellshock, combat fatigue or war neurosis. There was no real word used for what had happened to the dogs, although they showed the same symptoms as the soldiers. Later, service dogs from for example the Afghanistan War, and dogs serving with the police force, have been recognised as having PTSD. There is however little or limited research material, but for me, it was as clear as day and so easy to understand. I knew because I knew! These canine creatures that have lived alongside humans for thirty-two thousand years have an emotional pattern much closer to our own that one might think.

I knew first-hand what PTSD did; it took away you, the you that you knew, and in those moments when you were hit by a foreign force that you had no control over, even existing was painful. Shakespeare and I shared that knowledge.

When PTSD and physical pain had taken control of my life, after the car accident, I had forced myself to start breathing again. I had left Norway and gone to France. I had started a new life in the depths of the countryside where I could shield myself, where there was silence and birdsong. I had walked long walks every day, meditating and given myself time to heal and then meditated some more.

I had forced myself to breathe again and give myself time to grieve over the brokenness, and later I befriended my PTSD and accepted it would be a lifelong companion, sometimes taking up a lot of space.

Later, and in long periods, it would hibernate until it would strike again. But when it returned, I now had the knowledge on how to ride the waves.

This boy, Shakespeare, had however nowhere to go and he trusted no one to be his link to the outside world. He would without a question die in that corner unless someone helped him swim towards the light and embrace it. Embrace living.

This meeting was predestined. I knew that boy. I knew Shakespeare albeit I had never met him before.

As I sat on the cold floor in the early spring sun with my eyes closed, I was breathing calmly. I needed time to process who was inside the box. Part of my soul living in a dog. I knew – knew – he was in many ways my destiny.

He would live with me. He would spend the rest of his life with me – of that, I was sure. I just needed to figure out how.

Would they let me take him? What would Are say? Would he settle? Would he be aggressive toward my pack? Kill the cats?

My head was spinning.

I kept taking deep breaths reflecting on how some of us have a clearly lit path. Others have complicated life journeys. Some souls are kept apart in this life to be reunited in the next, whilst others get to meet repeatedly in every life.

I opened my book again and forced myself to read, and spent the whole day outside his box, reading to him. I did not peek back inside as I wanted to signal to him that he could trust me. I knew that if I overstepped his boundaries, he would never trust me, neither in the sanctuary nor later. The journey ahead had to be based on trust or we would not make it.

As it came closer to the time to leave for the day, and for me to get off the cold floor, I took my bag and pushed it into his box whilst still sitting on the floor. In my bag were a handful of packages of dry duck together with several packages of other dog treats, personal belongings, including a spare toothbrush. My passport and my wallet were left at the house so in the bag there was nothing that I could not replace.

I needed to see if Shakespeare were destructive and leaving my bag would give me the answer the next morning. If Shakespeare were destructive, it would tell me with high probability that he was also anxious whilst alone. Having a foreign object in his box would trigger that anxiety. There are many reasons why a dog can be destructive but in the case of Shakespeare I would suspect anxiety to be what would cause any destructive behaviour. It could of course be boredom but if he were bored, he would have chewed his bed and ripped his blanket that was already there, and he had not done so. If he chewed my bag, it would at least mean he was connected to his emotions. Any emotion. I pushed my bag further inside.

I will be back tomorrow morning Shakespeare, but I am leaving you my bag to watch over. No movement. I quietly got up from the cold floor and closed the gates behind me leaving my destiny in the corner of a concrete box.

> If I had my mouth, I would bite;
> if I had my liberty, I would do
> my liking: in the meantime,
> **let me be** that I am and seek not
> to alter me.
> -William Shakespeare, *Much Ado About Nothing*

It was still dark outside when I woke with a pounding heart and sweating. I had in the darkness of the Cypriot night revisited the car accident, and my time isolated in the hospital, two weeks after the spinal surgery. What started as a swelling had turned into a small golf ball size growth in the surgical wound that was on the front of my neck. The spinal surgery I underwent is done from the front and the incision wound where the stitches were, between my collar bone and base of my neck, were bulging and extremely painful. The doctor at the hospital I spoke to on the phone thought it was blood that had accumulated in a pocket but when I came to my GP to take out the stitches, he took one look at me and called the hospital, telling them they could expect me within thirty minutes. The hospital medical staff was unsure what to make of it, but as they removed the first stitch I passed out. The pressure released dark green pus in a projectile on to the wall behind the nurse who had clipped the stitch. I went down to the floor, and the last thing I remembered was someone shouting *get a bed*. I heard running feet.

I was put in full isolation, on an intravenous antibiotics drip, as the hospital was concerned it was Streptococcus pyogenes, the feared and dreaded flesh-eating bacteria. I was floating in and out of a strange dreamlike existence due to the pain relief they also gave me straight in my blood stream. On the door of the hospital room a hand written A4 page read "ISOLATION. All items leaving this room are to be burnt."

The doctors and nurses were wearing plastic aprons and masks. It was real and had all the makings of a daytime nightmare, but I was too ill to care.

Meeting Shakespeare took me back to the hospital room, a room filled with silent panic. In my dream I was flying, seeing Shakespeare drowning in fierce rising water. I needed to get to him before it was too late - it was a matter of minutes, seconds before he would be taken by the flood. I was trying to rip out the intravenous medication and get rid of what monitored my oxygen intake.

I woke, sweating and in a state of panic. I knew why I had revisited the time of my car accident. Meeting Shakespeare had taken me right back to that dark time.

It was during that hospital stay that I fully realised how bad my PTSD was. Although the nurses were moving around on rubber soles, talking in hushed voices in the hallway, my sensory system signalled to my brain that they were walking with metal heel caps, and shouting. I was hyper-alert. My body was in constant flight mode - every second. The only difference between Shakespeare and I was that he was frozen, and I was in flight.

I was so grateful for Lupin who was still fast asleep next to me. Her warm body and regular breathing helped me calm my mind and clear my spinning head. For a moment I was back to when I had adopted Captain Hastings just after our arrival in France. That calm regular breathing and the effect it had on my erratic body was the same.

I lay still, followed Lupin's breathing and within not too long I was breathing with my stomach, as I had learned to do - all those years back - in the pain clinic.

I had practised daily meditation since I arrived in France, and in those early morning hours in Cyprus, I was grateful for the gift of being able to breath and shake off the nightmare. After an hour of meditation, the panic had trickled away, and I was ready to get up before the tsunami of dogs knocked on the door.

I was excited to go back to the sanctuary and see Shakespeare and to check if he had been in my bag. Perhaps he had ripped it to shreds to get to what was inside but somehow, I was sure he had not. My money was on him not having touched the bag at all.

I pulled out one of my wool training tops from the suitcase, drew the curtains to check the weather, realising I needed to bring my rain jacket. Lupin was off the bed, wagging her tail as I dressed. I reached for some more duck treats.

Good morning beautiful. She wagged in response as she turned her head to "look" at me. The fact that a dog has no eyes does of course not mean it will not do the natural thing in "looking" up at you. She still detected my breath and listened to my voice that came from above. So even dogs born without sight will do it: look up at you. I stroked her and told her again about her new life awaiting her in a country far away.

It had been so cold sitting on the tiled floor the day before that I put an extra pair of training tights into a spare bag together with an extra jumper and a scarf. I knew I was in for another long day on the floor in Shakespeare small "courtyard" and the last thing I wanted to do was to catch a cold, or worse, so extra clothes were coming with me.

Urage, the volunteer at the sanctuary came each morning to C's house and as soon as he arrived and had helped clean up after the twenty-six dogs, most of them not house trained, we would be ready to go to the sanctuary.

Lupin, my darling, let us go to the kitchen and have some coffee. Coffee for me and a biscuit for you.

She looked back up at me and I bent down and kissed her on the head before I stroked her and opened the door to the awaiting dog crowd thrilled to see her.

Later, when we left the house, Lupin was on the dog-sofa in the hallway, and I stroked her again.

I will be back tonight sweetheart. She wagged her long black tail in response.

It was a grey day with drizzle in the air and I soon realised I could not sit in the courtyard during the day. I would somehow have to make it work with me sitting inside the box with Shakespeare, to avoid the rain.

Apart from having packed extra clothes, I had packed a cordless battery charger for my phone, and a quilted thick dog coat made by my rescue friend Hannah for Shakespeare before I had left France. I had also packed two different dog toys. I had ordered them express delivered after I had read what Suhair had sent me about Shakespeare. These toys are meant to stimulate dogs to think and seek solutions, of course involving rewards. The toys in my bag were by a Swedish designer called Nina Ottosson. I had used her dog puzzle toys for years to stimulate dogs. Would Shakespeare even look at them?

A good dog toy will challenge the dog to think, stimulate brain activity and the use of their sense of smell, and it can demand the energy equivalent to a good walk. Brain work tires dogs out and this is the reason service dogs in the police force and customs takes regular breaks. They have not walked far at all, but their brain has been extremely focused on the job at hand, and they get exhausted. Walking a dog is necessary for a dog's wellbeing and of course good for them but if you for some reason cannot walk them – they are recuperating after surgery - then a puzzle for dogs is such a good way to keep their mind stimulated.

The bag on the seat next to me was bulging with all I had packed for another day with Shakespeare, in his box, at the sanctuary.

On the car window raindrops were trickling like tears for Shakespeare and his broken soul. I was looking out reflecting over how different the landscape was, both in comparison to Bergen where I originally came from in Norway, and to where I lived in France, where the landscape was flat, and the eye could follow an everlasting horizon. I could breathe better there, at home in France, than anywhere else in the world and Shakespeare could find himself there. I knew he could, as I had.

The greeting from the dogs was just as enthusiastic as the day before, but that morning I went straight to Shakespeare's box without delay and was greeted by Billy and the former balcony-living German Shepard. Both were excited to see me, and Billy was up on his back paws before I had turned the corner of the concrete end wall of the rows of kennel boxes. For Billy, I equalled treats and someone to chat with, causing his tail to whip round.

Good morning boys! I sounded cheerful and carefree, despite my stomach being in a knot with anticipation as I stood outside Shakespeare's gate. I gave both dogs a treat and a stroke before I entered Shakespeare's courtyard. It truly was a miserable grey morning with slight fog and rain clouds descending over the sanctuary and even the cheerful sunny yellow tiles had lost their cheerfulness. The smell hanging in the air was that of wet dogs and wet vegetation. I entered and closed the gate behind me, crossed the courtyard without entering the box directly. Instead, I squatted down in the opening, leaning myself against the outside wall. I was on Shakespeare's level before I poked my head inside. My large bag was untouched at the same spot as I had left it the day before. My intuition had been right. The fact that my bag was untouched told me that Shakespeare was not curious, and certainly not destructive. I knew he had moved about and been outside in the night by the large pooh left in the courtyard close to the gate, so he certainly had passed my bag, but he had not touched it. It was of course good he was not destructive, but not so good that he was not curious. Curiosity is natural in humans and more so in dogs. Dogs are opportunists and a bag filled with treats would never go unnoticed and extremely rarely untouched. The fact that he had not touched my bag indicated he was not using his sensory system at all, even whilst alone, and that was less than good news.

The order of the different sensors in dogs is very different to that of humans. For dogs, the most important sense by far is smell, then hearing and thirdly it is touch, sight and then taste.

For humans it is sight, hearing, touch and then smell, and taste. Understanding the order of a dog's senses is the foundation of understanding a dog and its behaviour.

Good morning beautiful Shakespeare. I would from that moment onwards use his name as often as I could as it would be more than helpful if he knew it. I doubted he did. Dogs in shelters are often named as they arrive because they arrive without history. This means the dog has no connection to the name, and I strongly suspected that was also the case for Shakespeare.

Shakespeare did not acknowledge me apart from the same slight movements of his front paws indicating for me to go away.

Have you slept well. You must be freezing up against that wall.

No reaction. His eyes were in a fixed position, and he looked unreal in the grim, dim light. I tried to observe every little detail, even the details that normally would go unnoticed to the human eye. One of the nerves in Shakespeare's ear was twitching but was almost unnoticeable. I knew that everything I learnt about Shakespeare over the next days would be important for the future, so I was planning to use my time with him well and take mental notes of all details. I would also make a daily video of him, to watch later, to see if my phone camera noticed something my eyes missed.

Shakespeare will you let me come and sit inside your box with you? I promise I will not overstep your boundaries, but it will be wet and cold and miserable for me out here in the rain today.

There was of course no reaction at all apart from him signalling with his paws to not come close. I waited - sat still for a couple of minutes.

Shakespeare I would love to join you inside.

Again, absolutely no reaction to my voice. His nostrils did not vibrate at all. There simply was nothing. I got up, with no abrupt movements, and stepped inside the box. I did not approach him, and I kept my body half turned away from him as I opened the shopping bag and took out the extra clothes. Slowly,

I put my rain jacket down on the floor and put the other garments on top of the jacket to sit on, opened my bag and fished out the Agatha Christie book I had left the day before.

Having found a position, I could sit in for a while, I continued talking to him.

Shakespeare, shall I read for you like I did yesterday?

There was of course no response as I opened the book.

I tried to concentrate on what was on the page, but it was not easy as I could feel the cold in my back. For Shakespeare who had the whole side of his body glued to the wall it would be absolutely freezing. I knew that unless I could get Shakespeare warm, he would simply not be able to relax. The reason he was underweight was not lack of food, but that he was using all his energy to outmanoeuvre the consequences of his PTSD and the intense cold he was feeling from the concrete wall. Leaning against the wall gave him a sense of security. If a scared dog is in an open space, it will fight or seek flight. The other natural reaction of a scared dog is to seek to hide or as in Shakespeare's case lean against the wall as there was nowhere to hide in the bare concrete box that had been his home for so long. If I approached Shakespeare too soon, he would never trust me again. I had to choose the timing wisely, with only another five days to reach him.

C had told me there was a store of blankets near to the main entrance of the kennels, and I decided that within the day I would get him a blanket. The thin brick red blanket in his plastic bed had absolutely no function and it was far from clean.

When I heard Urage doing his feeding and cleaning I asked him to leave the food for Shakespeare outside in the courtyard, speaking from where I sat. I did not want anyone to come into the space Shakespeare and I were sharing. I did not want any distractions more than what was already there - Urage feeding and cleaning and being welcomed by barking dogs as he moved along the row.

To my surprise Shakespeare stopped moving his paws by midday, letting me know I could gently approach him. I moved about ten centimetres at a time towards him and I kept reading so that would hear my voice even if he would not look at me.

The rain outside made the space seem duller, greyer, and colder but it did not matter one bit as Shakespeare, and I were together in the same space.

I could feel his fear; it was still tangible, and I had to make a conscious decision not to get dragged into that fear, but every time I took a quick glance in his direction I wanted to cry, sob, and move over and hold him. Holding him is the human reaction and of course the nurturing mother gene in me, but for a dog like Shakespeare it would be violating his space.

All the other dogs had retracted inside due to the rain and the calmness of the sanctuary told me Urage and C had left.

On our drive to the sanctuary that morning I had asked C to come back and pick me up in the evening, and Shakespeare and I were now alone with around forty other dogs.

After having moved my rain jacket, bit by bit, I had by late afternoon come close enough to reach out and touch Shakespeare. He was staring straight ahead and my presence closer to him had not changed his posture, his facial expression, or his non-existent body language. This was good news as that indicated that he accepted having me there. He was neither more nor less frightened. I was close enough to be able to smell him. He did not smell of wet dog as he had not been outside in the rain, nor did he smell of any dog smell familiar to me. Shakespeare smelt of dust and dry dirt. On his elbow, on the left side facing me, he had a large cyst, from where he would squeeze himself between a concrete slab on the floor and the wall, In slow motion, he slides down exhausted from trying to keep himself sitting upright. I could also see he had two cysts on his short tail that had been docked at some stage, telling me that a human had been involved in his puppyhood. Shakespeare had not been born in the wild, where he had been caught as an adult dog of around two years. He had been at the sanctuary for almost five years meaning he would be around seven.

I decided to get some blankets before I touched him. I needed to move, as my metal-enforced neck did not take kindly to sitting in the same position for hours. I did not want to touch him before I could put a blanket around him at the same time. Slowly I stood upright leaving my book next to him. I wanted to signal I was coming back.

Outside the courtyard was slippery from the rain and there were puddles in the pathway that I tried to avoid by stepping over them. I did not have an extra pair of shoes with me and getting wet would mean freezing feet.

All the dogs were surprisingly calm with me passing their boxes.

They had sniffed me the day before and when I arrived that morning, and with me handing them all a treat, they thought of me as a positive addition to their day. Only a few barked as I passed but it was more out of boredom than anything else. I easily found the room with blankets, beds, and other equipment for the dogs, and I quickly chose two blue blankets. The dark blue was for me to sit on and put behind my back against the wall, and the white and blue was for Shakespeare. Back in the box, everything was exactly as I had left it. Shakespeare had not moved a millimetre. I sat down in the same spot I had left minutes earlier.

Shakespeare darling, I am going to touch you and I will put a blanket around you. That means I will have to unglue you from the wall, but it will only be for a short moment and then you can lean back in. It will just be for a minute, I promise, I just need to get the blanket around you, and you can lean against the wall again to feel safe.

I had of course no way of knowing what his reaction would be when I touched him, or what he would do when I tried to put the blanket around him. Shakespeare had had no close human interaction for many years, if ever, and he could react in several different ways. Aggression would be the worst as I was alone with him in a remote location so being attacked and bitten would be far from ideal.

My job with all dogs I deal with is to try to decipher the body language and signals, but I knew Shakespeare was not about to share his emotions. I would have to trust my experience but more so my gut instinct. I knew the risk of an attack was real, but somehow, I felt sure that would not be his reaction. I could of course be wrong. My life in the rescue world had taught me never to assume anything to be certain.

I know how cold you are, beautiful you, and you and I must change that. The cold is keeping you from relaxing. From breathing properly.

For many years after the accident and after I was diagnosed with PTSD, I had been constantly cold. I could not get warm no matter how many jumpers I put on. I slept with the minimum of two quilts in the night, under blankets.

It took years before I understood why this was so: if the body goes into shock, body temperature drops. Under normal circumstances heat is transferred through tissues and fat and is released at a rate depending on the environment but when the body is in shock the heat transmission is interrupted and blood flowing to arms and legs slows down. The blood supply is concentrated toward the torso and vital organs. Therefore, a blanket or emergency foil is provided to try to keep the body temperature stable after an accident or shock.

With PTSD the body will act as if it is in constant shock and the blood flow is redirected away from the extremities and concentrated in the torso to keep the vital organs going. It is the same process for dogs.

Shakespeare was certainly not helped in any way by the frozen concrete walls but the main reason he was cold, I suspected, was his PTSD.

Living with PTSD had made me understand shut down dogs on a different level, it had made me into a better rescuer, and amongst the first thing I would always do when faced with a shutdown dog was to make sure they had a blanket or even better a warm coat. My secret weapon under optimal circumstances was also a sheepskin. Sheepskins will give heat in a way no artificial material can, and sheep's wool has a calming effect on most dogs. Sheepskin contains lanolin and lanolin heals skin infection. A sheepskin has the magic ability to provide warmth but also to regulate the body temperature in a hot environment. I have saved several dogs over the years by having them lay on a sheepskin, covered by a blanket.

I would have to find out if I can get some sheepskins in Cyprus. Surely there must be some sheep farmers somewhere on the island, I thought.

As I put down the blue blanket on top of my rain jacket, I held on to the blanket meant for Shakespeare whilst I talking to him.

We will figure this out Shakespeare. You and I, we will figure this out. There is a life outside this box, and you are missing out on it all.

I looked at him and became completely overwhelmed again. Overwhelmed with sadness and a huge sense of loss for this broken boy with his life stolen from him. He had come to the sanctuary to be saved but instead the opposite had happened.

The captivity had broken him completely and in front of me was a soul alive only due to his beating heart and nothing else. Suhair had told me, and C had confirmed that no one had seen Shakespeare stand up or seen him eat for the whole time he had been in the box. He would only eat in the night when no humans were at the sanctuary.

I slowly, very slowly - reached out my hand to touch his neck. Just as I was about to touch him, I could feel I was trembling ever so slightly, so I retracted my hand and took a few minutes to breathe calmy. When I was relaxed, I reached out again.

Neither of us made a sound.

Everything around us seemed so fragile - this first touch, first contact, would define our onward journey forever. It was no longer Shakespeare that was frozen, it was time. I put the palm of my hand on his neck and simply left it there. I did not stroke. I did not move. The palm of my hand was warm, and the flesh under the short fur, under the palm, was ice, winter, freezing cold.

Dear God, how on earth have you managed to keep yourself alive? You must have the strongest heart of all dogs I have ever met.

As I spoke, Shakespeare flickered his eyelid and glanced sideways at me. It lasted a nano second of the physical time it takes for the pupil in the eye to move and the eyelid to blink. I realised it was the first time I had seen him blink since I had come inside the box. By him glancing over at me, even for the shortest blink of an eye, he had acknowledged my existence. It was his first acceptance of me being where I was, with my palm on his neck.

We did not move.

We sat utterly still, and I let the flesh under my palm be warmed by my body heat, transferred through my hand.

Shakespeare, I will be your human if you will let me. We will figure this out. You and me. You can come and live with me, with Are, he is a very nice man, and you will have seven dogs to support you and, oh and yes, four cats.

He was back to staring straight ahead.

I started to move my hand downwards on his neck, reaching his shoulder and then the side of his belly, and as I did so, I could feel that the nerve endings were shooting out small electric signals throughout his body, telling him he was in danger. I knew all too well how this worked. Signals like that had taken my sleep for the first years and still would when my PTSD flared up under stress. I could feel each "shot" through my hand, as he could feel them shooting off. I kneeled and reached out for the blanket next to me. I had already unfolded it, wanting to drape it around him.

As I put my hand over the ridge of his back, he forced his body, using all his muscle power, further against the wall. He could not physically get closer to the wall, but he was in panic that I was about to take away the only safety he had – a concrete wall - and he was not about to let me.

Shhhhhhh, please do not worry. We will do this when you are ready.

I stroked him over his spine, down the flank of his back leg, back up towards his neck until I reached the top of his head. I left my hand there at the same time as I used my other hand to wrap the blanket closer around him. I was not going to "unglue" him from the wall. It was too early, and he had clearly told me he was in the state of panic by me trying to get the blanket fully behind his body, so I simply pressed the edge of the blanket down behind him as you would do when you make a bed, when the mattress is too tight in the bedframe.

My hand was moving gently on top of the blanket. I tried to make sure his legs were covered as well as his body, whilst I stroked him on top of the blue and white blanket, in small circular movements.

Shakespeare, one day we will look back on this and know this was the beginning of something new. Something different. I promise you that you will get out of here and you will get to run in liberty again. I promise.

I sat close enough for him to feel me. I just sat still only moving my hand softly, and after a while I picked my book back up and kept on reading in a hushed, monotone voice. I knew there would be no quick fix to anything: not to getting him to France, not to getting him to awake his senses, not to get him to trust me fully, nor to get him to understand that his life had changed forever. I also knew that I would never let him go.

It would take what it would take!

As the afternoon past we simply sat and as a sign of Shakespeare realising things were about to change, he did not force himself back into sitting position when he slid down on the concrete floor where he now, for the first time, laid on a blanket. I was sitting next to him leaned against the wall with the blue blanket at my back. When I had been in the storage room to pick up the blankets, I had seen some polystyrene that looked like it had come from a shipment of goods.

I was wondering if the polystyrene would fit between the concrete slab and the wall, insulating the floor, and stopping

Shakespeare from getting his elbows caught on the slab edge. I was also looking around trying to figure out how to get his box changed into a place of some comfort with what was at hand at the sanctuary. I had seen several pallets whilst I were in the storage room. If I lifted his bed onto one of the pallets that would get his bed off the floor making it less cold. I was however not at all sure he used his bed. He might be spending his nights laying directly on the floor but raising the bed was absolutely worth a try. I formed a plan for the following days - one thing at a time - and for the rest of that afternoon we simply sat together, sharing the same space whilst I was reading to him off and on. As the hours went and it was getting close to my time to leave for the night, I was toying with the idea of spending the night with him in the box. I did not want to leave him. I did however not have enough clothes with me. My phone had gone dead by this stage, and I had used up the extra battery I had brought with me to film Shakespeare and to document my journey with him.

I had to go back to C's house. Lupin was there, and Andreas, C's partner and I were having dinner together that evening. But - before it was time for me to leave for the night, I prepared the two toys, filling them with treats. Both toys are built so that the dog will either turn something or lift something to get to the treats. My blind dog, Miss Kathryn Grey absolutely loved both those toys as we had them at home, but I was not sure at all that Shakespeare would take to them. All I could do was try and wait for the result the following morning.

I left the toys metres apart and again, left my bag and now also my rain jacket on a hook to the left of Shakespeare's feeding bowl.

I placed the food Urage had left in the courtyard earlier in the morning, in the food holder attached to the wall where Shakespeare also had plenty of fresh water.

Shakespeare was still covered in the blanket, and he did not move his paws or signal he was scared when I was moving around. As I was about to leave, I stroked his head.

Shakespeare I will see you tomorrow morning. Tomorrow is a big day as we will rearrange your box. If Are was here he would tell you that you will have to get used to me rearranging the furniture. Are is a bit like you, he does not like changes, but I promise that you will feel so much better. Tomorrow is another day and in Norway we say that each day brings blank sheets of white paper and new colour pencils. I will be back tomorrow my darling.

I bent down and kissed him on his head and there was no trembling.

Incredible!

I felt like dancing.

> There are **no tricks** in plain and simple faith.
> -William Shakespeare, *Julius Caesar*

I am not a religious person. I presume I fall in the category of those described as spiritual. The fact that I am not religious does however not mean I am without faith, far from it.

Finding God has simply just never happened to or for me but being without a God does not mean being without faith. I strongly and with all my being believe in the force of good. I have a solid faith in the force of light.

I believe kindness to be our strongest currency, and the best thing is that it is free. I believe in paying it forward and I believe that kindness spreads like ripples in the water after the silent jump of a fish. I believe that shining light in dark corners brings clarity.

I also believe in signs and that if you are open to them, they find you. Always!

I was sitting in the dog-crowded kitchen in C's home after we had come back from the sanctuary. Andreas had been out picking wild asparagus near the sanctuary and we were having a truly lovely evening meal, chatting easily, in a surprisingly calm kitchen taking into consideration there were twenty-six dogs present. I was curious about Shakespeare's history, what C knew about him, if anything. She explained Shakespeare had been caught on the riverbank where he lived with his partner and their pups.

Is she still at the sanctuary, I asked.

No. Sadly Agatha died. She was bitten by a snake and there was nothing we could do.

I had just lifted my wine glass to take a sip but put it back down onto the table without having put my lips to the rim.

Agatha? Was she named Agatha? Agatha who?

Somehow, I knew the answer before C said: *Agatha Christie.*

I could not believe it. Shakespeare had spent his life in liberty with a dog named after the same lady, the author, who had given names to all my animals and to my rescue association, Miss Marple's Universe.

I tried to ask how she got the name, but the topic was left by C, and I never got to know any more about their names – Shakespeare and Agatha. I wanted to dig and ask more, but I was a guest in her home.

Later that night I lay awake thinking about what could seem like an incredible coincidence, but here is the thing: I do not believe in coincidences.

> I'll follow thee and
> **make a heaven of hell**.
> -William Shakespeare, *A Midsummer Night's Dream*

It is amazing how quickly one can settle into a routine, and as my third morning in Cyprus arrived, Lupin and I were out of bed before the dogs went crazy. I was so excited about going back to the sanctuary to see if Shakespeare had touched his toys. I also wanted to change his box by putting his bed on top of a pallet and I desperately wanted sheepskins. They would not be from a local sheep farmer, as there were none, but there was an IKEA in Limassol. I would be going there later in the day and would bring them to Shakespeare the following morning. I had such a belief that I could get Shakespeare into his bed with the simple trick of keeping him warm. I have been surer of fewer things in life.

It felt like my childhood's anticipation before Christmas as I walked towards Shakespeare's box and before I had reached the gate, I could see the toys had been brought out into the courtyard.

Shakespeare had used the toys! He had taken the red tops off the small chambers and found the treats. He had pushed or lifted the toys outside, and he had evidently interacted with both toys and had eaten all the treats. I started to cry. This was so much more than I had dared to hope for. Crying and wanting to jump for joy at the same time, I handed Billy and the GSD a treat each before I entered Shakespeare's tiny courtyard. I kept talking to Billy, who was up at his back legs with a wagging tail, so that Shakespeare knew I had arrived.

Good morning, Shakespeare. You have no idea how happy I am that you like your new toys. It is simply wonderful that you also like the duck treats. They are good, are they not? Countess Elena insists that they are the best treats ever. You will like my Countess Elena when you get to meet her. She is my big girl waiting for us in France. She is born almost deaf, and her sight is not good, but you will love her. I promise you. You will.

As the morning before, Shakespeare had not touched my bag, nor had he touched my jacket. The weather had changed to sunshine with just a light breeze, and the forecast indicated I would not need my rain jacket anymore.

Shakespeare gave no signals of welcome when I entered the box, but he did something I knew to be a huge step for him; he glanced over at me and by that acknowledged me. If it had been a stranger, he would have gazed straight ahead as he had done when I first arrived. He was still completely motionless, but his glance made my heartbeat faster. He knew me! At least he knew me as the women who had spent the last days with him in his box.

Shakespeare, I would like for you to get your new coat on today. This means I will unglue you from the wall so I can get your coat on. I know you will like the coat.

There was of course no response, but I stroked him along his spine to see if he would push himself closer to the wall, and he did. The coat I had left the day before with my other belongings was left untouched on top of my bag.

Shakespeare, I will be back.

The polystyrene was easy to find. I carried that back, together with a large black plastic double pallet. I left the pallet against the wall in the courtyard and entered the box again. Carefully I lowered the polystyrene in front of Shakespeare to see if the width would fit between the wall and the slab and it looked like it would be a perfect fit. Two things needed to happen at the same time. I would fit Shakespeare with his new jacket, and I needed to lift him up so I could get the polystyrene sheet under him. I was sure Shakespeare would resist his coat and resist me lifting him up, but there was no other way to do this.

Listen darling, I will try to do this as gently as I can but there is simply no way of doing this without scaring you.

I kept stroking him as I removed the blanket I had wrapped round him. I forced my hand between Shakespeare and the wall. He was pushing back as I was gently pulling him away from the wall. It was like trying to handle a dog after rigor mortis had set in. Shakespeare was frozen in a fixed position, and I knew he did not move because he simply was not capable of it at that stage. His PTSD had taken over, telling him that if he moved, he would die. Being frozen was his only option for survival. My heart was breaking yet again but I had to try to use the situation to my advantage to get his coat on. There was of course a possibility that Shakespeare's PTSD would send new signals to his brain telling him to fight, but I considered that possibility to be slim.

In my experience, when the body has found it option of survival it tends not to change it in an instant, as the chosen option has meant life thus far - if he were to bite me or attack me, it would only be when I denied him the safety of leaning against the wall.

I unglued him by muscle power, mine winning over his. I slipped the coat on him as I released him, quickly letting him lean back against the wall. The fact that I had unglued him caused him to slide into panic, but there was absolutely no sign of aggression. He was however trembling, shaking in convulsion-like movements.

Shhhhhhh, you will be ok darling. Please do not worry. You will feel better in a bit. Please just sit still and let me do the rest of what we need to do. I pulled the coat under his belly and fastened it with the large piece of Velcro that was luckily facing towards me. As I lifted him to push the polystyrene under him, I made sure to hold him as tight as I physically could, to give him some sense of security as he could not feel the wall. I had decided against standing up whilst handling him because I would be towering over him, so everything had to happen with me on my knees. I lifted him and pushed the sheet simultaneously under him with my knee. Shakespeare was not a small dog, but I did not have the luxury of faffing about. My adrenaline helped give me extra strength for the lift-and-move motion. It was done in seconds. Shakespeare was back leaning towards the wall dressed now in a thick, neon-coloured padded coat, sitting on a snow-white polystyrene sheet that lifted him off the floor at the same height as the concrete slab.

His facial expression gave away nothing, but I could feel his confusion. He was questioning me, my presence, and my action, but he was not going to share that with me. He was back into his own safety zone of leaning against the wall, but his breathing showed me lifting him had challenged his very existence. Shakespeare was breathing erratically and trembling. I knew that all we could do was wait it out. There was nothing I could do to sooth him apart from keeping my energy level calm. I closed my eyes and focused on deep, diaphragmatic breathing, inhaling through my nose, and breathing out through my mouth accepting the present moment for what it was; two of us sharing the same space, focussing on what we had achieved in such a short time. In my mind we were walking next to each other through the woods near to my home in France, and soon his erratic breathing subsided. Then, Shakespeare showed no signs of panic nor of discomfort and soon, to my astonishment he unglued his head from the wall. Not by much but I could fit the palm of my hand between his head and the ice-cold wall.

The heat from the jacket was starting to do its job and his legs were ever so slowly starting to feel less frozen. He turned and looked at me - a miniscule fleeting glance. He had moved his head!

That afternoon's trip to IKEA provided the required bounty; two sheepskins. They were white, not the most sensible choice for a dog in a rescue sanctuary but what did it matter? I had grown up sleeping on sheepskins and after my accident, when I could not get warm, I started to sleep on sheepskins again. Sheepskins help to regulate the body temperature and the skin has a moisture-wicking quality, absorbing humidity without feeling humid or wet. Prefect for a damp box in a sanctuary and just what we needed to hopefully move us forward.

Courage and comfort!
All shall yet go well.
-William Shakespeare,
King John

C, Urage and I arrived at the sanctuary a bit earlier on my fourth day at the sanctuary. C was going off to an afternoon meeting. I would not be picked up before the evening, leaving me another full day with Shakespeare. I had my battery charger, more clothes, the sheepskins of course, water for me and some chocolate. More treats for Billy, the GSD, and all the other dogs, and a packet of IKEA ginger cookies. My happiness level was elevated when I came around the corner to see that Shakespeare had yet again brought the two toys into the courtyard after I had filled them with treats and left them inside his box the day before.

Morning Shakespeare.

Unhurriedly I walked inside his concrete box and unpacked my bag leaving the different items spread on the floor. Unlike any healthy dog, Shakespeare showed no interest at all in any of the items, but he did quickly look towards me, before he locked himself back into a stare.

Darling today is our big, big day. Today you are leaving your corner. I know it will be absolutely petrifying for you, but I will be here with you, next to you, as we journey forward on this first massive leap. You have no idea how scared I was when I first started moving around after my accident. Actually, you absolutely do know. Today is your day to take that first step.

I sat by him, and for a third day running Urage left Shakespeare's food in the courtyard. Shakespeare was trembling as Urage went by and on to Billy's enclosure, whilst Billy expressed his utter joy at seeing Urage, who spoke to Billy in his native language. There was absolutely no need for Shakespeare to fear Urage. He was a kind and gentle young man. But common sense is not involved with PTSD.

I read to Shakespeare whilst stroking him under his jacket. Amazingly he had kept it on since the day before, and again, he had not touched any of my belongings. He had emptied the toys to get to the dried duck treats. I was slightly baffled by the fact that my bag was still untouched, as I would certainly have thought that by now it was so familiar to him that he would have helped himself to the treats still left in there. But he had not.

The two of us sat close together in Shakespeare's preferred corner, me reading to him and him staring straight ahead but glancing over at me, in a split-second eye movement, three times during the morning. I felt like he was saying: *Who are you? I know you from somewhere, but I cannot place you. Where did we meet?*

By lunch time there was not a sound in the kennels. All was so calm it was hard to believe how many dogs there were around us. The sun was throwing sunbeams into the box making it seem almost cheerful. I could smell the soil, mountains and whiffs of unfamiliar vegetation and early spring. The blue and white blanket together with the blue one I had used to sit on, were in Shakespeare's black plastic bed. I could see the bed had been used in the night and that was good news in connection to the next move - getting Shakespeare into his bed.

I got myself off the floor and took the few steps into the courtyard where I had left the pallet the day before. It was easy to move the few metres into the box, to the left side corner, opposite where Shakespeare sat frozen. I lifted the large bed onto it, placing it across the pallet at an angle. It worked out perfectly as the pallet was big enough to leave some space for me to sit on the edge of it, despite the huge bed. Shakespeare would now be able look into the courtyard if he were laying in the bed and that was my intention. I took the blankets, refolded them and put them in the bottom of the bed and put the two sheepskins on top. What a transformation!

The bed was off the cold floor and the bed was now hidden under two large sheepskins making me think of The Princess and The Pea. I smiled.

Shakespeare, look at your new bed. I could hear the excitement in my own voice.

No reaction.

I went back into his corner and sat down next to him whilst I massaged his ear trying to think how to best lift him.

Shakespeare I am going to move you from this corner and onto your new bed. You will be warm and when you are warm you can breathe. You can sleep if you like. I will be here with you. I will not leave you, so you do not have to be worried. I know it is ridiculous me saying you do not have to be worried or scared, because I know how petrified you are, but I promise we will be ok. You will be ok.

Now is as good time as any, I thought, and as I stroked him, I put my left arm under him. It was the only way for me to be able to lift him. I got halfway up and lifted him with me. He was heavy as any dead weight is, but he did not move at all. He was the same rigor mortis dog I had found in the corner when I first arrived.

It was all done in seconds as the bed was three steps behind me, and there he was on his new sheepskin bed. In that moment I was utterly grateful that Shakespeare's chosen PTSD survival choice was freeze, not flight, as he simply stayed where I had put him. I kept stroking him.

Shakespeare darling. I am now going to stretch your legs under you so that you will lay down on your bed.

Carefully I touched one leg as you would run your hand down the leg of a horse to get it to lift its leg to clean its hoof. As I held one hand around one ankle, I carefully repeated the motion on his other leg. Slowly, gently, I lifted both legs at the same time and I stretched his legs. He surrendered into a laying position without any protests or interest. There was no reaction - he simply stayed.

Sitting on the edge of the pallet, leaning up against his bed, I kept stroking him, and after less than an hour, as by a miracle, I could feel him relaxing under his coat where my hand was still on his spine. I could feel the tension leaving as one muscle after the other simply released its tension. I saw his right front paw twitch. His breathing went from slightly erratic to regular. His ears were relaxing, now hanging down the side of his skull. His head kept drooping forward and he nodded off a couple of times before his eyes finally closed - staying closed with his head resting on the sheepskin. Within another thirty minutes, Shakespeare was fast asleep next to me on his sheepskins. I was holding my breath scared that the sacred moment would shatter, but he was in a deep, seemingly dreamless sleep, and there were absolutely no signs that he was worried I would not watch over him. His facial expression had changed. Gone was the haunted look and he looked absolutely at peace. He had moved to laying on his side with all paws away from under him, meaning he was not in a state of alert. He was simply perfectly relaxed. I kept looking at him, absorbing every detail of the change in him.

He was an aesthetically incredibly beautiful dog but the beauty I saw was that of him letting go and daring to trust a human for the first time ever. He had just unlocked his own prison. I cried in admiration of this incredible being that had let me share this life-changing moment with him.

Eventually I sloped forward and fell in a light sleep half on top of him and half next to him. I knew what it felt like, to become warm again, after having been cold for so long. The experience of being there when he went to sleep filled me with gratitude in its simplest form.

It all gave me such hope for the future. Our future!

> **They say miracles are past**; and we have our philosophical persons, to make modern and familiar, things supernatural and causeless.
> -William Shakespeare, *All's Well That Ends Well*

It had been a sleepless night. I had been tossing and restless, trying to decide when would be a good time to ask the ladies of SPDC if I could bring Shakespeare to France. I had spoken to Lupin in the night in my attempt to go through all the possible scenarios. Lupin had picked up on my restlessness and had simply moved herself closer to me. I was scared they would say no to my request that he come to France. It was not because I did not think they trusted me. It was actually not linked to me at all, but to Shakespeare. When a rescue association has a dog like Shakespeare in their care it becomes so difficult to see any shimmer of hope and the path certainly is neither straight nor clearly lit. I knew I would have to get all the women to agree as they all took decisions on behalf of the dogs.

I had met Katy and Elena outside C's house the morning after my arrival. It had been a very brief meeting as we were all heading off in different directions but today, they would come to the sanctuary, so today would be the day.

When a rescue association has a case like Shakespeare it is heart-breaking, and no one truly knows what the best solution is. I knew there was a real risk of them saying no, as it would involve a long journey. I was of course convinced that the only solution was for Shakespeare to come to live with me and my pack, but that was my personal opinion and that might not matter in this situation.

C, Urage and I arrived at the sanctuary in the morning to be greeted by Billy as it had been his turn at night watchman. He met us with elated joy. It was hard to believe that after Shakespeare, Billy was the second longest resident at the sanctuary. He knew me and he also knew that I had treats in my pocket. This black and gentle giant of a dog nuzzled my pocket for a treat, making me laugh and defusing my nervousness of the upcoming day and the conversation I had prepared for overnight.

It goes without saying I gave into Billy and gave him several treats. His tail was rotating in gratitude both for the attention and the treats. As I was going to Shakespeare's box, I took Billy with me to return him to his. He came willingly and easily and was of course rewarded with another treat.

I glanced into Shakespeare's courtyard and the toys were back out in the yard. He had played with the toys and lifted each red lid to get to the duck treats. Some lids were scattered, others were gaping open. My body responded to the sight with exultation.

Walking past the toys I looked into the box. I saw Shakespeare was not in his, but back in his corner. Moving unhurriedly, I entered the box catching Shakespeare trembling in the left corner, staring straight ahead.

Good morning, Shakespeare. My voice was hushed as to not startle him.

I can see you have played with the toys, and I can see you have slept in your bed. I am so sorry you are so scared you needed to go back into your corner, but please my darling, do not worry. Every day we can start over if we have to. Start over until you realise life is changing for the better.

I sat down next to him without him moving his paws. He simply just let me come into his personal space without any reaction. Lack of reaction was the best I could hope for at that stage. No reaction was actually fantastic as it meant he was not scared of me anymore.

I put my hand on his neck. He was ice cold again. I got up and got the blanket from under his sheepskins. He still had on the neon-coloured coat and there was no question it helped, but nevertheless I wrapped the blanket around him again and he soon sank into a lying position on the floor whilst I was stroking him.

Right my dear, I will lift you back onto your bed as it is so much better for you to lay on there. I can sit with you on the pallet.

I did not wait. I put my arm under his belly to get a grip of him and he did not resist. He did not try to force his body closer to the wall. I simply lifted him and put him on the sheepskin, repeating the stretching of his legs from the day before.

He seemed indifferent but there were nanoscopic movements in his neck muscles as he started to relax. Then he turned his head and looked straight at me.

It was overwhelming. Shakespeare had an intense presence that filled the box. When he looked at me all his energy and presence were focusing on me. A dog like Shakespeare will normally never look at you as part of their avoidance behaviour, and yet, here he was looking straight at me as to ask me again: *Who are you? Where did you come from? What took you so long? Do we know each other?*

As I responded, I tried my best to answer all his questions and as I spoke, he drifted off to sleep. I opened my book and read to him. I so wanted him to know my voice. I sat on the edge of the black pallet, stroking him, reading *The Body in the Library*, my favourite Agatha Christie story. I knew it by heart. My hand was resting on Shakespeare's chest under his coat, and I could feel his heart beating. His facial expression had changed. The haunted look he had when I first arrived was replaced with softness in his facial muscles and closed eye lids as if he were sleeping. But just under the surface he was surveying what was going on outside the box.

Then - the alarm went.

When forty dogs bark at the same time it is not as if it is possible to ignore the message that a car was approaching the sanctuary. I assumed it was Elena and Katy. Shakespeare was trembling under my hand, but he stayed in his bed, surprising us both. I leaned forward and kissed his head.

Please wish me luck. I will talk to them about letting you travel. I got up and walked outside into the intense sunlight, making me squint, shielding my eyes with my hand. The two women came walking towards me on the narrow path that passes all the boxes. It was such an easy and uncomplicated reunion.

Elena was a petite woman with beautiful kind eyes, curly dark hair and such a soft smile. Katy was a tall slinky blond woman with the body of an athlete and a relaxed happy energy. Elena was one of the founders of SPDC whilst Katy joined the team a bit later. Whilst both women are native to Cyprus their appearance is so opposite that they confirm the diversity of humans on this island.

The conversation was easy and all my plans on how to present my wish to bring Shakespeare home had suddenly evaporated. I told them about the progress Shakespeare had made. Then, in the midst of a sentence: *I so want to bring him home*. Elena did not even flinch, and her response was immediate.

Of course, you can bring him home!

I can? I heard the surprise in my voice.

Of course, you can. Leave it all with me. He is going home to you. To France. Just like that - it had been decided that Shakespeare was coming home.

I wanted to cry but decided to wait until I could share the news with Shakespeare. Katy was the association's photographer and had photos of dogs to take to update the dogs for adoption list. Elena was off to a meeting, so I returned to Shakespeare wondering why I had been awake the whole night before, intimidated about asking. I had in reality not even had to ask, but to state I wanted him to come home. I was not capable of jumping into the air to do a split jump for joy, but I did several mental ones as I walked back to Shakespeare's box.

Shakespeare you are coming home. My voice was bubbling.

He was back in his corner. I sat down by him, stroked him before we again went through the same procedure of me lifting him onto the sheepskins where he soon settled down again.

You are coming home Shakespeare and then the tears came, yet again.

My head was racing with plans and question that no one but the future could answer.

As the afternoon passed the temperature was dropping inside the box but Shakespeare was snuggled up on his sheepskins wearing his jacket and covered with a blanket. I sat on the edge of the pallet stroking him under his coat and down his legs, as the afternoon headed towards evening. There was one human at the sanctuary, me, and most of the other dogs did not even know I was there as I did not move from Shakespeare's side. It was a strange feeling as the light dimmed more and more until it was absolutely pitch black inside the box. Outside it was dark but there was a new moon behind scattered moving clouds.

I could at least see the outline of the fencing and landscape around the sanctuary, whilst inside it was not possible to see anything. My phone had died and yet again, I had no more battery on the spare.

In reality I was completely isolated at the sanctuary, in the middle of nowhere until C would come and get me. It was such a rare and unique opportunity to be still and feel the energy from the boy next to me. We could not see each other but we both felt the others' presence. I was breathing calmly as was he. As it was not possible to see anything at all inside the box, it felt like I was in a different zone to all humans who were not in that box with us. My voice was low as to not break the magic and then, suddenly, Shakespeare moved. In several surprising moves, he got up. I could not see him, but my hand was on his back and there was no question he was standing on all-fours.

My brain was having the strangest conversation with itself:

What do you mean he has got up? No one has seen this dog walk since he got to the sanctuary. He cannot be standing up as you are here and you are a human, like the ones he fears....

I was trying to take it all in. By not having light and not being able to see him I had to use my sense of hearing as my primary sense and there in a flash of sensory change I could relate to how Shakespeare perceive the outside world. He was not physically in the dark during the day but yet he was, as he could not see anything around him. This was why he depended totally on the bark from the female by the gate, to warn him of danger. I had never sat in complete darkness with any of my dogs as I sat with Shakespeare that evening, but it taught me a lot about how we unconsciously pick up on energy.

Before the light had left us inside, I had prepared the toys with duck treats and Shakespeare now, in the pitch-black dark, went over to one of the toys and pushed it with his nose into the courtyard. He did not open the lids, but he certainly pushed it. I heard him walking across the tiny courtyard to do a wee. I was holding my breath sitting completely still on the edge of the pallet wondering if I should follow him. I decided to walk the few steps towards the opening of the box and as I approached it, the light changed from black to dark blue. The scattered clouds sailed by and disappeared. leaving the sky clear for some minutes, with the new moon sharing its light with us.

I was holding my breath as to not break the moment of watching Shakespeare move around the courtyard of his box. He seemed taller than expected, with long slinky legs. Billy appeared on the wall with his paws looking like a silhouette in the moonlight. I stood mesmerized watching Shakespeare moving freely around and watching Billy watching him.

Did they have some kind of interaction when humans were not around?

Did they "speak" and exchange stories about their confinement and about their mundane life? Did they support each other like human cellmates would?

I felt honoured to be given a glimpse into their night-time.

Shakespeare graciously got up on his hind legs to look over the shrubs that were growing across the path on the other side of the fence.

Was he dreaming of the times he could run free? Dreaming of when he had a life with Agatha and their pups? Was that the place by the fence ahead of him where Agatha would visit him with only metres dividing their worlds? A wave of grief for him made the tears come back. All this dog had lost. He seemed so utterly alone, so lonely, as he stood on his back legs whilst his claws were holding on to the mesh in the gate, staring towards the horizon. Gazing into the dark evening, towards liberty.

The moment was broken by the headlights of a car climbing in the distance and I knew it was C. No one else would come to the plateau at that time of the evening as there was nothing to come there for. Before any of the dogs could react, Shakespeare grazed my leg, shooting back into his box and into the corner.

I felt my way around and went and sat by him, stroked him, and as on cue the female at the gate started barking.

Leaning forward, kissing Shakespeare on his head I whispered

Please go and curl up on your bed when I have gone.

I love you and you will come home to France to a new life; A life filled with fields to run and no mesh between you and the horizon. I promise. I will see you tomorrow.

> **My Crown is in my heart, not on my head**:
> Not deck'd with Diamonds, and Indian stones:
> Nor to be seen: my Crown is call'd Content,
> A Crown it is, that seldom Kings enjoy.
> -William Shakespeare, *Henry VI*

Half way through my stay, C and I had been on a mission to rescue five pups that had been discarded in the freezing mountains - thrown out like garbage and left to die. It is very rare that I get angry as anger steals my focus but that night, I had been angry. How could anyone do this?

It was a local farmer that had been in the mountainside to look for wild asparagus that had heard the pups and called C. I think everyone on the island knew of C and SPDC as the go-to place when it came to abandoned dogs. The farmer had met us by the roadside to show us where he had heard the petrified high squeaks. C and I split up searching in different directions following the sounds - the cries of babies freezing to death. They had not managed to stay together, and the two weakest ones had been separated from the others. C found three pups in the sloping terrain, and I found two under low vegetation where the landscape was flat. They were skeletons. They carried the smell of fear. The small bodies were trembling and shaking. They were all in shock and in a state of panic as they were searching for their mum who of course were nowhere to be found. They had been driven into the mountains to die.

All the pups were desperate, but a tiny one was in worst condition then the rest and closer to death. A little girl. She was dying from hypothermia. I unzipped my thermo jumper and put her inside next to my skin.

We returned to C's house where there in reality was no room but C who always sought solutions to every situation made room in the basement and with that, added another five dogs to care for.

The pups were flea-infested to a degree I had never seen before and as we bathed the little girl to get rid of some of the fleas, we were both overwhelmed with grief for these small creatures that had not been on this earth more than six weeks and already had experienced such a dreadful reality. The pups were fed with high-quality emergency puppy milk and high-quality food.

All but one curled up and went to sleep under a heat lamp Andreas had rigged for them, but C and I brought the little girl into the kitchen. There, we put her in a fur bucket I had brought from France.

The fur buckets are made from real fur from old coats donated to different associations in France, who then gave the coats to my association. There, the coats are cut up and sewn into buckets with real fur on the inside, and fabric on the outside. This simple trick of recycling the fur of animals that had given their life for the fashion industry, to rescue living animals, carried some poetic justice. So many pups and kittens have been saved this way and the bucket without question saved the life of that little girl that evening. It lay on the kitchen table with the pup inside and like an awakening, life slowly returned. Later in the evening Lupin and I were joined in the bed by the pup, still in the fur-bucket. She was still weak, and as the night progressed, I checked her every hour until dawn – she was still alive.

This tiny pup who showed every sign of surviving, who I had carried inside my jumper, had left me with a terrible allergic reaction to flea bites. The whole of my upper body was covered in lumps. I was itching like crazy and running a fever. I contacted my GP in France who told me what I needed to buy.

I needed a pharmacy, and it was decided I would hitch a lift with C who kindly dropped me off by Ledra Street, in the middle of the old city in Nicosia. It was ten in the morning and C would be back to pick me up just after lunch. This way I would get to be tourist for a couple of hours whilst C went to clear travel documents for SPDC dogs that were leaving the island to travel to their new homes.

It was a grey cold morning as I walked down the famous shopping street with bars, boutiques, chain stores, independent shops, and restaurants in search of a pharmacy. There was little that reminded me of the bustling city of summer tourism. The pharmacy was easily spotted by the green neon cross on the wall, flashing happily in the cold wind. The pharmacist was kind and gave me what I needed with some added recommendations. From there I headed for to the closest café, to have warm chocolate and water to swallow the small arsenal of tablets from the pharmacy bag.

It was a simple little café with odd chairs and Lebanese music and suddenly I felt very far away from home. I missed my husband and my pack.

The young girl who brought me hot chocolate and a bottle of Perrier was stunningly beautiful, with olive skin and dark long wavy hair and a film-star smile. We chatted before I pulled out my phone to check emails and messages.

I had not kept on top of all my messages because I had been with Shakespeare for so much of the time, and there were close to no cell phone coverage at the sanctuary, and to be honest - I was emotionally exhausted. Meeting Shakespeare had taken its toll.

My rescue association was in reality only me and a few foster homes. This meant I did all the work myself, answering queries, pre-adoption interviews, home visits pre-adoption, contact with vets, payment of vet bills, follow up of adoption families, often transporting the dog home over long distances. I also helped families that had adopted blind or shut down dogs from other associations who were struggling to make it work. I had supported families in UK, US, Germany, Italy, Portugal, Sweden, and as far away as Australia and of course in France. Before I had left France to go to Cyprus, I had cleared my calendar but that did of course not mean people did not contact me. One of the messages I saw immediately was from my friend Monika-Andrea Kovacs, an extraordinary rescuer based in North Romania. I knew Monika well and we had worked together on several occasions. If she came across a blind dog, she would contact me.

I opened the message with trepidation as to what I would find. The photo made me gulp for air. I was trying not to cry but it was to no avail. The tears came as I looked at the photo again. It was a picture of a dog in the gutter amongst beer bottles and garbage. The dog that looked like a German Shepherd mix was half sitting, looking to have given up on life. Monika's message read.

This is Baxter. He was hit by a car and left to die in the gutters. He is blind. The lady who found him said he was silently asking to be put out of his misery and pain.

Can you take him?

It was one of those situations where I did not need time to reflect.

I typed.

Dear Monika

This is beyond heart-breaking. Of course, I will take him, and I will find him a home. I am in Cyprus at the moment but please do whatever he needs, and I will fundraise for the cost.

I could see by the small dot that came up to the right of my response that she was online, and she responded immediately.

He is suffering from trichiasis. His leg is damaged.

I typed back, *Just have the surgery done and I will forward money to cover it.*

Trichiasis means in-growing eye lashes. It is overly represented in some breeds and when Monika said she thought he was a Shar Pei and GSD mix that made perfect sense as trichiasis is over-represented in Shar Pei bred together with Pekingese, English Cocker Spaniels, Bulldogs and Pugs, although not exclusive to these breeds. The surgery is so easy and quick, but this dog had suffered - with every blink of his eyes taking him closer to blindness until he had stepped out in the road, blind, and a car had hit him. Instead of helping the dog, the driver had dumped him unconscious in the gutter.

Monika and I chatted a bit more on Messenger. She already had Baxter with her and between us his life would become better than he could ever have dreamt of. He was already on pain medication and the surgery would happen the following week.

The girl at the café must have seen me cry as she brought me another warm chocolate and by the cup was a homemade biscuit. *From my mum* she said and nudged her head in the direction of the open kitchen door. The act of kindness did not stop my tears, rather the opposite as her gesture deeply touched me. It felt like the young lady and her mum had shown me, just in that moment when I needed it the most, that there are always kind humans out there.

I did not answer any more messages or open my email app. I had been shaken by the photo of Baxter. I felt fragile and all I really wanted was to go and see Shakespeare as my time in Cyprus was running out.

The course of true love
never did run smooth.
-William Shakespeare, *A Midsummer Night's Dream*

The plane was filled to the last seat. The familiar routine of getting settled into a flight seat and out of the way, so that my fellow passengers could also settle, was an automatic motion. I had spent so much time onboard planes in my former business life that I easily could be on auto pilot. Habitually, I had booked a window seat where I sat motionless staring at the tarmac. I did not hear nor see anyone around me. I was numb and had no excitement for this journey.

I also felt sadness over the fact that I had no joy over the accomplished mission of being safely onboard the flight with three blind dogs in the aeroplane belly beneath my feet, as it truly was an incredible mission completed. I had left my own cats, dogs, and my husband, for a week to do this - get the three blind dogs to France, but I only felt sorrow. Deep intense sorrow for leaving Shakespeare behind. I felt as if I were letting him down in the worst way possible. I had showed him there could be a connection and then, then, I had walked away without the possibility to make him understand I would come back for him. To make him understand I was not abandoning him. When I walked away it was with the knowledge he would soon be back in his emotionally black hole. Alone!

The evening before my return flight, I had sat next to Shakespeare stroking him.

He had curled up, taken a deep sigh, and gone to sleep again. I knew how huge it was. Him sleeping next to me was one of the biggest compliments I would ever be granted.

By his action Shakespeare was showing me that he trusted me. He trusted I would never harm him and that I would warn him should any danger arise. He felt safe on my watch.

I had got to know Shakespeare a bit during those days I spent with him, and I knew, trust was something Shakespeare rarely, if ever, shared with anyone.

Shakespeare had sat in a corner for five years without moving. No one had ever seen him stand up. He had never communicated or interacted with any human. He would tremble by the sound and sight of a human, and yet, there he was - curled up lying next to me sleeping as I stroked him and spoke to him in whispers.

Shakespeare had never eaten whilst humans were on the property. He only ate during the night and yet, the last afternoon, he had taken a small piece of dried duck out of my hand. He had not chewed it as to let his taste buds come alive, he had swallowed the small piece without even moving his jaws, or making the piece touch his teeth. It felt like he took the dried duck for my sake and not because he wanted it. He only took that one small piece and nothing more, but it felt like such a generous gesture. He had not looked at me nor had he expressed any joy, but it was a huge breakthrough.

Shakespeare had left his bed, stood up and walked out into the courtyard when he and I had sat in the dark after night fall on the fifth evening. He had told me in so many ways he trusted me.

Whilst sitting with him I had tried to imagine Shakespeare and Agatha getting caught together with their pups, taken from their life in liberty, separated, and later for Agatha to manage to escape her captivity at the sanctuary only to refuse to leave. Agatha stayed because her beloved Shakespeare was still there, enclosed in a concrete box, in solitude, still in captivity. Her choice to stay, to be close to him had cost her, her life.

Killed by the bite of snake.

Did Shakespeare know she was dead? Was his grief over her death one of the reasons he had given up on life? Did his will to live die with Agatha? I truly believed it was a part of the answer.

I kept looking at him sleeping. This stunningly beautiful maroon coloured dog, with white spotted knee socks and amber eyes, had stood up in my presence - had taken a tiny treat out of my hand and had gone to sleep next to me, was somehow now a part of me.

I leaned forward and kissed his head; *I will be back for you. I promise. You will come to France to live with me, with Captain Hastings, Japp, Hercule, Lady Eileen Bundle Brent. Lady will know you as she will know your fear. Countess Elena will be there, Isabel and Miss Grey and the cats also. You will meet Miss Marple, Miss Lemon, Mrs Oliver, and Mademoiselle Milesi. You will live with Are who is an extraordinary and kind man, and you will have your own large garden. We will watch days become night and seasons silently float into each other. You will have a life. I promise. I will do whatever it takes. I promise!*

Kneeling next to his bed, as I had done so many times during those days I had been in his presence, I kept promising, as I unknotted my pink and white bandana and put it in his bed before I got up.

I was shaking and moved in a daze, leaving him behind as I walked towards the gate of his enclosure. One foot in front of the other, creating distance. As I closed the second gate behind me, I wanted to run back and open the first gate again. Open it with such force that the gate hinges would come off the pole. Then rush back, rip off the second gate, the one that kept Shakespeare confined and scoop him up and hold him. Hold him tight and tell him it would be OK. Everything would change. After, I would carry him to the car, and he would travel home to France with me.

It was of course impossible.

Shakespeare was a large petrified, broken dog who was not going anywhere on that late winters' day.

I wanted to throw up. I wanted to scream, but instead I sat quietly in the car with nothing to say, concentrating on holding back my tears, leaving the sanctuary behind us, one kilometre at a time. I did not want supper and went straight to the bedroom carrying the pup in the fur-bucket, with Lupin walking next to me. We curled up into a ball and I cried into the fur of Lupins back, with a pup snuggled up inside the fur bucket resting by my pillow. Lupin lay completely still.

I cried for her, that she had lost her eyes because someone had shot her in her face. I cried for Shakespeare who had been caught and separated from Agatha. I cried for the fact that I had to leave without taking him with me. I cried for the pups, and for Baxter that had been thrown away like garbage. I cried for all the neglect, abuse, and horrific suffering every rescuer saw every day in our rescue lives.

Lupin's fur was wet from tears that trickled down onto the pillow and soon the pillowcase was wet as well.

The trail of tears had no end. I knew that when I left Shakespeare, he would sink back into his black hole. It would not even be a matter of days. He was already back in his own darkness. The breakthroughs Shakespeare had had with me in his concrete box at the sanctuary, on the beautiful mountain plateau in Cyprus, had no value at all. As all I had done was show him there could be a connection, and then I walked away. How was I ever to get him to trust me?

I sobbed, at first with sound and then a whisper of despair. Later, at some point the emotional exhaustion got the better of me and it all subsided into regular breathing. Lupin was snoring and I could hear the pup's regular soft breathing.

We laid curled up together without moving until the alarm went off at four am and it was time for Lupin, Sir Henry, and Andy to get into their flight crates and for us all to head for the airport. Time for the pup to join the others under the heat lamp in C's basement.

It was hard to let go.

Sir Henry who had been in a foster home arrived as we were getting the small van belonging to SPDC ready for the airport run - and by this the focus was shifted. It was a cold, crisp, starlit night without the rain that had greeted me when I arrived in Cyprus only a week earlier. It seemed like a lifetime ago. The dogs all went to sleep in their crates in the back of the car. We were alone in the universe: two women in a car with a cargo of three blind dogs.

As dawn broke, we checked in at the airport.

I opened the first crate and took out Sir Henry, the puppy Pocket Pointer.

Sir Henry was a most beautiful chocolate brown pup with silk ears. I did not know why he was blind, but I suspected trauma to his head, but I would find out at the specialist animal hospital in Bordeaux after I was safely back in France. He licked my face as I held him, sending his crate through the metal detector. I could hear the airport crew utter *Aaaaa* at the sight of the beautiful pup. Sir Henry went for another lick and for the first time since leaving Shakespeare I smiled. No one can ever be licked by a pup, smelling of that wonderful, sweet smell only babies carry, filled with enthusiasm for life, and not feel like giggling to join in the joy.

The crate passed through the metal detector without any alarms and as soon as it had been lifted back onto the floor, Sir Henry, still licking my face, could go back in. I returned and opened Lupin's crate. Lupin knew me and did not even hesitate as she stepped out. She willingly followed me through the airport metal detector, using her front paws to feel the surface. She trusted me explicitly so there was little hesitation as to the unfamiliar environment. Some researchers have found that dogs that are blind will develop new and more nerves in their paws making them capable of picking up the most minute changes to the surface they walk on.

Her crate went through another detector.

The airport crew was astonished that she so evidently did not have any eyes and in awe of how easily she moved around staying close to me.

Only once leaning slightly towards my leg for guidance. She wanted to stay with me and not go back in her crate but with some gentle guidance she gave in. I sat down on the floor and with her crate door open I stroked her and told her it would not be long before we were in Paris, and I would be there waiting for her.

I went back out for the last crate. Andy was a beautiful Springer Spaniel that C had rescued from the public pound. Andy had lived with C since the day she met him and C had named him Andy after her partner Andreas, to soften the blow of her bringing back yet another dog. In an act of selflessness C had asked me to find a home for him as her days were extremely busy and the steady stream of new rescue dogs that needed her attention, often of the medical kind, made it hard for her to give Andy the one-to-one attention she so desperately wanted for him. It is always a compliment when a fellow rescuer asks you to find a home for their dog, but it is also nerve-wracking as you do not want to get it wrong. C was crying. It was extremely hard for her to let her boy go, but she also knew that if she wanted the best possible life for Andy, he would have to live in another home where there was more time for him. She said goodbye to him with tears streaming down her cheeks from behind her glasses.

I handed over the crates to the handling crew that would make sure the dogs were well taken care of until I would see them again at Charles de Gaulle Airport in Paris. The crates were all each clearly marked "blind dog" and as the dogs were transported onboard the plane, I hugged Constantine goodbye leaving her with my promise.

The first thing I will do when I get home is to book a return flight, so that I can come back to pick up Shakespeare.

I did of course not know that it was a promise I would not be able to keep.

> Doubt thou the stars are fire;
> Doubt that the sun doth move;
> Doubt truth to be a liar;
> But **never doubt I love**.
> - William Shakespeare, *Hamlet*

The trip to Athens, for connection to Paris, was uneventful and everything seemed to happen in slow motion. I would not be seeing Lupin, Andy, or Sir Henry before we landed in Paris. At the airport in Athens - an airport I knew well from past travels - I walked toward the toilets furthest away from the crowds as I wanted to take simple steps to keep myself from getting the Covid virus that had now spread to Europe. Few people were wearing masks and mostly the virus was something that did not concern the greater masses. On my return – only a week after my departure - there did however seem to be a stronger underlying nervousness amongst travellers. No one really knew what this new virus meant. The news headlines were competing in worst case scenario death numbers, but looking back it was still the "quiet" before the storm. I found toilets that were unused as the cleaner left as I entered. I splashed my face with cold water, put on some lipstick in an attempt to make myself feel somewhat better. This was slightly ridiculous because the lipstick did not cover up the fact that my eyes were read and puffed after I had been crying most of the way from Larnaca to Athens.

I had two hours before my flight to Paris and in that time, I had two missions: to check availability on return flight to Cyprus and at some point, find someone who was willing to help me push three large dog crates through customs upon arrival in Paris. It was simply not physically possible for me to push three trollies by myself. I bought a black coffee in a thin paper cup, and, fingers burning, headed for a quiet corner near the departure lounge where I could charge my mobile.

I miss you so and I cannot wait to see you. I love you xxx

The text message left my phone with a swoosh and seconds later the phone released a cheerful pling with the response from Are.

I have missed you so much too. I love you. We are getting closer to Paris. All is well. See you soon. Safe flight xxx

The "we" in the message was Are driving one of our cars, and Amanda and Tim, Lupin's new parents driving their own car to pick up Lupin. There was no way any ordinary hatchback could have room for three huge flight crates, so Amanda and Tim would come and pick up Lupin straight from the airport.

In between eating a sandwich and drinking my coffee I switched my attention to the Aegean Airlines app on my phone. If I flew out on an early morning flight via Athens, I would be able to go straight to the sanctuary and simply just stay in Shakespeare's box with him and fly back late the next day. Or I could stay for a couple of days. I still was not sure how we would get him into a flight crate, but I knew there would be a solution. C, Katy, and Elena prepped dogs for flights all the time and whilst Shakespeare was far from an ordinary case, I knew it would solve itself.

Today was the 28th of February 2020. I could see there was a flight Athens - Bordeaux on the 2nd of April.

The first flight of the summer season. That would be thirty-four days wait to get him home. I would fly out of Paris some days before and fly back to Bordeaux. In the winter season there were only flights to and from Paris but come summer, the itinerary changed. It would make sense to wait for the flight to Bordeaux - only two hours' drive from home -instead of the five hours' drive from Paris. If I waited until 2nd April, it would give me time to settle things at home, block my rescue calendar and stay at home with Shakespeare after his arrival. I had several rescue cases waiting for me upon my return with Lupin and the others. My to-do list included finding Sir Henry and Baxter their permanent homes. Sir Henry was staying with us until he was adopted and finding him his permanent home could easily take a month. April 2nd it was.

As I was in line to board the plane to Paris, I started to look around for a dog lover - someone who would help me push a trolley through the customs to meet Are, Amanda and Tim on the other side. The person standing next to me was a cool, hip young man of African descent and as the queue of passengers moved forward to board we started chatting. First about how slow the queue was moving, then about where we had been. He asked me if I had enjoyed my holiday in Cyprus. I smiled and responded by telling him about my mission of bringing the three blind dogs back to France with me.

Three blind dogs? He sounded like he could not believe it.

Are they on the plane? Now? On the same plane as us?

I laughed by the shocked expression on his face. He even removed his large headphones that he had hanging round his neck. I had a clear feeling he did this to make sure he truly heard what I said and that he was not misunderstanding me. *Yes, they are in the belly of the plane, in the cargo area, but not together with the suitcases*, I smiled. I went on to explain that they were in what is called "Hold 5", a fit-for-purpose compartment at the rear of the plane for carrying animals. The dogs have the same temperature and pressure as in the cabin. I assured him that most dogs curl up and go to sleep. I smiled, trying to make him relax and understand that it was safe for the dogs to travel this way. After he was over the initial shock, he asked me question about how to recognise if a dog would be aggressive towards a human, and in between he smiled the most beautiful smile. I explained to him what signs to look for in a dog that was warning you: holding ears erect or flattening them along their skull, snapping, low growling, having the tail erect, moving from side to side or circling you, snarling, trying to stare you down. I also told him that with some dogs there would be no warning before they would bite. *If your gut instinct is telling you to stay clear, that is exactly what you should do. Never go against your instinct in interactions with animals* I told him. He thanked me. *It is so important that we all respect each other, humans, and animals alike as we share this planet.*

I wanted to clone him, and he made it easy to ask him if he would help me push the trolleys with the crates. In response he smiled another beautiful smile.

Yes of course I will.

I wanted to hug him, before I cloned him, but I restrained myself, and simply squeezed his arm and thanked him.

See you in Paris I said as we headed to our seats onboard the flight.

Bien sur, he smiled in return still looking a bit baffled over the conversation we had just had.

Three blind dogs I heard him murmur to himself, as he moved his head from one side to another. I smiled. My blind dog rescue often had that effect on people. We touched down in Paris in the same freezing cold winds but at least there was sunshine, trying its hardest to send some warmth.

The dogs arrived without any hiccoughs or delay at the airport's baggage claim section. They were all calm and had obviously been sleeping. They made no fuss until they heard my voice and Lupin barked one bark to say hello. People were of course curious as to these large flight crates all so clearly marked "Blind Dog." The young man and I pushed the trolleys through without any effort, helped by someone from the airport staff, meaning one trolley each. Safely out on the other side, I bid my travel companion farewell after having met his family who was there to pick him up. His mother, a stunningly beautiful woman in a citrus yellow African costume, brought the warmth the sun could not deliver. I secretly did not think his mum quite believed I was travelling with three blind dogs, until her son pulled her by the arm over to the crates parked side by side. Then Are, Amanda and Tim were there. I was exhausted but felt such a spurt of joy at seeing them. Are held me, hugging me tight. Soon I would be home.

I sat down in front of Lupin's crate and opened the door.

Hello darlin girl, welcome to France. Soon you will be home sweetheart. You mum and dad are here to greet you.

Lupin put her nose in the air and vibrated her nostrils. Where her eyes once had been, before someone shot her in the face and she had undergone the enucleation surgery, there was now fur but still visible scars from the stitches. Shot gun pellets remained in her skull. It had been too dangerous to remove them. The hope was that they would stay put and not wander. This girl with the most incredible will to live, put one paw in front of the other and stepped out of her crate. It took two steps for her body to be out of the crate and she touched my knee with her nose. I lifted her up and put my face into her fur. The smell of her, her story, my journey to get her home, the warmth of her company in Cyprus would always stay with me.

I kept my promise to you Lupin. You will be going home to the most wonderful life. I was emotionally completely overwhelmed, exhausted after the trip and no sleep for the last thirty-six hours. I kissed her on her head, and she turned her nose towards me and as she did, I handed her to Amanda. With my phone I took one of my absolute favourite rescue photos. It shows Amanda holding Lupin, the black girl with the silky soft fur and no eyes, with such care and affection as if scared Lupin would break. It was a moment revealing fragility, longing, generosity, and   tenderness.

The photo sums up what rescue is truly all about: hope, love, and new beginnings.

> My soul is **in the sky**.
> -William Shakespeare,
> *A Midsummer Night's Dream*

It was wonderful to be back home and what a welcome - wagging tails, licking tongues, paws holding on to me. Captain Hastings tried to climb on my lap as soon as I sat down like he always did, thinking he was a lap dog, at forty-three kilos. Endless sniffing as to determine where I had been and with whom, but they eventually settled on their beds scattered in the kitchen. Are had prepared the most wonderful seafood meal before leaving for Paris to pick me up, and now he opened a bottle of champagne as a welcome home. It was wonderful to be back with my pack. I was worried I would break the magic as I needed to tell Are that Shakespeare would be coming home. The topic of bringing another dog permanently into a household, where one party, in this case me, had promised not to increase the number of animals, was a balancing act. The difference this time was that it was not one of the bargaining situations where I would back down.

I started by showing Are a photo of Shakespeare sloped over in his box and I saw Are tear up. *What on earth*? I showed him all the photos and some of the videos, and he simply said: *let us do it. Let us bring him home*! My husband is an easy man to love.

As if the stars were aligned for Shakespeare's homecoming, my beautiful friend Verity sent me money for the plane ticket, from a memorial fund in the name of her daughter Madeleine Maria – Maddie - who had tragically died a few years before, at the tender age of eleven years old. Verity had always been my mentor in the rescue world. She had always supported my work and had followed my journey with Shakespeare closer than anyone else, as I had sent her video updates from Cyprus every day. Verity had cried with me, and she truly understood more than anyone why Shakespeare belonged with me in France.

On the 30th of January 2020, before I had even left France for Cyprus, the WHO had declared the COVID virus a public health emergency of international concern. I booked my return flight ticket to Cyprus, confirmed 2nd April 2020 crossing all I had that COVID would not throw spanners in my travel wheels.

Katy from SPDC booked me a room with a neighbour in Cyprus for a couple of nights and I would hire a car at the airport so I could easily go back and forth to the sanctuary to be with Shakespeare. I would spend my days with him in his box when I was there, and we would travel home together. I tried not to pay close attention to the news headlines about COVID that now started talking about flight restrictions. I had a busy schedule both with rescue and at home, and I was determined to focus on the tasks at hand and not pay attention to the growing uneasiness and the fear I was feeling.

I had several emergency rescues after I arrived home from Cyprus and I went to pick up the biggest Pointer I had ever met, a stunningly beautiful blind boy that came from Monika-Andrea Kovacs in North Romania, who had Baxter. I had found the Pointer later named Brunsky, a wonderful home in France. I also had Sir Henry staying with me. Sir Henry was happy with us, but having a new blind pup around demanded my presence. I already had a blind dog, one with limited sight, two born deaf dogs and some emotionally damaged dogs. Bringing a new pup into the equation restructured the pack with some of my wilful females wanting to mother Sir Henry, so it was impossible to leave them all alone together even under the guidance of Captain Hastings.

I actively wrote posts about Sir Henry on my rescue page, in my search for his forever family, and a friend of an earlier adopter stepped forward. Sir Henry found his new family in England. I was absolutely thrilled, and so happy that he now would go on to live a long happy life. All I had to do was to find a way of getting Sir Henry from France to England and again, things just fell into place with my friend Stuart being at his summer house in our hamlet. On 11th March 2020, WHO declared COVID to be a pandemic and the talk about shutting everything down and closing the borders was now on every news broadcast. It was decided that Stuart would take Sir Henry back to England with him in the early morning hours of 17th March 2020. When Sir Henry crossed into England, he just managed to get his tail inside the border before everything slammed shut. On the evening of the same day, it was announced that all airports around the world would close for two weeks. I hurriedly rebooked my flight ticket to Cyprus, not knowing I would rebook the same journey six times - and would never get to go.

Over the next days and weeks, I contacted friends and former colleagues in the airline industry to see if they knew more than the public.

It was a dramatic situation playing out live, minute by minute, and the insiders in the airline industry knew as little or as much as us all. There was no drill. It was unreal! When I spoke to former contacts and I told them that I was desperate to get to Cyprus to bring a dog back to France, every single one, without fail, had the same reaction: *What do you mean a dog? A dog?*

I knew that it was impossible for people to understand that for me, getting Shakespeare out almost felt like a matter of life and death.

As the weeks passed and the airports did not open, I kept rebooking my ticket. I also started to investigate the option of cargo transport for Shakespeare. I spoke to lots and lots of cargo flight handlers, and they all said the same. Impossible!

There simply was no ordinary cargo traffic either. My last attempt was to contact someone I know who has his own private plane. He patiently explained that no take-off or landing permission was granted for anyone, so there would be no solution. As supermarket shelves were emptied and people were being confined at home, there was a tangible fear everywhere. The number of dead was rising by the hour, but I only had one thought in my head; to get Shakespeare home.

I even looked at driving to Cyprus. One can of course not drive to an island without crossing the water, so boat or ferry was needed - there simply was no solution and even I, with my immense determination and huge network could not change or solve this. My PTSD flared up, not because of COVID as that situation by itself was something I handled well, but because I could not get Shakespeare out. I had promised him. I had promised!

I remember, even writing to Katy in Cyprus that I was petrified Shakespeare would die before I could get him out. Katy, who of course had not lost her mind, calmly responded: *Why would he die?* I knew I did not make sense, but my fear truly was that if he were to die, I would not be able to live with myself as I could have gone back the day after I had first returned from Cyprus. By trying to be sensible, in planning my return 2nd April, I had not prioritised him enough.

I felt like I was going crazy and somehow love does that to you.

It makes you crazy!

> **But where there is true friendship**, there needs none.
> -William Shakespeare, *Timon of Athens*

Parallel to trying to find a solution to getting Shakespeare home I had my own dogs to care for: Captain Hastings, Hercule Poirot, Inspector James D. Japp, Miss Kathryn Grey, Lady Eileen Bundle Brent, Isabel Duveen, and Countess Elena. I also had my cats: Miss Lemon, Mrs Adriana Oliver, Miss Marple and Mademoiselle Milesi and as always, my pack of seven dogs and four cats were my balance. I would get up early to walk my dogs. Everyone else was in confinement during those early months of 2020 and so were we, but if you had dogs you were permitted to walk them. In France, you could walk in a radius of a kilometre from your home and the walk had to be limited to an hour, twice a day. I had three different walking routes I always took. One was ten kilometres and would take me in a loop through the farmers' fields and through a large woodland. The second was a five-kilometres route that would also take me in a loop but through the vines. The third alternative was up the tractor track and through the woods that had given name to our address and that had been the backdrop of our wedding photos. I knew those woods like I knew my inner landscape. It was a two-kilometre loop.

I opted for the longest walk daily. I needed to keep busy. Our home was so remote that during the months of confinement I just once saw a farmer, who I waved to from a distance. Apart from him, I saw or met no one. Are and I tried to get on top of odd jobs at home and there were many of them. We lived on a large property from the 1800s, and although we had totally renovated the house, there were enough jobs to keep us busy for months to come.

I liked the confinement apart from the stress of not being able to bring Shakespeare home. I started baking bread again, getting yeast and flour from a local baker, as there had been none in the shops for weeks. I baked cakes and scones. Baking has always been one of my favourite hobbies, as I find the whole process soothing. I loved every minute of those slow days but so wished Shakespeare were confined with us, at home in France, and not confined in his concrete box in Cyprus.

Are and I shared space and time with our pack and the cats and even started baking pizza, delivering to our elderly neighbours in the hamlet. It was a way of checking our neighbours were doing ok in those strangest of times.

There were no demands, nowhere to go, no one to see.

The rescue world was of course in panic when everything closed, but the French government was quick to put regulations in place, so I could still transport animals within France, and I did. Several dogs were adopted but I was as always extremely strict as I was fully aware that many would adopt during the confinement but an eventual return to work and ordinary life might leave the dogs destitute. I am happy to say that all the dogs I adopted out during the times of confinement - amongst them, born deaf Lieutenant Morris -have all stayed with their lovely families.

My dialogue with C, Katy and Elena in Cyprus was close and they were as eager to get dogs out as I was desperate to get Shakespeare home. And then, in the beginning of May, Elena contacted me with the news. Shakespeare was coming home. I could not stop crying and as Are walked through the door he looked panic stricken by the sight of me standing straight up and down with my mobile in my hand, sobbing. He thought I had had news that someone had passed. I simply could not stop crying. It was months of unreleased frustration, sadness and anxiety for Shakespeare that surfaced with a force I had not been prepared for.

He is coming home.

Christ all mighty. You scared me, Are said as he opened the fridge and pulled out a bottle of champagne.

Next morning it was time for me to tell my pack they would have a new brother named Shakespeare, arriving in Belgium on 18th May.

This meant going to the barn with seven dogs in tow, to find one of the large crates I had stacked against the wall. I moved some chairs in the hallway and put the crate up in a small nook by the toilet door and filled the crate with soft vintage feather down. On top of the crate, I put two dog coats I had made for Shakespeare sewn in the softest fleece material, two sheepskins, extra blankets, and Shakespeare's new water bowl.

The pack all followed me around, watching, sniffing. They knew what this meant and with everything set up it was time for the pack to visit the crate, sniff around and to take in the changes to the hallway. They all knew that a crate meant a new family member.

The only thing I would not let them do was to go asleep inside the crate as that could mean ownership and I did not want there to be any unclear reflections on whose crate this was: the crate belonged to Shakespeare, and it would be his den.

None of my dogs are crate-trained or have ever used a crate, but for a foster pup or foster kittens it can be a safe place to retract to, so I always had a crate or five at hand. For Shakespeare, a crate would be essential as there was no way he would be able to handle the overwhelming change of coming out of his box after five years and into a home environment without a place that belonged to him, where he could retreat. How long he would need the crate was not up to me but to him. It would be his decision and a decision in which I would not interfere.

I trust my pack explicitly and I had absolutely no concerns whatsoever about bringing Shakespeare home. Captain Hastings was the clear alpha, and he would rarely raise his voice but when he did - like when the lion roars before it dozily puts its head back on its paw - the pack would listen. Hastings and I were intertwined and all it took was a glance and he would sort out any problems that might arise. I left so much of the pack structure to Hastings, and I would rarely truly intervene. When I did step in, it would only be after I had let the natural interaction runs its course. I had learnt a long while back not to fear the worst outcome as that would make me step into a situation far too early and not let them figure it out amongst themselves. When you live with a pack of seven dogs there are of course challenges, and when you live with a pack of born blind, born deaf and broken-spirited dogs there are more challenges about boundaries than in an ordinary pack. But if the dogs are to teach each other boundaries, they need to *"feel each other's teeth"* as we say in Norway. My job was to hover over and observe and only step in if things were about to escalate out of control. It was rare I had to say anything and normally a *"Hey!"* would be enough.

Are and I spoke a lot about how we thought the alliances in the pack would change when Shakespeare arrived.

We both thought that Shakespeare would seek support from two of the dogs, Lady Eileen Bundle Brent, and Countess Elena. Shakespeare and Lady would intuitively know each other because they both suffer from PTSD. Lady was our Bruno de Jura mix - an ancient breed directly related to the Saint-Hubert Hound, better known as the English Bloodhound. Both breeds are scent hounds, and the Bruno de Jura comes from the Jura region of France, originally used for game hunting.

Lady had been found abandoned in a forest where she had dug a hole so that she could give birth to her pups. She was alone and tried to fend for the pups the best she could. One of the pups, later named Lola, followed another dog home, and sat in the courtyard crying. The local refuge was alerted, and they caught Lady and her pups. I met Lady at the refuge where she had been for around two years. Her name then was Lulu. She was a petrified dog who no one could touch. I fell intensely in love with her and brought her home.

We were convinced that Lady would offer Shakespeare emotional support of the kind none of the others could. She would help him back on his feet.

Countess Elena is our forty-five kilos Dogo Argentino. She was born with very limited hearing due to the hereditary congenital white gene (CSD) and in Elena's case she also had limited vision. Dogo Argentino is a pure white Mastiff dog that originates from the planes of Argentina and is an illegal breed in many countries. The breed originates with the mix of Great Dane and a strong Pitbull-terrier-like breed that no longer exists. The result is a white muscled dog that looks like a Pitbull in XXL!

Elena had been dumped over the fence of a refuge as a week-old pup, in a different part of France to me, on a cold December night some years before. She came to us for me to evaluate her as she was diagnosed as permanently blind and deaf. She arrived and simply never left and was raised by our Staffie-mix Miss Kathryn Grey, our dog born without eyes.

With time Elena gained some very limited sight and hearing but the vets still considered her deaf as the hearing was very limited.

Elena was an obvious choice for Shakespeare to make an alliance with as she was by far the physically strongest dog in the pack with her forty-five kilos of muscle mass. Elena was also the peacekeeper - always defending the weakest part in any confrontation, something any dog would quickly observe. If there was anything brewing, she would follow Captain Hastings example and physically go in between to defuse the situation. No one argued with her.

Both Are and I suspected Countess Elena was the future pack leader, but Hastings did not think she was ready and nor did we. She did have some amazing qualities about her despite - or maybe because of her deafness and lack of sight, that one day would make her into a fantastic pack leader.

On the morning of 17th May 2020, on Norway's National Day and Miss Kathryn Grey's birthday, I said goodbye to the pack and Are, and drove my car away from our property in the lush, green vine growing nowhere, heading for Belgium, and Liege Airport to pick up Shakespeare. Our boy was finally coming home!

> **I have a journey, sir**,
> shortly to go;
> My master calls me, I
> must not say no.
> -William
> Shakespeare, *King Lear*

I sat in line in my car, waiting at the closed border between France and Belgium. Europe were just over two months into the COVID pandemic, and everything felt uneasy, unreal, and unfamiliar. I was in a line with three cars in front, and several cars behind me. There were police officers present at a makeshift border control check point. The police officers were all wearing firearms and masks, making the whole situation seem dramatic. I had come through here many times before and on several occasions, crossed the border without even knowing I had gone from one country to another. Normally the traffic was free-flowing, but COVID had changed all that, as it had so many things. It was no longer ordinary times.

My heart was almost leaping out of my chest. I was emotionally and physically exhausted. After months of waiting to get Shakespeare home, my seven-hour drive to the border, and lack of sleep, I had arrived at this exact border point moment.

Behind me, seven-hundred kilometres on ghost-like, empty motorway. If I were lucky enough to get across, I would still have another two-hundred kilometre to get to my destination at Liege Airport. Everything felt unreal. As there still was a travel ban in France, I had not seen more car than you could count on two hands after I had entered the motorway about twenty-five minutes from home. Apart from random police cars parked on the hard shoulders, the motorway was empty.

Each time I did pass one of the police cars I expected them to give chase and flag me down, but no one seemed interested in a small, champagne coloured A-class Mercedes with a Norwegian women on a journey to bring her beloved Shakespeare home.

It had been a long seven hours, where I had tried my best not to think what would happen if the police would not let me cross the border. I had been given a permit by the French officials to cross so I could go to Liege Airport and collect Shakespeare who was arriving on a cargo plane from Cyprus. But I also knew all too well that if the border police did not agree with the permit, they would not let me pass. This was France after all!

The police officers were taking their time with each of the three cars in front. Only essential travel was permitted and to cross the border, official permission or proof of transporting goods or livestock - that normally would have free flow between EU countries - now needed a permit. Early in the pandemic the French government had placed a transport permission in place for animal transport and my small non-profit association fell into the transport permit bracket. I had become good at reading the French governmental rules and exceptions and to fill out the continuously changing forms for transport of dogs during confinement, but no documents had been more important than the one in the file sitting on the seat next to me.

After I had got the confirmation from Elena in Cyprus that Shakespeare would arrive at Liege Airport, Belgium, on 18th

May, I started to prepare for that crossing. I had commented to Are that I did not care if I had to illegally walk across the border and continue on foot to the airport.

What I would do there, after Shakespeare had arrived, I had not figured out, but I was sure I would come up with a plan. In Norway we say, *"nudity quickly teaches a woman to yarn."*

The first of the cars in front moved forward, and after a couple of minutes did a U-turn heading back into France. He had not been granted permission to cross. My heart sank. The same happened to the second car. The car in front of me was a dark royal blue Volvo hatchback and I could see two children in the back seat. It had French license plates from the North coastal region. It was an eternity before the Volvo moved forward before it did the same U-turn back into France. Through the Volvo's side window, I could see the driver's angry face and one of the children obviously crying in the back seat.

I was holding my breath as my car aligned with the heavily armed police officer. The officer was standing alone whilst five mask-free colleagues had gathered on the lawn stones-throw away, for a coffee and cigarette break.

Bonjour Madame, quelle est votre destination finale ? I responded in French and before he could ask me too many questions, I handed him the folder of documents I had spent the last five days preparing. In the file was every document I had been able to think of. The first page was the all-important permit from the public office in France, giving me permission to cross the border to go to Liege Airport, in Belgium, to pick up a dog. Shakespeare was considered livestock; hence he was under the exception of travel ban rules.

There were official stamped documents showing the legal status of my association and copies of my passport, stamped by the mayor of our village confirming my identity and that I was the president of my association.

I had also included a copy of my driving licence more so to make the file look as thick as possible.

He glanced at the first documents but did not turn the page to look at the other documents. Holding the folder open he looked at me with curiosity.

What will you be doing at Liege airport, Madam.

He had friendly eyes above a black mask, and he caught himself leaning forward towards me as he asked the question, but pulled himself back in reflex, remembering there was a pandemic, and I could potentially be carrying the virus. We were all getting used to this new virus that had already killed so many. From behind my own mask, I welled up, trying to hold back my tears as I quickly told him the story of how I had waited for Shakespeare to arrive. How I had met him in Cyprus when I was there to pick up the blind dogs.

Blind dogs? The officer looked baffled, whilst I carried on talking, explaining I ran an association specialised in helping blind dogs. I quickly thought that if I needed to, I would say Shakespeare was blind. At that point I found I would have been willing to say anything to get across the border. I simply could not turn back.

With trembling hands, I reached into my bag and pulled out my phone and with a swipe on the screen up came a photo of Shakespeare. It was one of the photos of Shakespeare sloped over against the wall of his concrete box, broken, looking more dead than alive.

The police officer took my phone and looked at the photo as he did not quite believe what he saw.

The expression in his eyes softened and I suspected he had a dog at home or had had a dog growing up.

He handed me back my file of documents, all neatly held in a pink folder with the words "Dream like a unicorn" in gold letters printed on the front.

The police officer also handed me my phone back and simply said *I wish you and your beautiful dog a lot of happiness together. Bon courage et bon voyage.* His eyes smiled. He stepped back as he tapped the roof of my car and waved me through, before stopping the car behind me.

Some hundred metres into Belgium I pressed record with a shaking hand and recorded a video message to Are and Verity, telling them I had crossed the border. After the message was sent, my journey continued on empty roads.

I had booked a hotel room at the SAS Hotel at Liege Airport as Shakespeare would not arrive before the next day. It would be impossible to drive eighteen hours roundtrip nonstop, and I wanted to grant myself plenty of time for the journey in case of border disruptions. My plan had then been to find another border crossing if needed and for that I would have needed extra travel time. I would have tried every single crossing existing, but there I was, having arrived safely without any hiccoughs whatsoever. Tired but filled with hope I parked in front of the hotel. The car park held just two cars. Like the motorways, the hotel was empty. I had a whole floor to myself.

In the night I kept waking up checking the time impatiently waiting for it to become the morning of the day Shakespeare and I would be back together.

The next morning finally arrived, with sunshine and breakfast served in a paper bag outside my door by an invisible person. All restaurants in Europe were closed and that included the breakfast room of any hotel. The breakfast bag contained an apple, yogurt and a wrapped sandwich that came with a cup of coffee in a paper cup.
In my previous career I had spent more hours in hotels around the world then I cared to remember, not always having time to enjoy luxury during quick overnight stops, but that morning I loved the quietness around me. It felt exclusive, and the bathroom boasted a huge bathtub.

I had all day ahead, as the flight would arrive at 21.30 in the evening.

I tied my jogging shoes and ventured outside. I could see the different terminals in the distance, and I knew the flight would arrive at the terminal marked Horse Inn. As I got closer, I easily found the building placed between the glass main terminal and the aviation tower on a completely deserted airport. I was the only human around. I messaged the transport group set up by Elena in Cyprus and told the transport drivers where the terminal was. They would be there to pick up the other dogs arriving on the same flight. Now all I could do was wait and check for flight updates. I had the flight number, so the flight app on my phone would show when the flight took off from Cyprus. I did however see early on that the flight would be delayed.

It was late leaving Dubai where the cargo plane had picked up horses for transport to Liege, before the plane would be picking up the dogs in Cyprus. Loading the dogs would also take time. I went back to the hotel to do what I had done so much during those months before: wait.

> **A victory is twice itself**
> when the achiever brings
> home full numbers.
> - William Shakespeare,
> *Much Ado About Nothing*

I had left Shakespeare behind on the 28th of February 2020, and he was coming home today – the 18Th of May 2020.

Eighty days. I had waited eighty days.

One-thousand-nine-hundred-and-twenty hours after I had left him in Cyprus, thinking I soon would be back for him, the moment of reunion was finally there.

The large cargo plane with Shakespeare and other dogs and horses onboard, touched down at Liege Airport at 23.38.

It was a surprisingly freezing night considering it was May, and I was shivering in the cold despite being sensibly dressed. My car was parked inside the large metal gates of the entrance to the terminal together with several professional transporters.

I was anxious, excited, scared, happy, elated all in one go. The last couple of hours since the flight had taken off from Larnaca I had held my breath. I had not eaten anything, so my body was hungry, but my mind kept ignoring any physical wants and needs. I only had one goal and that was to hold it together for when I could touch Shakespeare. As I stood shivering, pulling my jacket closer around my neck nothing else mattered.

It was eerily quiet. Normally an airport would be buzzling with the traffic of passengers coming and going, freight flights, people going from terminals to the airport hotel, but tonight, there was nothing. Just one lone plane with its belly full of animals would touch-down. I knew this flight had been politically sensitive as there were those who claimed one should not make animals any priority under COVID. I did of course respect their opinion, but I strongly disagreed as animals that were supposed to leave just as COVID closed all airspace were trapped in sanctuaries and refuges making it impossible for any rescuer to help other animals. With this flight now carrying animals towards their families across Europe, rescuers could get themselves reorganised within the shortest time and save more lives.

I heard the first trailer with the dog crates coming at the same time as a horse handler came around the corner of the building with six stunning Islandic ponies, three leads in each hand. The horses were showing clear signs of distress and the handler, a man with his chest pushed as far out as humanly possible, was raising his voice, swearing at the horses. I had spoken to the man when I first arrived, and my gut instinct was that of keeping my distance as he made me feel uncomfortable. I could not pinpoint what it was, but the horses and I were aligned. The man made us all nervous. In sharp contrast was the man from a former east European country who came closely behind the first man. This man had four horses who walked by him, two on each side, walking with him completely relaxed as if the five of them had known each other since birth. I had also spoken to that man when I first drove through the gate. He had a soft expression - kind brown eyes and his broken English gave him a certain charm as he was trying to explain to me from what direction the large transport trailers with the dogs would come from. His colleague had abruptly interrupted him and told him to stop hanging around.

I touched the man's arm and thanked him for explaining and handed him one of the large chocolate bars that was on the seat of my car. He smiled and put the chocolate in his pocket before he headed off to pick up the horses.

As the two men passed me with the horses, the gentle man with the deep brown eye looked at me, and we exchanged a glance that said *even the horses think he is an idiot* - and we both smiled.

The large transport trailer that was pulled by small trucks, now arrived with more dogs, parking the trailers side by side. On each trailer there was flight crate after flight crate. Curious, scared and some indifferent eyes were looking at us through the crate doors. Not a single dog made a sound. The first dogs I recognised were the Beagle pups that I had met whilst visiting Katy in Cyprus. Katy did not only work as a volunteer and as a huge part of the SPDC team, but she and her husband Paul also fostered pups and dogs from the sanctuary. The Beagle pups were the cutest, softest most wonderful pups and here they were, two in each crate, having travelled together on a long journey to bring them home to their new families in England.

Each of the professional DEFRA-approved drivers were waiting in lines to get "their" dogs. The organisation required any flight transport of this magnitude is of such a standard that some of the women behind the execution could run a country, and Elena from SPDC was no exception.

She had organisation skills that I as a former overseas manager in the tour operations world simply had to bow to. Each crate was clearly marked with name, age, chip number and destination of each dog and this information was now to be checked against the transport list that each transporter had.

Automatically I started to help the different transporters finding the different crates that was on their list. The more quickly we could load each dog into the right transport-van, the more quickly the dogs could go home. I was by the trailer reading numbers and the ground crew helped carry the crates into the right van. Many were going to UK, to Belgium, some to Germany and Scotland. As I worked my way through the different crates, I was looking for Shakespeare, but I could not see him. My heart was racing and as we lifted the last dog off the second trailer, I panicked. What if he was not there? I knew he was on board the plane as I had video of him in his crate being loaded. I was simply not capable of being rational and for a couple of seconds I was sure he was not on the remaining trailer. He was left on the plane. They had forgotten him. I walked towards the last trailer thinking Shakespeare would not be there. The panic must have been showing on my face as one of the ground crew turned to me and said *Your dog's name was Shakespeare, wasn't it?* He did not wait for my response.

He is here. It is the crate with the green funnel.

I was scared to look. What if it really was not him. I had lost my mind again!

With a leap of faith, I walked towards the trailer and saw the crate with the bright green funnel used to pour water into the water dispenser. The crate was marked: *High Flight Risk. Do NOT open crate door!* It was dark and despite the yellow light beaming from the streetlamps outside the terminal I could only see the contours of a dog lying inside the crate.

It was too dark to see any facial expression. The dog inside the crate was completely still, silent, huddled up in the back corner. Standing in the cold night in front of Shakespeare's crate, I felt tired to the bones of me and all I wanted was to take him home. Two men from the ground crew kindly helped me carry the large crate into my car, facing the door of the crate towards my seat. The whole of the crate filled the back of my car. I almost did not dare to look at Shakespeare. After all this time I was worried he would evaporate into thin air. He was frozen and I had not expected anything else.

He was like he had been those first days at the sanctuary, staring into space, past me. There were no vibrations of his nostrils, no movement of his eyes. No expression, no sound. He still smelt of dust.

I headed away from the airport, seeing the light of the animal arrival terminal getting smaller in my mirror. I continued driving until I found a quiet place, by the roadside, to park. I got up on my knees on the driver's seat and faced him. He was lying motionless, with his legs pulled up under him, in a ready to run position. I carefully opened the crate door and there was absolutely no reaction from him. He continued staring past me, into the night.

Hello Shakespeare, you are almost home. All we need to do is drive until we reach the house in the vine-growing nowhere, and you will be truly home, with your siblings and your dad.

My whispering voice was trembling and my hands shaking as I offered both my hands into the crate at the same time, with open palms, as if my open palms were holding a gift. I have no idea why I did this, but as my hands moved forward, Shakespeare very and ever so carefully put his head forward and put his head in the palm of my hands. Then, he let go. The weight of his head rested in my hands.

He did not look at me but as he placed his head in my hands, he closed his eyes for a moment as if to say, breathe, and by this we were reunited as if no time had passed. We sat like that, by the roadside, alone in the dark, just the two of us breathing in the same space - alone in the universe - and I felt a connection to Shakespeare even deeper than ever before, something I had not thought possible. *I will drive us home* I whispered, and he lifted his head and pulled it back as if he knew what I said.

We had a drive of around eight hours ahead of us, a trip that in fact would end up taking thirteen hours due to a mortal accident involving a multi axle lorry that flipped round in the air not far in front of me on the motorway. Another driver, who reached the lorry that was on its roof, minutes before me just shook his head after he had checked the driver. It truly was a night of fragility on the pitch-black motorways leading home.

Shakespeare slept silently the whole way home as if he were too exhausted to begin to process where he was. When we finally parked up outside, on our top land, we were welcomed by balloons on the metal gate and a sign saying, *"Welcome home to Shakespeare and mum."*

> Words are easy, like the wind;
> **faithful friends** are hard to find.
> - William Shakespeare, *The Passionate Pilgrim*

Are and I had agreed that we would introduce each dog individually to Shakespeare outside the gate. Under normal circumstances I would walk the new dog together with each one of the dogs individually, so that the acceptance or rejection was not a pack decision. I could however not walk Shakespeare. He would freeze, and not be able to walk anywhere. Even if he would, he was far too high a flight risk to be let out of his crate on a lead. I also suspected Shakespeare had never been on a lead in his life. My suspicion was later confirmed.

I had parked the car under the hazelnut trees. It was a glorious sunny early summer's day and as we lifted Shakespeare's flight crate and put it on the green grass in dappled shade, I felt again completely emotionally overwhelmed. I had been down to the house to spend ten minutes with the pack before we were to introduce Shakespeare. Without this, the dogs would only have focused on me and not on meeting the new pack member. I went back up to stay with Shakespeare; Are would bring the dogs up one by one.

Captain Hastings, the alpha, would be introduced first. As Shakespeare and I waited for Hastings to arrive, I sat down on the ground next to his crate, and watched as his eyes followed the moving sunlight on the grass. He was completely fixated. He moved his eyes and followed the sun beams.

He followed the shadow as the branches and the leaves of the hazelnut tree moved. It made me cry, again, as it hit me with full force that he had of course only seen the same flat light for the time he had been at the sanctuary. There had been no dancing leaves or dappled shade playing on the grass, as there was no grass in his concrete corner. There was daylight, darkness and concrete but nothing more. And now, there he was seeing dancing light for the first time in five years. It was in many ways incomprehensible but his reaction to the light said it all!

Each dog met Shakespeare one by one, and Shakespeare stretched his neck to sniff each one quickly before he went back to follow the light of the dancing leaves. He was spellbound. It was heart breaking but so beautiful to watch him trying to take in that he was out of his box.

After Are had brought our born-deaf American Cocker Spaniel Japp, as the last dog to meet and greet, I sat with Shakespeare a while longer so he could enjoy the playing light and the smell of grass, daisies, and the aroma of the French spring.

Later, we lifted his flight-crate between us, and he was safely inside the hallway in a matter of minutes, with the whole pack following like a tail. All the dogs were utterly curious as to who this new fellow was, and I had to close the door to the hallway for a moment. Shakespeare had gone back to frozen mode, and I knew he would not walk out of the flight crate, so I simply unclicked and lifted the top, leaving him exposed. He sat for a couple of seconds assessing his options, looking like a dog in a boat, and then carefully I tilted the bottom half of the crate. Shakespeare immediately left the open space and hurried the few steps into his awaiting crate.

He, of course, sought a corner, the left corner, the same corner he had chosen in his box in Cyprus. He was staring straight ahead and as before, there was no vibration in his nostrils as would have been natural for a dog who entered a new environment.

Shakespeare you are home. You are safe and nothing bad will ever happen again. We made it! We did it Shakespeare! You are truly home. I stroked him softly as I spoke, and I observed his ears twitching ever so slightly. It was the only true sign of life apart from the beating heart I could feel under my palm.

I opened the door to the dining room and the awaiting pack poured into the large hallway, where Shakespeare's crate shared the space with a billiard table and two chairs. I was now to witness something that made my heart swell. Each of the pack members went over to Shakespeare and through the open door of the crate they all met Shakespeare again, face to face, without any crate door in-between. Lady gave him a lick on his nose and Shakespeare looked confused. Hastings came to me for reassurance, and I sat holding him as Countess Elena sat herself down by the opening of the crate and stretched her neck out to smell Shakespeare. Elena then did the thing that is her "trademark." As a deaf dog, raised by a blind dog, she communicates slightly differently to the others. She stretched her paw into the crate and touched Shakespeare. Shakespeare seemed baffled, confused by the physical touch of Elena's paw, but he did not show any signs of wanting to disappear. Instead, he seemed quietly and reservedly curious in his own extremely cautious way. Shakespeare exchanged a long moment of eye contact with Elena as if to ask: *Who are you?* Elena gave a perfect Elena response: *Come and play and I will show you.*

I kept stroking Hastings and taking it all in.

You know Hastings, I got him home. That was my part, now you need to do your part, and make sure he is included and loved. We need to love life back into him. I know you will make sure it happens. I have such faith in you. I love you so. I kissed his head.

They all came, gathered around and one by one they quietly laid down in a half circle around the crate. It was all so gentle, and completely quiet. There were no sudden movement and no squabble or fuss. They were simply there to lend support to who they already perceived to be a broken dog. Within ten minutes, everyone was asleep. I watched how Shakespeare lay down and went to sleep as well, mirroring the behaviour of the pack. This dog that never relaxed felt the safety the others were offering him. It was animal magic at its most humbling and within twenty-four hours we had settled into a new routine. None of the dogs asked to be taken for walks or made a fuss about anything. They had their meals in the kitchen, with the exception of Lady Eileen Bundle Brent who had her breakfast and dinner served outside Shakespeare's crate whilst Shakespeare had his meals served inside his crate, as he was far too scared to leave. He would not touch the food if I were in the hallway but when I returned ten minutes later, I could pick up two empty food bowls. After the meals and a trip into the garden for toilet activities the whole pack went back to their half circle in support of Shakespeare.

Shakespeare would sneak out of his crate in the night to go to the toilet in the corner of the tiled hallway. I did not mind one bit as house training a rescue dog is all part of the journey. Shakespeare would become the easiest dog I have ever housetrained, once he dared to leave his crate.

We all lived in the slowest lane those first weeks. Are was at home with us all due to COVID restrictions, so nothing disrupted our everyday life. We were going nowhere. It was utterly peaceful. We spent time together on the floor, me reading a book resting on two cushions against the wall and Are coming and going. On day three Shakespeare moved his head to watch what was going on, still frozen much of the time but briefly dipping into companionship with the other dogs as we moved slowly around.

On day four I woke to find Lady and Shakespeare sleeping together, nestled up, inside his crate. Shakespeare was laying in front, half on his side and Lady was nestled up behind him with her head on his back.

She was not Agatha, but she was another girl who knew Shakespeare as they shared the fear that is caused by trauma. They knew each other in a way only they could, and the bond that was already there, after the shortest time, will remain until the end of their days.

Early on the morning of day five, I came downstairs to a completely quiet house. The courtyard was soon bathing in sunlight after a colourful, soft, sunrise. All the dogs had had their breakfast, as if they had collectively decided to move slowly and without any noise. Miss Marple was sunbathing by one of the terracotta flowers pots, stretching her legs and washing her paws. Miss Kathryn Grey was walking around in the orchard under the fruit trees. I was sitting outside having my morning coffee and a croissant, under the large sea blue canvas sails which gave shade over an eggshell white vintage cast-iron table and chairs, just outside the kitchen doors. There were duck-egg blue cushions, with bird drawings in the chairs and I could see Japp under the glass table.

I had coffee in my old French chocolate saucer, soaking in the quiet morning, reflecting on how lovely it was to sit in a chair and not on the floor where I had spent all my time since Shakespeare came home. Amazing that there are eight dogs here, I thought, as there was not a sound apart from birdsong. Behind me there was hectic bird activity, nests being built by the second lots of birds having come home to nest, as they did every year. The sky was still free from evaporation trails from planes and the grass still intensely green before the summer heat would burn it brown. I was still sleep-deprived after Shakespeare's homecoming and I wondered if I might nod off in the corner, on the floor, in the hallway. For now, I just wanted to inhale the peace.

I was so used to worrying about Shakespeare that my body had not got the memo that he was home. So far everything had run without incident. All the dogs kept supporting Shakespeare by gathering around, sleeping with him, or simply just lying in the hallway with him. The three cats, Mrs Oliver, Miss Lemon, and Mademoiselle Milesi had all walked through the hallway and Shakespeare had followed them with his eyes but as none of the other dogs were bothered, neither was he. Shakespeare had yet to meet Miss Marple, the cat born without eyes, as she simply did not wander into the hallway, but they would meet when they met.

I was not worried. Shakespeare slept, and that was the absolute best way for him to decompress and it was such a huge compliment to both the pack and us, as he would not be able to sleep if he did not feel safe.

He had stopped seeking a corner in his crate and that was all down to the dog's empathy and support. Any sound still startled him, and he would tremble, but he would settle back down more quickly than I had dared hope. I did not touch him at all for the first three days to let him relax completely. I could sit on the floor by his crate without him being worried, and I would now touch him and stroke him gently. If Are came near him he would panic, so Are left him be. So far Shakespeare had not been out of the crate in the daytime, and I was reflecting on how long it would be before he dared to step outside this safe space. I kept blankets on the top to muffle any sounds going on in the house.

The main entrance door to the hallway was open and the olive trees that were just outside the door cast a moving shadow on the floor as they swayed gently in the breeze.

Just as I moved from the warm oak flooring to the cool tiles in the hallway, I stopped mid-step. Straight ahead of me was Countess Elena looking slightly confused. I knew that look, and I knew something was going on that I could not yet see, as the fireplace in the hallway restricted my view to the crate. I reached for my phone, pressed the camera function before I crept around the corner to find Shakespeare with his head and neck stretched outside the crate. He was staring straight ahead and from what I could judge he was watching the movement of the olive tree shade on the floor. I stood still with my camera recording, and this is how I got to film how Shakespeare, with ghost like movements, put one paw in front of the other and stepped outside his secure zone. He stepped out and crossed the floor, one paw after another, passing Countess Elena by centimetres, walking into the sunlight.

Countess Elena looked at me as if to say: *Did you expect that? I certainly did not*!

I was overwhelmed. In the dark at the sanctuary, I had not been able to see any details of how he moved but now I was here, in my own hallway, in flooding sunlight, watching my boy cross the floor. He was elegant, regal in his movements despite his head being carried low. He had the distinct movement of a Pointer, but after having seen him move, I wondered if there might be some Cypriot sighthound in there somewhere!

I hardly dared to breathe. Elena and I exchanged looks again and together followed Shakespeare outside.

Just across from the entrance door there is a large flower bed with the two tall olive trees. At the far end there are lilac trees in a line, hiding a narrow original pathway that I had found when we had cleared the property for debris left by the former owners. Around each olive tree there is lavender, with the rest of the large bed filled with non-edible sage and ornamental perennial foliage in different colours, all releasing individual perfumes as Shakespeare was moving through the thick growth of it all.

Shakespeare was feeling soil under his paws for the first time in five years.

The shrubs in the flower bed were Shakespeare's height or taller so he had almost full coverage. The other dogs came to investigate what he was up to, and it soon became evident that he was digging himself a den. When the ten-minute digging job was done, Shakespeare rested himself in his newly-acquired safe place, under the olive tree, under the lavender. I could see him, but I did not approach him. The dogs visited him under the bushes but none of them seem to understand why Shakespeare would not prefer the comfortable outdoor sofas and many bed options to a hiding-spot on soil under an olive tree. They let him be. We all spent the day in the garden, me with odd jobs and reading part of the afternoon, and the dogs lazing.

I wanted Shakespeare to understand that outside was also a safe place and the absolute best way to do that was to let him stay in his hiding spot from where he could observe us all. He stayed under the lavender until early evening when he snuck back into his crate when I was in the kitchen preparing the evening meal for all the dogs.

During the next weeks there would be numerous dens dug and tested but Shakespeare, a creature of habit, old or new, kept going back to the first den he had dug. From there he had perfect view of what was going on in the courtyard and he could see us moving in and out of the kitchen, meaning he could perfectly time when to sneak back into the hallway. The second he was out of his crate I could not touch him and trying to approach him was like trying to approach a feral cat. Little did I know that it would be like that for many seasons to come.

> **One touch of nature** makes the whole world kin.
> -William Shakespeare, *Troilus and Cressida*

During those first weeks I did not walk the dogs and I could see that for Elena especially, it was starting to wear on her with lots of built-up energy. It was time to start walking again. I split the pack in two, and took with me Elena, Hercule, Lady and Miss Grey for my first walk since my return from Belgium. The rest of the pack would stay at home, and I would take Captain Hastings, Inspector Japp and Isabel Duveen with me on shorter walks. Shakespeare could not come yet. It was still too early to bring him without a lead, and I knew that was impossible.

I had seen Shakespeare leave the safe place of his den under the olive tree, checking out the parameters of our property, testing to see if there was any place he could easily escape. There were none, but he had shown interest in the corner where the stone wall met the fencing, so Are secured it further. To ensure that I would be able to find him should he be able to get out, Shakespeare was wearing a GPS tracker on his collar.

We settled into the new routine of split walks. Shakespeare was monitoring my every move, and I made sure not to open the gate if he were too close, wondering how long it would take before he could come for a walk with me. At some stage I would have to trust him and let him come but I wanted to be able to touch him outside his crate before I let him out.

It was seven weeks after Shakespeare had come home, and I was getting ready for my first morning walk. Shakespeare was in the garden at a good distance, observing us leave.

I felt bad for not letting him come, but I simply had no way of capturing him should he run off.

Lady, Elena, Hercule and Miss Grey were expressing their joy with loud barks, elated and exuberantly happy as we walked out the gate in the orchard, for the liberty of running. I felt their joy and was also so pleased on my own behalf as I absolutely loved my daily walks with the pack. It was not only good physical exercise, but it was part of keeping my mind healthy and my PTSD at bay.

I saw so much horrendous abuse and neglect in my rescue work that my daily walks were my time to reflect and try to shake some of the most disturbing images and experiences.

A few steps from the gate and I was on the tractor track that runs parallel to our walled garden and orchard. I had not walked more than a couple of hundred metres, when I saw that Elena, who was in front of me, was squinting at something behind me. I turned and there was Shakespeare, happily jumping like a stallion bucking.

How on earth…

My mobile rang as on cue.

I simply do not believe this. I was standing in the garden, and I watched Shakespeare jump the wall, the one with the fencing on top. Jesus, I cannot believe that it is even physically possible. He even had clearance over the top.

Are sounded shocked. I was less so, as I had seen dog climb and jump heights you would never think possible. But still, I was also surprised.

Well, he is here with me. The happiest dog ever. I laughed.

All the dogs had run back to greet him, welcoming him like a long-lost family member. Shakespeare was wagging his stub of a tail and the whole of his bum. It was as if the whole dog was oozing happiness and joy. He had a different softer facial expression and his body had gone from staccato movements to a gentler flow and stretch.

As all five dogs came running towards me, I laughed again. *Welcome to the walk Shakespeare. Can you fly?* No response other than a glance and I settled for that. Shakespeare ran, every muscle moving, alive with the others and seeming so perfectly at ease, like he had done this walk many times before. Shakespeare had not run for five years, apart from in our garden and orchard. He had lived five years without being able to just set off, heading in whatever direction he wanted.

The dogs were walking in togetherness as a pack when Shakespeare started trotting. I watched as he changed over to a canter and before long, they were all galloping over the farmer's huge field.

I stood perfectly still, shielding my eyes from the sun with my hand, crying with the immense joy of watching Shakespeare coming alive. Even Miss Grey who has no eyes was picking up on the happiness and was barking in joy.

Elena and Lady took turns in running alongside Shakespeare over the fields. There was a slight wind brushing the air but no agitation or obstruction as we entered the woods. Like the wind, the dogs were unconstrained and entangled with one another and with the landscape that surrounded us.

My dogs know every track and every path, waterhole, and foxhole in their landscape. They know the wild boar tracks and where the wild rabbits feed.

It was as if they were in a hurry to show Shakespeare everything all at once. Elena and Lady could not contain their jubilation at having Shakespeare running with them.

Hercule was observing it all and chose to stay close to me with Miss Grey returning and checking in as she always did. I would randomly put my hand into my pocket to give Hercule a treat to reinforce Shakespeare joining us was a positive experience for Hercule, who is nervous by nature and does not like change either. Hercule was still unsure what to make of Shakespeare, as he was not an easy dog to read. I kept talking to Hercule, telling him everything was going to be ok, whilst keeping an eye on Shakespeare and the girls. Watching them was delightful and I felt so joyous for him and with them, but I could not help being slightly worried: would he follow me the whole route or would he take off? Only one way to find out: I kept walking.

Where the tractor track took a bend to the right, I lost sight of Shakespeare and Elena. I knew Elena would not go far and that she would, if I did not appear, come and look for me but I also knew that even a loyal dog like Elena could be tempted to be led astray. To my relief they both stood still waiting as I came round the bend. They had the sun behind them making them glow in the sunlight. Hercule, Miss Grey and I walked, and Elena, Lady and Shakespeare kept running, stopping occasionally for a minute to interact with each other. Despite his liberty, it was clear that Shakespeare did not use his nose. He was following the other dogs as they were running, disappearing into the vines, and reappearing a little further ahead.

It was almost impossible to comprehend the changes in the seven weeks Shakespeare had been home.

At home he would now test and try out the dog beds around the house, only staying if no one moved, but he by far preferred the huge dog bed I had placed for him under the billiard table in the hallway.

I had removed his crate a week earlier after I had spent hours with him as he was sleeping in the crate. On some days I had even crawled into the crate and laid with him whilst I was meditating.

The balancing act of getting him to trust me, seeking the company of the other dogs and wanting to stay with us instead of seeking solitude was hard. I had used the knowledge I had of him from the time I spent with him in his kennel box in Cyprus and the constant observations I made of him after he arrived home.

Many decisions I took were based on experience but to be honest, with Shakespeare, most were based on gut instinct. When to leave him alone and when to push him. It had become evident in those seven weeks - his trauma was not going to let go quickly. I had also confirmed my immediate suspicion in Cyprus, that Shakespeare must have been taken away from his mum at an extremely early age as he had no coping mechanism. For a pup to grow up and turn into a healthy well-balanced dog they should follow a certain pattern in their first few weeks - sleep around ninety percent of the time and feed the rest. In the first two weeks, a pup will normally double their body weight.

At the two - four weeks stage several things will happen. Eyes will open after ten – twelve days. Ears will open after about fourteen – twenty-one days. This is of course no exact science but an average indication.

In the timespan of two - four weeks the pup will take their first wobbly steps. By the end of a puppy's third week, they enter the socializing period. They start playing with their siblings and will as part of their socializing interact with mum. At this stage puppies will form attachments they will remember for the rest of their lives. Around the time the pups are four weeks, mum's milk production will drop, and pups can start eating solid food. The time between six and eight weeks is crucial. This is when they learn to accept others. When a puppy is around fifty days old their brain waves appear like those of an adult dog, but their brain is not fully developed. This is the time when environment starts playing a significant role. A puppy is normally weaned by week eight and by week ten - twelve is ready for adoption. A dog is normally not fully developed before the age of eighteen months and some as late as four years.

I would take a stab at the fact that Shakespeare would not have been in contact with his mum or siblings after he was four weeks old, or maybe never, maybe the mother had died during delivery. This could explain his lack of coping mechanism.

Another reason I was sure he had not spent time with mum and siblings after the age of four weeks was Shakespeare's utter lack of social etiquette. He simply had no idea how to be a dog.

Dogs have a codex they work by - a set of rules that is basic dog etiquette. I had observed Shakespeare displaying behaviour that for sure would have got him killed if he had lived with a pack in the wild. One day he had been spooked and he had simply physically sat himself on top of Captain Hastings' back whilst Hastings was chewing on a bone. Hastings growled - a long, deep warning growl, but there was absolutely no response from Shakespeare who simply kept sitting. It was an absurd situation, and I must admit quite funny, but it could have ended up in a serious dog fight if Hastings had not been Hastings. Most dogs would not have come up with the idea of sitting themselves on top of another dog in the first place, and they would certainly have moved with the growl Hastings released to tell Shakespeare he was overstepping all boundaries. But Shakespeare had no way of deciphering the message. It was a perfect combination of lack of knowledge and understanding and PTSD that made Shakespeare react completely irrationally.

Shakespeare also had no concept of personal space. He would invade that space of the other dogs without even reflecting. My pack is placid, and they got along because they all obeyed ordinary interaction dog-rules. Otherwise, there would be anarchy and placing Shakespeare in their midst certainly had tested their coping skills. It was of course concerning that Shakespeare had no basic knowledge, and almost five years in solitude with no interaction with other dogs, had certainly reinforced this. It was obvious that I would have to teach Shakespeare how to be a dog, in parallel with helping him handle his PTSD – but first I needed to get him to walk back home with me.

Our ten-kilometre walk had come full circle, and we were homeward bound on the sandstone white tractor track. There were workers in one of the huge fields of vines but apart from that there are no other humans around. The dogs were bouncing, the energy level had not subsided, and there was no indication of the dogs being tired apart from Miss Grey who had slowed down.

A blind dog uses far more energy on a walk as they filter the landscape and every step through their nose, so I was happy for Miss Grey that we were almost home.

My phone rang. It was Are. He had watched our walk on the screen of his phone, delivered by the GPS tracker Shakespeare was wearing.

I see you are almost home. I have left the top gate open so hopefully Shakespeare will follow you back in.

I know all too well that having eight dogs and four cats had never been part of his dreams for us, but he loved me, and would support me in whatever I did. He also loved the animals dearly once they had arrived. I crossed over the meadow at the top of our land heading for the gate and as I did, Shakespeare came to an extremely unsure anxious halt. In a split second he had gone from happy and carefree, with a soft facial expression, to having that anxious look and stiff body language I knew all too well. I slowed down to try to ease Shakespeare's obvious anxiety as we approached the gate. I turned slightly to the left and walked out on the tractor track and back over our land. Same reaction. As I got closer to the gate, Shakespeare came to a halt.

Was he scared of losing his liberty? Was he scared of the gate opening itself? Did he think that if he came in, I would not let him back out?

The questions were flying through my head as I tried to read every little sign of his body language. Shakespeare had, however and yet again, confined his emotion and was standing motionless still. Elena and Lady kept looking at me as if to seek advice on how to handle Shakespeare's sudden change, but I had no advice to offer as I felt somewhat lost myself.

I decided to walk all the way into the courtyard with Lady, Elena, Miss Grey and Hercule and see how Shakespeare would react.

There are two gates to pass through. The first, a large double metal gate on solid sandstone gateposts is as old as the house, leading from the outside into the orchard. A wide path then leads through the orchard, with fruit trees on the right-hand side. The path goes in a straight line until the double wide wooden thyme coloured gate that will lead straight into the courtyard.

It is possible to stand in the opening of the top gate and see the bottom gate, but from the first gate it is not possible to see the door opening to the kitchen, nor the main door. Shakespeare stood frozen watching me as I walked towards the house. Captain Hastings, Inspector Japp and Isabel Duveen were waiting for me and were overjoyed as they knew it was their turn to walk. Between wagging tails and dog glam I switched dogs and left within minutes.

Shakespeare was standing where I had left him and as Hastings ran towards him, he came back to life, bucking, rabbit jumping and wagging the whole of his body.

The juxtaposition in one and the same dog was hard to fully take onboard. I walked with the four of them and despite Hastings starting to become an elderly gentleman I decided to walk a longer route than I would normally take him with the aim to ease Shakespeare in to coming back in with us. The landscape was peaceful, with shades of green interrupted by the wheat and barley crop that was swaying slightly in the light breeze.

Except for a bright green tractor belonging to a distant neighbour moving in the landscape, there were now no one else around.

Hastings was happy to spend time with Shakespeare as he was to spend time with any dog. Inspector Japp was running alongside the two of them. Isabel Duveen was in her bright Christmas red harness on a lead clasped around my waist. Isabel could not be trusted off lead. Her extreme sense of smell made it possible for her to follow a trail for hundreds of kilometres.

With Isabel - all the efforts and hours I had put in to training her recall had been to absolutely no avail. If she were off-lead and got on the trail of something she thought interesting, she would glue her nose to the ground and go into her own zone - and she would not look back. Five-six hours later she would stand in the middle of a woods howling like mad for me to get her, suddenly changed from the mighty tracker she was, to my soft loving Isabel who wanted her mum. Lady and I had been on so many rescue missions with her howling and crying at the top of her voice because she was scared and lost. She would sit herself down and wait for us to get her. Lady would roll her eyes at me as to say, *There she goes again. We better get her out.*

Isabel also had this funny notion that she could only walk forward and not turn to any side - unless she was on a trail of course. Her funny antics made me giggle and I had learn to accept her quirky side at the same time as I tried to teach her that she could choose several options, like walking to the left or right and even actually turning around. She loved Shakespeare and could relate to his PTSD.

I had rescued Isabel after she had been through the most horrendous abuse and neglect, which ended with the owner chaining her inside an abandoned car wreck, leaving her to die by starving her to death. To this day Isabel will trade her food for a hug any time.

The thought of her abandoned, alone and left to die makes me feel dark grey.

If Isabel's reaction in the aftermath of her horrendous abuse is anything to go by, the solitude had been the torturous part for her. Solitude is incredibly hard on a human and there is no reason to believe that for a dog left to die of starvation, it is any "easier." A pack is not only a social gathering amongst dogs, but an emotional support system. The other pack members have your back, and they are the ones on which you can lean. Solitary confinement was part of her torture and Isabel will always carry the emotional scars of what she has been through. She will often use her front legs to physically hold onto my or Are's leg to prevent us from leaving her, or just to tell us she wants to belong. She will use any opportunity for physical contact for reassurance in a manic way, looking at us *Please never leave me. Please love me.* And love her we do! We try to reassure her every day that she will never be left behind, never be alone again.

She has come such a long way and as I sat down in the field with her, she curled up to me and we sat watching Shakespeare, Hastings and Japp running before they came to join us. Here we all lowered our energy levels before heading home. Isabel cuddled, Hastings came and laid right next to me as was fit for an alpha and Inspector Japp, the cutest kid in town, lay next to Hastings who was his world.

As Japp is born deaf he relied so heavily on Hastings to warn him if anything was up. Japp was Hastings' dog shaped little shadow.

I wanted to observe Shakespeare when we all just sat and did nothing. I watched him closely as he came and laid himself about ten meters away from us. I knew why. He did not want me to have any chance of catching him. I had to accept that it was like that, and I had promised Shakespeare that I would give him his life back, so I had to meet his needs. I had not rescued Shakespeare to fulfil a void in myself. I did not "need" any more dogs and I had certainly not rescued him because I could not get hold of any other rescue dogs. I waded in rescue dogs! But only Shakespeare was Shakespeare and he belonged with me. I cannot explain it, but every dog in my pack with exception of Japp who Are had fallen in love with, had all come to live with us because I had fallen in love and felt a strong connection with each one, before they even lived with us. Shakespeare was in many ways just like my other rescue stories of abandonment, and yet he was different, as his PTSD in combination with his total lack of coping skills made him in a worse position than most.

If he had not come to live with us, he would have died in that corner where I had met him. That did however not give me any right to push him to fit me.

He needed to figure out who he was and where he wanted to be and in a little while he would tell me if he was prepared to come back inside or not.

We walked calmy back towards the house with Hastings and Shakespeare trotting side by side but before we reached the gate, Shakespeare simply stopped. Hastings was confused and looked to me for answers.

Darling, I do not know why he does not want to come back in, but I know we must give him time. He needs time to figure himself out and to realise he is home.

I walked through the gates leaving Shakespeare after I tried to coax him inside, but he stood completely unresponsive without even looking at me. I knew there was nothing I could do to explain to him that it would be safe to pass the gate and he would be let back out for his daily walks.

I kept walking, opened the kitchen door so all the dogs could be together in the courtyard. It took only seconds for the pack to gather at the bottom gate, staring at Shakespeare standing in the opening of the top gate. My hope was of course that Shakespeare would come and join the pack. He did not.

As the hours passed Are and I sat watching the yellow line on the GPS tracker on the phone screen, indicating every step Shakespeare took. He walked off our land and over to our neighbour's barn. He walked over the junk yard where there were a gazillion hiding places for a street-smart dog. He went through the vines just outside our house before he returned to the junk yard. Then he backtracked the routes – before he repeated it all, all over again.

We decided to go and look for him by sunset, bringing Lady, Elena, and Hastings. It is minutes' walk from our gate to the back of the junk yard that is hidden behind the vines. There were old tractors with missing wheels, a wreck of a poplar green Citroen from the 1950s. Old water tanks, a dilapidated lorry and metal junk in heaps. There was also heavy undergrowth of briars and brambles.

I could see on my screen that Shakespeare was under one of the large metal heaps, having penetrated the thick wall of briars and brambles with large thorns. I sat down to talk to him even if I could not see him. Lady tried to get through the briars as she so obviously could smell him, but she gave up and backed back out.

Shakespeare had the huge advantage that his adrenaline production now was through the roof so he would not feel any pain caused by the thorns on brambles until much later. It was a magical bright pink sunset in sharp contrast to the ugly rusted metal at the junk yard. Hastings, Elena, and Lady were all looking at me; *what now?*

I turned to Are. *Darling, let us go home.*

He looked at me in disbelief.

Go home and just leave him?

Yes. Tonight, Shakespeare will have to make the most important decision of his life. If he wants to stay with me, with us, or if he does not. I cannot force him to be with us and to let us love him. We have done everything possible to show him how loved he is. It is now up to him. He now has the liberty to run and never come back. I have kept my promise to us both, I brought him home. I cannot imprison him. He needs to decide if he wants to stay.

I stretched out my hand towards Are's. His met mine halfway, warm, and safe as always.

Are you sure about this darling? He asked again.

I am sure. If we do everything we can, to catch him now all that will happen is that he will never trust us again.

He will live through the same experience as he had when he was caught in Cyprus all those years ago. He will think we are catching him to confine him. His PTSD will go through the roof and there will be nothing I can do for him. There will come a time where he will have to decide that he wants to stay with us. It may sound strange, but it is time. It has arrived sooner then I prepared for, this decision time, but tonight, he must decide if he will physically leave or stay.

I felt a calmness I had not felt since I first met Shakespeare that day in Cyprus. For some reason I was sure he would not leave me by going anywhere, like I had been sure about him not touching my bag in Cyprus. Do not ask me to explain how I thought I knew, I just did.

We crossed the junk yard with the dogs rushing in front of us, knowing where we were heading. The sunset-sharp pink sky was gone, and we walked home as the stars were coming out.

When it gets dark in the countryside it is almost instant, like flipping a switch. The dogs seemed baffled about leaving Shakespeare behind and I could see them turning to look over their shoulders.

As if she could not get her head around why we did not stay until Shakespeare came out of hiding, Elena turned and looked at me.

I know darling but we simply must hurry up and sleep and find out if he is here tomorrow morning. He must decide. We cannot decide for him.

Are squeezed my hand.

We walked the last meters to reach the courtyard, leaving Shakespeare behind under a heap of overgrown metal junk in a junk yard. I had no idea what would await the next morning - or what destiny was to hold for years to come.

> It's not in the stars
> **to hold our destiny**
> but in ourselves.
> -William Shakespeare,
> *Julius Cesar*

I fell asleep quickly, taking into consideration that Shakespeare was sleeping outside by himself, but at five o'clock the next morning I was wide awake. I saw the soft yellow light from the downlights we had along the house façade. Behind them, in the orchard, there was a wall of black night. We live where there is no light pollution. When it is dark it is pitch black unless the moon and stars are out, then the night is dark blue. I snuck out of bed and down the stairs. Hastings lifted his head expecting me to do whatever I needed to do and go back to bed. The other dogs did not even bother to look up. I checked my phone to see what the GPS indicated. The dot was in the same spot as the night before. Either Shakespeare had not moved, or the GPS tracker had come undone from his collar as he had hidden himself under the heap of junk through the brambles. If that were the case Shakespeare could be anywhere. Long gone!

I walked across the wide oak floorboards where I had stencilled a pattern with mandala circles in white and moss green. The stencilling was a substitute for a carpet under the kitchen table and the six vintage chairs, as carpets needed hoovering and that was an ungratifying job when one has a large pack of dogs and four cats.

I filled the kettle and removed it from the stove before the flute signalled the water was hot, as to not wake Are. With a large cup of coffee in hand, still in my dressing gown, I unhooked a winter jacket and crept out to the courtyard. Elena had realised I was up to something and almost tiptoed in-between the dog beds to join me. She looked at me as if to ask: *what are we doing mum?*

We are going to see if we can see Shakespeare. We need to see if he is still there. Do you think he has left? I did not want to interpret the fact that Elena was not wagging her tail. We were on the tractor track in less than a minute. I was walking whilst sipping my coffee trying to prepare myself for the fact that he would be gone, but somehow, I did not think that was the case. I did not feel his absence. Stop being ridiculous, I told myself.

We entered the junkyard, me stepping over, Elena jumping high and graceful over the large metal beam that was laid across the entrance to stop vehicles from entering to steal metal.

I left my coffee cup on the edge of the beam in case I had to get down on my knees to crawl under something, and with Elena ahead of me, walked to where the GPS had marked Shakespeare the night before. I had not brought my phone as I had experienced dogs losing GPS trackers several times and I did not want to get my mind stuck on the thought that Shakespeare and the tracker would be in the same place, as the night before. Or in the same place at all.

Everything was quiet, and Elana's bleached white fur seemed to sparkle in the dark. I became hesitant. What if he was not there? What if he had left never to return? I swallowed the lump and continued walking, calling him.

Shakespeare. Shakespeare?

My mouth was dry. *Shakespeare?*

Elena was circling the heap of metal I suspected Shakespeare to be under.

Please, please, please my inner voice kept repeating. *Please!*

Shakespeare? I caught the anticipation in my own voice.

I kept looking around and glimpsed the eyes of a cat rushing into an old bus wreck at the far end of the yard, but apart from that there were no movements. I could hear a mouse hawk over the field behind me and smell the early morning sweetness of summer. Soon the sun would be up and maybe I would find out that Shakespeare was gone. I swallowed another lump in my throat and tried to swipe the whole junk yard with my eyes. At the far end of the yard there was an open hay barn: maybe Shakespeare was inside? Maybe he had slept there?

Just as my thought process was about to go into another circling loop, I saw a shadow. In reflex I held my breath. I could not see it was him, but I could hear the metal ID tag on his collar making that familiar sound. Elena's reaction gave instant confirmation! She was jumping in circler movements, and her tail was swishing with such force I thought she might get airborne.

Shakespeare? It was him. He was wagging his short stump of a tail, dancing with Elena.

You stayed I said as the tears came. *You stayed!*

I stood still, straight up and down, absorbing the emotions and the fact that he had not left and with that came the knowledge he would never leave no matter how long he stayed outside. Shakespeare would not leave me!

My thought went to the words of one of the most amazing rescue women I know, who told me when Lady disappeared for four days: *dogs like Lady form a bond with one person and that bond stays with them forever. Lady will be back.*

Nanou had been right. Lady had come back, and she had never left me since. Shakespeare and Lady also had this in common. They form that bond, and it makes them stay.

I walked back to where I had left my coffee. I sat down on the metal beam with my back to the junkyard, facing the huge field that soon would be filled with a crop of some sort. Sunflowers maybe? The two dogs had ventured into the field running, going up on the hind legs like two boxers in the ring, Elena jumping over Shakespeare's back using him as cavaletti bars. Shakespeare was showing signs of unfiltered happiness by barking and engaging Elena to further play with him, doing his play bows, stretching his long front legs out in front with his bottom in the air. I sat watching them, letting the gratitude for Shakespeare still being here sink in as the sun appeared in the east. There was no wind and it felt like I could hear the incredible colours that the sun carefully released into the open, early morning landscape. It was peaceful, as if nothing bad could ever happen. I sipped the rest of my cold coffee wondering if Shakespeare would come back in with me. If he did not, I would have to accept that, and we would have to find a way forward until he was ready to come in.

Shakespeare was still wearing his GPS, but he had not come out from under the heap that the tracking app had indicated. I suspected that the GPS-signal had been lost under all the rubble at the junk yard not indicating he had moved in the night, something he for sure had done.

As I got closer to the gate Shakespeare stopped in the same spot as he had stopped the night before.

Come on Elena. We will go home. I kept walking.

I had already decided, that if he did not come back in with me, I would go straight back home to feed the other dogs' breakfast before I would go back out to feed Shakespeare.

Later I would take all the dogs for a walk with Shakespeare. Maybe if we walked as a pack, he would come to realise he could live inside with us and keep some form of liberty.

In Shakespeare's world everything seemed black, white, and flat, it was my job to put colour and nuance into his perception of the world and make the images 3D.

.

> There are **many events in the womb of time** which will be delivered.
> - William Shakespeare, *Othello*

Yet again, we settled into a different daily routine centred around Shakespeare.

In the beginning I would try to feed Shakespeare just outside the gate, but he would not come anywhere near the food bowl. It was obvious he thought I was using the food bowl to trick him, and I suspected that food had been used to catch him in Cyprus. The second problem I had was that Shakespeare would not eat with humans around. I knew that if I were ever to reach Shakespeare, and for him ever to truly trust me, I would have to change this.

I picked a spot in the vines about fifty metres away from the top gate, and I decided that would be his feeding spot. It was in between the first and the second row of vines. This way he was able to feel safe and he would have full view to the track and anyone passing. It could be days and sometimes weeks between someone passing but it did happen and for Shakespeare to feel safer he needed to have full view of his surroundings. The first day I put down his food bowl on the chosen spot he stood for almost two hours watching the bowl with me sitting ten metres away before he finally gave in and came to have his breakfast, moving with the body language of a thief in the night. It was so sad to see how scared and worried he was. I knew there would be no quick fix to anything in regard to this dog. It was all a question of Time! Time! Time!

As I sat watching him, one of my cats, the small, soft, grey, and black tiger striped, Miss Lemon came for a snuggle.

Miss Lemon was an outdoor cat from early spring to late autumn and judging from Shakespeare's reaction when he saw Miss Lemon, they already knew each other, and better than simply their brief encounters after Shakespeare had arrived. The two animals exchange looks as if to say *Oh hello there you are*! An idea formed in my head.

What if I fed the two of them together? It had been evident when Shakespeare was living inside that he felt safer in the company of other dogs, so why not a cat? It was worth a try.

The same evening after having fed the others, I left the house.

In my hands I had Shakespeare's large yellow and blue metal bowl, with dry biscuits sprinkled with fish oil topped with wet dogs' food. The smell of the fish oil reminded me of the cod-liver oil my mum made us take every morning growing up. I was hoping the oil would help the cracks and wounds Shakespeare had on his elbows. All the years without moving properly had made the skin lose its elasticity. and the wounds were sometimes raw. This worried me.

In my other hand I had a small porcelain bowl with pink cat paw prints, with two sachets of Miss Lamon's favourite cat food. A huge dog bone stuck out of the righthand pocket of my skort.

Shakespeare! Dinner!

Miss Lemon came from nowhere, purring softly and draping herself in between my feet. She at least liked the idea of dinner in the vines. Shakespeare soon appeared from the hedge - just his head and neck but slowly he moved his whole body onto the tractor track, standing still, observing, and sceptical. I followed his eyes and saw he was watching Miss Lemon, not me. I walked the extra few metres and put down Shakespeare's bowl where he could see it and where I would be able to see him.

I picked up Miss Lemon to sit on my shoulder as I squatted down to prepare her meal. I glanced over at Shakespeare, without moving my head or making a point of looking at him; he was still focusing on Miss Lemon.

Miss Lemon was purring up against the back of my head. As I put her bowl down, she elegantly and weightlessly jumped down and started to eat. It was like Shakespeare took that as a sign - and in snail-motion he started to walk towards his bowl. After a few metres he stopped to let me move, looked to the left and right to make sure it was not a trap, moved forward and started to eat. In-between every mouthful he would stop and listen, but there were no sounds of alarming barking dogs.

Over the next months I would feed the two together. I would put down a bowl of cat food for Miss Lemon halfway between where I would sit, and Shakespeare's bowl. Shakespeare would stand and observe me as I came with the food, and he would go to his bowl immediately after Miss Lemon had started to eat. It was like Shakespeare took the fact that Miss Lemon would come bouncing over the field to have breakfast or dinner as a sign of him being safe.

It was magical to watch the effect Miss Lemon's presence had on Shakespeare and within two months I could feed them side by side whilst I sat only a few metres away. After dinner I would give Shakespeare a bone that he would carry with him into the field and I would watch him from a distance chewing in total, unspoilt liberty. At night he would find somewhere to sleep, and I now started to walk in the night when there was moonlight on top of two daily walks. We walked a minimum of seventeen kilometres a day that summer, but often up to double that distance.

The walk always ended the same way, with Shakespeare stopping by the gate. He would be back early every morning barking to make his presence known to the other dogs who would be overjoyed to see him. But he would not walk past the top gate.

That summer we walked the equivalent of the distance from my home in Southwest France to the Vatican in Rome and half way back. We lived as one pack with me running an outdoor food service for Shakespeare and Miss Lemon.

For me, being able to sit and observe him eat was such a pleasure and I knew what an immense compliment it that Shakespeare was letting me stay when he was eating. He would still stop and listen between the mouthfuls – a habit he would never loose. In spite of the progress, not once during those months could I get close to him. In an attempt to change that I cut back on his breakfast portions and as we walked the first and the second walk of the day, I would stop at the same spot every day, and offer him a handful of food. In a matter of days Shakespeare would take my food offering without hesitation, spurred on by the positive enforcement of the other dog's reactions. But if I lifted my other hand to stroke him, he would bolt. I had no physical contact with Shakespeare at all that summer apart from him eating out of my hand, but we kept walking, and we kept stopping for mouthfuls of dried biscuits. We were bonding and that was all-important.

Every evening, he would stop at the same spot outside the gate as we walked in and every morning, he would be waiting for us. He was always within ears' reach and I could call him any time and he would come bouncing. Always so delighted to see me and the pack.

We walked and rested together, and Shakespeare taught the other dogs to dig – hunting for field mice. None of my other dogs had ever been diggers but boy did they enjoy the new shared   digging experience.

Field mice are small rodents with a long-pointed nose that digs burrows in the ground for nesting, hiding, and resting. They are sandy brown in colour and slightly bigger than the grey house mouse. When it came to hunting them, Shakespeare was in his element as these rodents are hunted on the high-pitched sound they release, and Shakespeare had finely- tuned hearing after all the years in the corner of the box in Cyprus. In the beginning, especially Elena did not understand what they were digging for as she could of course not hear any sound, but she was extremely happy to participate in the digging together with Shakespeare and later Lady and Hercule. Soil would splatter to both sides as they would dig with such speed - leaving great big holes in the farmers' fields. These were such joyful days. We all also learnt to accept the fact that Shakespeare was living outside. We spent time with him on his terms and I spent my time simply observing minute signs of progress.

Any signs of Shakespeare daring to do something he had not done before, like laying closer to the pack when I stopped to rest and lower the energy in the pack. This brought such a sense of joy and achievement on his and my behalf. It was during such a stop I saw Shakespeare wash himself for the first time. We were all sitting in a green meadow filled with daisies with Isabel and Lady both flat out sunbathing. I was leaned up against the silver trunk of a birch tree, Hastings was keeping an eye out for any quails - his favourite chase. Hercule was on my lap with Miss Grey and Japp close by.

Shakespeare was lying closer than usual and as if something simply clicked into place, he started licking his paws, then his legs and the flank of his back legs. I was mesmerised by this. I had never seen him wash himself, but it was as if the fact that his fur had now been washed by the rain had awoken something in him. Docile, he kept repeating the circler motion with his pink tongue. I hugged Hercule and whispered *Look Hercule, Shakespeare is starting to realise he is a dog.*

We had just crossed another threshold.

> Ay, but to die, **and go we know not where**; To lie in cold obstruction and to rot.
> - William Shakespeare, *Measure for Measure*

Shakespeare had now been home hundred-and-sixty-eight days and autumn had arrived in all its glory with the woods painted ochre, yellow, red, and orange. Every morning the temperature had dropped a bit more and the winds had that distinct autumn chill. It was liberating after the scorching hot summer that had given us more than fifty degrees in the courtyard - but I was starting to worry.

Our region of Southwest France normally has mild autumns but Shakespeare's first autumn in France would be different. As the cranes flew further south to the backdrop of pale blue skies, the cold spells arrived. With autumn came hunting season and I was worried that Shakespeare would be shot, mistaken for wildlife. I tried everything I could think of to get him to come inside but he would not pass that same spot before the gate, where he had stopped since the day he flew over the fence. I could still not get closer to him than arms' length, unless I was hand- feeding him - and even then, I could still not touch him.

The bad weather arrived much earlier than we were used to, with sleet and non-stop heavy rain. Still, we walked twice a day whilst I tried to keep my life and routines as normal as possible. I had problems concentrating when the rain was whipping against the windows at the large double kitchen doors at night. I could only hope Shakespeare was curled up warm somewhere, like the neighbour's haybarn.

I would feel more at ease when there were clear crisp days, but these were hunting days.

However rainy days were the worst by far. To see Shakespeare standing soaking wet, looking longingly at us as we walked back in through the gate was heart wrenching - but his fear of the gate, of inside, or maybe fear of losing of his liberty, would always win. We would return from our long walk, where he was so happily one of us, and as we got closer to the always open gate, Shakespeare would slow until his feet no longer moved forward. Most days Elena or Lady would return to him, standing chiselled still, and they would individually, or together, encourage him to come with us.

Elena especially would return again and again, looking from Shakespeare to me, asking why he wouldn't move all the way into the garden gate and onwards to inside the house, to a place in front of the fire. I would talk softly to Elena and try to explain why Shakespeare was not capable of following her all the way to the safe, warm home that we all loved so much.

I had to keep reminding myself that I had promised Shakespeare he could take as long as he needed to find his footing. I knew that if I forced him, all he would do would be to look for ways to escape to regain his liberty.

Elena looked at me in a begging way, wanting me to solve a situation that weighed so heavily on us all. But I was not going to risk breaking the only bond Shakespeare had ever had with a human. Shakespeare needed to find the strength to join us inside the garden gates.

You see Elena, Shakespeare has never trusted or loved any human before he came home, and Shakespeare still does not understand we will never abandon him or break his trust. He will one day come inside, but it will not be today.

I could tell she did not understand how he could choose to be outside alone instead of inside with us. She found it confusing!

I had not rescued Shakespeare to fulfil some void within myself. I had brought Shakespeare to France to give him back his liberty, his dignity, his life, which had been taken away from him for so many years. He was here to have a life before it was his time to die for real. I knew from the first moment we met, that Shakespeare would never belong *to* me, but he belonged *with* me. Shakespeare would never be *my* dog, but I would always be his human. I was the tool for him to be given what he should have had all along: a life. We belonged together.

Wise, wonderful Captain Hastings would also look at me with his large hazel eyes to ask; *Why? Why is he not coming inside?* My response was always the same.

He will come inside when he is ready darling, but I do not know when that will be, but it will be one day. For now, we need to give him the gift of time.

All seven dogs would – in the afternoon or at night - be curled up in front of the fire in the dining room or the hallway, or the open fire in the living room. There were dog beds scattered everywhere, each with soft mattresses and blankets.

I would sit reading or writing in the blue and white armchair in the dining room under the chandelier, or at the large dining table that was painted in a soft light cream white. I felt constantly uneasy that Shakespeare was missing from us. We were incomplete without him.

We were all sad and I was starting to think that one day, I would have to drug him to get him inside. As it turned out, that day was to come sooner than any of us anticipated!

If I were out on a rescue, picking up a dog that needed to find a new life, or - on a rare occasion - out for lunch with a friend, I could not relax or concentrate properly because my mind was with Shakespeare in the rain or worrying about the hunters. I was losing sleep, and I was losing weight. I knew I had to try to turn myself around or I would be no good for Are, the other animals nor myself.

On the Thursday of a second week of pouring rain I had walked in the wet, freezing morning. Shakespeare had been waiting by the gate as always. He looked tired, sad, and old. His head was lower than his body and because I knew him like I knew the back of my hand, I felt a rush of fear that he would give up. That he would simply lay down and die, truly die. That he would decide it was too hard. Too hard to choose life over death. He had his liberty. I had given him that, but I had failed to give him more. I cried as I walked back in through the gate leaving him in the pouring, grey rain. I looked back and he was walking away with the pace and motions of an old, sad dog. His running body was not running anywhere. He was moving as if his joints were aching.

My sadness was festering and all absorbing.

In dry clothes, I poked the fire and put more wood on the flames as the dogs settled. I went to my office to get a small parcel that I needed to take to the post office for shipment. Everyone was asleep and no one minded me as I walked through the hallway where Hastings and Japp slept flat out on a big rug in front of the dancing flames, passing through the dining room and into the kitchen where the rest of the dogs had each found a place to lie. Despite a rub down with a towel as we came back in, there was that distinct unmistakeable smell of wet dog. On the kitchen table Miss Marple was curled up into a soft white fluff-ball in her wine box lined with a sheepskin.

All so utterly peaceful.

A large bright yellow golf umbrella shielded me as I ran with long steps through the rain, jumping a puddle, to get to my car heading for the post office.

The road takes me past the north wall of our home, leading to farmers' fields on each side of the road. The wall and the landscape were grey matching the weather and my soul. Vision was limited as I turned up the heating in the car. I still felt cold after the walk and was trying to shake the sense of strong uneasiness that had not left me for days.

I reached out to turn on the radio to try to distract my wandering mind. My eyes were off the road for less than a second and I heard myself scream before I had time to reflect as to why. I hit the brakes, bringing the car to a screeching halt skidding slightly sideways on the wet asphalt.

Just in front of the car stood Shakespeare in the pouring rain. He was in the middle of the road as a ghost of himself. For a couple of seconds, we sat looking at each other through the windscreen wipers that was going full speed. I reached out and turned them off. I turned the key and silenced the engine. With every move I was afraid of breaking the moment, scaring Shakespeare so that he would run off. Slowly, ever so slowly I opened the door.

I did not really stand up but kept my body leaned forward as if I was trying to move against a storm. It was not a storm I was leaning towards; it was Shakespeare.

I had never seen him in the middle of the road before.

He locked me into his gaze. He was shaking from the cold. It was like convulsions, and I could see he could not control it despite his efforts. He kept looking at me asking silently for help. Everything was intensely fragile. I reached out my hand and his eyes responded, *No, please do not reach out as I will have to run.* I spoke to him, telling him he would be ok. We would be ok. I would find a way. I did not know how, but I would find a way forward. For him - for us all. As I looked at him, he seemed grey, like the light inside the beautiful shining copper-brown fur was dimming and he was losing his glow. It was all grey apart from four open wounds on his legs that were blood red. Shakespeare had lost all elasticity in his skin after years on the concrete floor. Every time he moved, the skin over his elbows and on both hocky-joints on his back legs would break open. Every day on our walk I would take photos of his legs and compare the photos to those of the days before and by that I could keep a close eye on the wounds to see if it were getting worse or better and act accordingly with painkillers and antibiotics.

I also kept adding fish oil to his food. After the temperature had dropped, I would also give him almost double portions of food, and yet, he had lost weight. He was using all his energy to try to keep warm, but he simply could not. His PTSD was telling him he was in acute danger causing him to produce constant adrenaline.

I was crying. The only warmth in the ice-cold rain was from the tears that trickled, warm on my cold cheeks. As the water of the tears jumbled with the water from the sky I sat on the cold asphalt, soaked to my skeleton with Shakespeare standing only a couple of metres away from me. He could not be further away if he were back in Cyprus. I knew, and he knew, that his fear of life was bigger than anything I could offer him right there and then, so we simply stayed still in the freezing rain, until he could stand still no more because he was shaking so badly.

As he turned and walked away, I knew in the depth of me he would die that night if I did not do something immediately. He turned and looked at me several times as he walked away, silently reaching out asking for me to help him. I was sobbing. I knew Shakespeare loved me and trusted me more than he had ever loved or trusted any human, but his fear was all consuming and no matter how much he wanted to walk towards me, he simply could not.

He kept turning back to look at me.

I would not make the post office - I got back in the car and reversed the few metres home. None of the dogs acknowledged my return. For the second time that day I got myself out of soaking clothes. I searched my closet for my Norwegian thermal underwear, and I found a woollen jumper. In the laundry room I found my thick raincoat and hat. I grabbed the phone as I opened the kitchen drawer where I kept emergency drugs for the animals - anything from compression bandages to cortisone and ear cleaning remedies. My hand found the packet of sleeping tablets.

Are picked up the phone almost immediately. I explained what had happened and asked if he could come home on short notice. He did not ask for details but simply said, *Of course.*

I counted the sleeping tablets. I would have to give Shakespeare higher dosage than what was indicated as his adrenaline production was constant and high. From the shelf in the laundry room, I got two tins of wet food that I emptied into Shakespeare's food bowl. The tablets were small and easily disguised. This plan could go horribly wrong as I knew that the tablets would take a long time to work, and Shakespeare would be on the move until the medication kicked in.

If I lost him out of sight between him eating the drug and until they worked, I would have signed his death warrant, as he would not survive drugged in the cold. If I did nothing he would also die for sure.

You just must make sure not to lose him, I told myself, but I did of course know there was a chance I could do just that.

I gently woke Elena by stroking her and giving her a signal to follow me. I could not take Lady for this mission as Lady was too easily spooked should anything happen. Sleep-drunk Elena got on her feet and looked curious as to where we were going. We left through the laundry room as that way the others would not understand we were leaving the property. If they did catch on, they would try to tear down the door to join in any walk. Elena and I slipped out the side gate.

Safely outside I told Elena that she needed to help me to keep Shakespeare close. *We cannot lose him out of sight after he has taken the medication.* She wagged in response to us being alone without the pack: alone time was a treat. She looked up at me through her milky dark eyes.

I slipped a lead on her and together we walked towards the spot in the vines where Shakespeare would have his food every day. The rain had changed to drizzle, and the temperature had dropped further. It truly was a miserable day.

Shakespeare stood at the end of our land watching my every move as I walked towards his feeding spot. I put down his bowl and stepped back with Elena looking up at me wondering why I would feed Shakespeare and not her. I gave her a treat out of my pocket to compensate and she calmy sat herself next to me as we waited under the large oak tree for Shakespeare.

He was sceptical as this was not his normal feeding time, and Miss Lemon who came bouncing in between the vines wanting to be fed as well, had no food bowl. The sight of Miss Lemon seemed to ease Shakespeare's scepticism, but I was worried that Miss Lemon would eat from Shakespeare's bowl, and I had a flash of a mental image of Miss Lemon curled up asleep for the next weeks after having eaten medicated food. Miss Lemon liked dog food, so I was relieved when I saw her just sit still observing. She had seen Elena and knew Elena would chase her if she discovered her, so she kept her distance.

We all stood watching whilst Shakespeare ate his food, lifting his head to listen for danger between every mouthful.

As soon as the doctored food was gone, I released Elena from her lead. She showed such happiness in greeting Shakespeare, but I could see she was worried for her close friend. She circled around him and licked his face before she turned and looked at me. *What is wrong with him, mum?*

Miss Lemon had climbed a tree as I started to walk towards the woods. My plan was to walk until I could see the effect of the medication and then - slow right down in the hope Shakespeare would lie down. From there, I would have to play it by ear. Drugging a dog like Shakespeare who produces constant adrenaline and is in constant flight mode is like trying to drug a rhinoceros. I knew I was in for a wait.

The rain picked up, coming in buckets at us and the horizons were dark grey. The woods seemed to have lost its colours and the ground was muddy. The smell of decaying, decomposing leaves and lack of hope made the day seem like the most miserable of all days, only brightened by Elena's shining white fur and her bouncing steps in her efforts to cheer Shakespeare up. She was the single sparkle during it all. We walked in the rain for almost two hours before there was any sign of effects of the drug. Shakespeare had now become unsteady on his feet, but he refused to give in. Like a drunk sailor he was fighting the effect of the drugs with all his might and kept going until we came to the opening of his favourite spot in the woods. It was where we would stop every day for a treat. He went off track and circled around on the soft moss a couple of times before he lay down. I held my breath, but he was soon back on his feet, now seriously unsteady to the point of falling over. He was too cold to lay still. His survival instinct was telling him not to fall asleep and I was truly scared he would fall over and injure himself or manage to ride off the drug and I would lose him. If I could not catch him before dark, my plan would have failed, and the effect of the drug would knock him out after dark when I could no longer see him.

I love living in a place without lights or light pollution but when it gets dark it happens quickly. I would not stand a chance in following him after dark: he would blend in one with the woods and I would have seen him for the very last time. I was concentrating so hard as to not panic - breathing in through my nose and out through my mouth to keep my heart from going crazy. I could hear my blood drumming in my ears. When I thought neither Shakespeare nor I could take any more, he finally, after another hour, caved in. He circled round, fell over, and curled up.

Neither Elena nor I moved. It was like Elena by now had understood that we were waiting for Shakespeare to lay down.

We sat on the muddy ground and waited for a couple of minutes before I fished my phone out of my soaked pocket and called Are, utterly grateful for speed dial as my fingers were frozen solid.

We are in the woods. Can you come in from the north side? We are in the middle. Every minute seemed like hours. I was watching Shakespeare as he was fighting the drugs and fighting the cold. Elena and I were sitting on the ground a couple of metres away and as I heard the car, I slowly pulled myself out of my sodden rain-jacket, got on all four and crawled across the muddy forest path. Elena looked utterly confused but I had to trust that she would stay and not think this was a game. If she did Shakespeare would get spooked and spring to his feet, drugged or not. As if I was granted a small miracle, she understood something was wrong and that this was no time to play. She stayed with my jacket and hat as I moved forward.

I was intensely cold after hours in the rain, but I was determined to do this. The dog I loved more than anyone could fully understand, might die if I did not pull this off. It had to come together. It just had to!

As I was less than half a meter away, Shakespeare opened his eyes and looked straight at me. It was like he was filtering the information through his foggy brain - he tried to get up. I stretched my hand and got hold of his collar. I grabbed as hard as I could with my frozen fingers holding on for his life. I got halfway up and put my body on top of him, like a gravity blanket - and just then Shakespeare threw his head back in a reflex movement. His long canine tooth, the pointed teeth dogs have in the top and bottom jaw that are used to puncture and hold on to things, did its job. I could feel the sticky blood gushing down my face. In that instant, Shakespeare looked at me with a shocked expression. I had been prepared for something like this to happen and I was determined to not let go, come what may. If he wanted me to let go, he would have to fight me, big time. He would have to rip me to shreds and not just graze me by accident. It was a breaking point moment and we both knew it. I could see it in his eyes as he looked at me through the fog. He had not in any way intended to hurt me and I truly did not care. My focus was on saving him from the hell he was in.

I will let you back out when you are well. I promise. I will. I kept whispering to him and I quietly sobbed, with blood running down my face, down my neck and making a path down my wet jumper. I was crying for him and not for myself. Under the weight of me I could feel him giving in. We were both so utterly exhausted.

Shakespeare took a deep breath and relaxed his body as if he knew what I was telling him was true. On that Thursday afternoon we were a woman and her dog as one, on the muddy, soaking wet grounds, in a small forest in France.

Are had driven the car close enough to where he could see me, and I released one arm to wave. It took seconds for the car to park up next to us.

Shakespeare did a last attempt to get loose, but I was not letting go. I held Shakespeare in a dead lock and Are and I lifted him into the back of the car whilst Are was looking at my blood-stained face and top. *I am ok*, I said, *we need to get Shakespeare home.* How I got myself up whilst lifting Shakespeare I will never know. The back door of the car was closed with a soft click as Are did all he could not to make any abrupt movements or create any sudden sounds. I was in the back of the car holding onto Shakespeare telling him we would be ok. Elena on the front seat next to Are. Her sparkling white fur was black after all the hours in the rain and mud. The car was warm and felt safe and Shakespeare was finally breathing regularly. He gazed up at me and held my eyes. I stroked him and whispered; *I know darling. I know.* We had got out of the woods without getting stuck and as we drove through the gates, only minutes later, the darkness had arrived. I had got hold of him just in time!

Later that evening Shakespeare was fast asleep in front of the fire in the hallway, on top of two new sheepskins that I had bought for him. I had covered him with a soft baby blue blanket, and he looked like a dog without a care in the world. I sat next to him with all the other dogs gathered round. I was exhausted beyond belief and every part of my body was aching. I was still in my wet clothes, with the blood-stained jumper, now in a state of damp and whilst I looked at him, I knew I would keep my promise and let him go again but for now he was in to stay for the winter. I would not let him back out before spring arrived and I knew he would be ok. I would treat the wounds on his legs and make sure he was fit and healthy before he was to live back outside.

Would we ever live permanently together? I wondered, as I climbed the stairs to our bedroom and a warm bath making a mental note that I needed to call my GP the next morning for some antibiotics for the puncture in my chin.

> To die, to sleep -
> To sleep, perchance to dream - ay,
> there's the rub, **For in this sleep of
> death what dreams may come**...
> - William Shakespeare, *Hamlet*

From spending my life walking upright as all humans do, I came to spending hours, days, weeks, and later months on the floor with Shakespeare to connect with him, to help him. For him to understand that he could fully trust me. I wanted him to know me.

Life on the floor also gave me such a unique opportunity to practice deep meditation and stillness, thus helping my own PTSD to subside. In the years after the accident, I had often wished to go on a silent retreat, to get closer to myself. As I was attempting to get closer to Shakespeare, my wish was being granted, without me having to travel anywhere.

My dreaming pattern in the night changed, from flying off the bike to moving in beautiful landscapes. Often, I felt a closeness to Shakespeare that I cannot explain. I mean, I am close to all my animals but with Shakespeare there was something I could not name. It just was.

After Shakespeare's arrival I had become more aware, more present. I paid attention to my energy level, to my breathing. I was wary of the tone in my voice. I also discovered that when speaking with a hushed voice to the dogs, both Shakespeare and the others were paying closer attention. Because I spent my days fully present, things changed for the pack and me. We learned to be still together, and we also learned, all of us, to pay more attention to what was going on.

In our interaction as a pack, small signals that I so easily could have overlooked before became eminently clear. I watched Shakespeare's broken brain slowly, very slowly, with minute sometimes almost undetectable steps, move towards healing. Through our togetherness we shared moments of intense closeness, like we were intertwined. We had a silent communication – as if our brains floated into each other. I was on my stomach one afternoon on the checkered blue and light-colored tiles in the entrance hall. The floor was cold against my body, although I was warmly dressed. The wood in the log burner was gave off muffled bangs of microscopic explosions set off by air pockets in the wood, shooting sparkles.

The hall was warm and cozy in contrast to the floor where I lay. It was a rare moment where we were alone with closed doors. Are was in the kitchen with the others. Shakespeare was in his bed under the billiard table. He was resting on top of the sheep skins and thick teddy blankets, all atop an old fashion heavy wool blanket. His bed was Great Dane size and could so easily fit two dogs his size, as it often did when Lady curled up with him.

Shakespeare was facing the wood burner, and I was facing him. Only in those last couple of days had the sound of the wood burning stopped sending him into trembles. Shakespeare had never been inside a house before he arrived in France and his lack of coping mechanism made adapting to inside life extremely hard for him. It was now three weeks since I had drugged him and brought him inside. My head was resting on the cross bar under the billiard table. I was facing Shakespeare nose to nose with only centimeters distance. How different he smelled. When I first sat close to him in his box in the sanctuary, he smelt of old dirt and dust. Crusted over.

The smell of grief, sadness, and confinement. The smell of a dog that had not cleaned himself for years. As I now laid close to him, I could smell earth. Shakespeare was softly licking one of his front paws - his fur was no longer dusty. Hours spent outside in the rain had washed him again and again, sleeping under the stars and in the moonlight. I could smell that he had been sleeping in the woods, in the hedge and in brambles. He smelt like no other dog. The smell of Shakespeare mixed with the smoky smell from the wood burner. I was inhaling, memorizing the smell to erase the smell from the corner in Cyprus. The smell of someone more dead than alive. Now, Shakespeare smelt of a beating heart and of liberty. I glanced across the floor behind him. I had handpicked the tiles in our hallway, choosing them to give the hallway a feeling of time gone by. There are three doors leading away, one to the living room, one to the dining room and one to a guest toilet. The door to the toilet is painted in mat charcoal black. I had made the wallpaper in the toilet. It is hand painted with Napoleonic bees and from the ceiling there is a lamp filled with crystals, spreading dappled light patterns on to the bees. Above the door are two replicas of theater masks from the Roman era. I bought those in Athens once on a work trip in the nineteen nineties. I could see them from where I was lying. How different everything looks from the floor.

To the left a staircase goes up to the guest bedrooms. I turned my head slightly as I detected movement on the stairs. I saw the chat noir, Mademoiselle Milesi sitting on the third top step watching us. She would sometimes come down the stairs stretching her legs.

She walks so elegantly. My nickname for her - Miss Ballerina - is so fitting.

When she stands still, she looks like her paws are fixed in the first ballet dancer position, heels together and toes pointed outwards. She is elegant and gracefully moves across the floor. She is so beautiful with her huge green eyes and her intense black shiny fur, like a miniature panther. Mademoiselle Milesi is unrecognizable to the cat I rescued after she had been thrown out of a car, which had driven through our hamlet. No claws, a broken tail and a broken spirit made her unpredictable and aggressive. Now she loved nothing more than physical contact.

She had made a routine of climbing on to my back, curling up and going to sleep as I was lying on the floor in the company of Shakespeare and the other dogs. She would purr, enjoying the warmth from me and the wood burner. But not that day. Today she was content just watching Shakespeare and I resting under the table. I do not know if it was the warmth of the fire, the fact that Shakespeare was breathing easily or me being tired, or a combination of all, but despite the uncomfortable position, I drifted off. Years of meditation does that to you. It is possible to be completely relaxed, mind over matter, even on a cold floor in an uncomfortable position.

I was drifting. My body had no weight, and my mind was empty. I was taking in every little sound from the fire, Shakespeare's breathing, the cat on the stairs, the sound of a car passing the house, Inspector Japp barking outside. I heard a door into the kitchen open and close.

I drifted further away.

I walked through the valley of the shadow of death.

The voice was near but still distant. I was in a different space. I was visiting as an observer. In front of me was an intense green hill. The ground was covered with dead dogs. Butchered dogs. I could clearly see the beaten and battered bodies.

All dead!

I could touch them if I wanted as that is how close I was. At the same time, I was at a distance. Space had no meaning. A beautiful cinnamon colored female had had her skull split in two. Her dead eyes were filled with terror.

I was not scared. I was not worried, nor did I feel the urge to escape. I was simply observing a scene I was meant to see. It was information given to me. I was floating in space. I tried to count the dogs, but I knew there would not be enough time. There were too many. I saw the souls of the dogs floating above the corpses. like beautiful colors in shades of bright green, yellow, pink, dappled with white. I do not know how long I stayed but I knew when it was time to leave. I lifted my hands and blew the souls the light that was in the palm of my hands. My hands were open, with my palms up, like when I first offered Shakespeare my hands after he arrived in Belgium. I turned and I sensed the souls following me. As in an intertwined motion I departed from one space to arrive in another. I was awake, back in the present with Shakespeare in the hallway. I stretched out my hand to find Shakespeare's head - as I softly touched him, he moved his head slightly and then he screamed. It was a scream like nothing I had ever heard. A sound that came from the depth of him. A scream filled with fear, grief, sorrow, misery, anguish, broken-heartedness, despair, and bereavement.

I did not move my body, nor my mind. I somehow knew I

needed to be motionless not to disturb him. He was letting go. A sense of relief and immense gratitude swept through me.

He was moving forward.

When I was a child, my mother would take me to church on random occasions. The church was a white wooden building with a high spire and a deep red door. It was a place where I felt uneasy. Whilst there I would keep my mind occupied with the light-beams as they hit the green in the stained-glass windows. I fixed my eyes on the colors to forget where I was. I remember those words - by the angry priest, the man who always sounded like he was shouting to punish people for being just who they were, *walking through the shadows of the valley of death.*

The priest sounded like everyone present could benefit from a whipping. I always wondered about those words, where was that valley, the valley of death? Now fifty years later I knew - it is where Shakespeare had lived. I crept under the billiard table into Shakespeare's bed. I curled myself around him. I held him. Like that, Shakespeare was wrapped by his human, and he let me. This is how we became one lump of two souls under a billiard table in the French countryside. In the hallway of a house from another century, we are forcing ourselves to the surface to meet the light and the air, like the pool toy that shoots to the surface if you try to suppress it.

We were letting go to move forward. How long we laid like that I do not know.

There was no time, only space. We were both exhausted despite not having physically moved - at some point, we drifted off to sleep. I was woken by the fire dying out. It was not cold, but the soft warmth given by the burning wood was gone. I crawled out of the dog bed and Shakespeare got out behind me. He stretches his beautiful long legs with white knee socks with maroon spots. I closed my hand around the wood basket handle and noticed that Shakespeare was not showing any signs of being worried over my movements. He kept stretching as he was looking at me. He seemed peaceful. I opened the door to the dining room, then the kitchen, and seven dogs were showing their delight over seeing us both. There were eight wagging tails.

We all passed through the kitchen door. The cold air was refreshing. It felt like I was breathing for the first time - in a very long time. It felt like we had just returned after a long journey, whilst we had only been gone for some hours.
There were more wagging tails and happy sounds. As I walked back in with the wood basket filled with heavy wood Shakespeare passed me. He brushed against my leg. Again, as so often before, something in our relationship had shifted. We shared something I cannot explain, nor do I feel the need to analyze it. It is what it is, and all I know is that it was meant to be like this.

Later in the night as the full moon was shining over our home, I went out to light a candle. There was a candle holder in front of a large, round outdoor mirror, reflecting the moon. I lit the candle as part of my ancient Norwegian heritage where the flame lights the soul's path home.

They are all there. The souls I saw earlier in the day.

As I turned and walked back, crossing the courtyard with all the dogs watching me through the glass door, there was a sense of peace and utter calmness to our magical spot amongst the vines in Southwest France.

Nothing can come of nothing.
- William Shakespeare, *King Lear*

Was living inside too much for Shakespeare? The question was constant.

We had done so well, but then something shifter and things had taken turns for the worse. I was losing sleep and in the morning my body would turn itself toward the window in search of the morning light. There was none - it was still dark outside. My brain was seeking the surface trying to leave the unsettling unrest of the night behind. I knew I had to do something. I knew neither Shakespeare nor I could continue the path we somehow had turned down. I felt like we were sliding into darkness.

After so many steps forward, Shakespeare had regressed and was worse than he had ever been. His PTSD was back to being out of control and he would hide under the billiard table in the hallway, or under the counter in the kitchen or under the vintage French metal bed, so low he would injure himself. He would act in panic and adrenaline rush, when his brain signalled his life was in danger by his sheer existence. He would act on instinct, for survival and nothing else. I would watch him, and my heart would break, again and again. I could do nothing for him. If I tried to get closer to him, he would panic even more. If I left, he sometimes settled but also look for smaller spaces to hide in – putting himself in further danger. He spent most of his time hiding and I spent all of my time worrying for and about him. Nothing specific had caused the regression. There had been no incident but somehow his fear was out of control.

Shakespeare was trembling, shaking, and drooling. The other dogs tried to help him, but they could not reach him either.

Without a way forward, I had transported Shakespeare from Cyprus to France for him to just enter another storage box. A better looking one, with soft blankets and endless human and paw love, but still a storage box. A place filled with support, a huge garden, and a potential future but what good would that be if *he* in effect did not understand that everything had changed.

When I fell asleep, I felt exhausted. I felt completely disheartened. I felt overwhelming grief like a cold wave reaching every corner of my being.

I also felt anger on Shakespeare's behalf, for the suffering he was enduring. During the night, all my emotions had bundle themselves into a knot in my gut that could not be untangled. Grief. Heartbreak. It had all accumulated into a twitching in my spine. A twitching I knew all too well. It was a twitching calling me to action in response to a silent call for survival.

It was as if the lifeline attached to my dwindling hope of a full recovery for Shakespeare had grabbed me by my shoulders and was pulling me out of the quicksand experience the last months had become. After we had brought Shakespeare inside, his spurts of joy had made me so optimistic. But then he sank back into his own darkness. Shakespeare would shake, tremble, and look at me in panic like he had done the day he stood in the middle of the road. My heart broke many times each day. In juxtaposition, I was filled with deep gratitude to my pack that simply accepted Shakespeare and his fear; him hiding and they trying to comfort him by staying close and circling around at bedtime.

They willingly and generously shared me and my attention, and if I snuck down in the night, I could get a glimpse of Shakespeare surrounded by love. He would be curled up in the huge bed together with Lady who knew fear all too well. Fear, anxiety, and stress remained her travel companion too, but unlike Shakespeare she would let me sooth her. As I brushed me teeth, looking in the mirror at my baggy eyes, I talked silently to my reflection: *If there is a solution out there you will find it!* As if Shakespeare could feel the shift in my energy as I came down the stairs, he came out from under the billiard table and did one of his play bows. His beautiful body went down in the front by the longest stretch of his front legs and his back end was up in the air with his docked tail moving like a swirly whisk aiming to make cream from milk. His deep amber coloured eyes looked straight at me, and he did not retract his look like he normally would after less than a second. He kept his eyes interlocked with mine and with that we had passed yet another mile stone. It had taken months before he could look at me, but he would normally feel he had to glance away as to not challenge me. This morning was different. He kept looking and then he barked at me, or to me and I heard him loud and clear.

Mum, we will be ok.

I am so proud of you, I responded.

It was a statement!

He gave me another small bark and my heart was yet again filled with joy and hope.

Eight wagging tails, seven noses wanting to sniff and smell and make sure I had not changed in the night, that I was still me. I was still mum, and the love was shown by everyone wanting to have a cuddle and a stroke. Shakespeare climbed back into his bed under the table but the other seven plus Mademoiselle Milesi, who had appeared from nowhere, followed me to the kitchen. The whistle on the kettle is part of the morning ritual and this morning the kettle was left to whistle for a bit. Feeding time was back to being problematic for Shakespeare but not in the way it was when he first arrived. He did not mind me being in the room when he ate but when he chewed, he obviously could not hear as well because of the crunching in his mouth so he would constantly stop chewing and listen for danger whilst trembling, preparing himself for the worst possible outcome – that he could die.

I had already been to the laundry room to get all the porcelain feeding bowls and Shakespeare's metal bowl, the one with the sharp bright yellow outside and blue rubber ring on the bottom. All bowls were lined up in the order they were every morning, and the croquettes were there, prepared in a huge metal bowl ready to be dished out. Two tins of wet food were opened, croquettes ready in a large bowl, and boiled eggs from my wonderful neighbour Geneviève ready to top their breakfast. For dinner they would have vegetables on top. As the dogs were looking at me with longing breakfast eyes, I composed a message to my wonderful friend Dr D in London. In her adult years she had left her job and started on the long road to becoming a veterinarian. I trusted her completely and I knew she would give me sound advice on where to go from here. I added a video clip of Shakespeare at his most joyful and some of him in his everyday state hiding under something. I silenced the whistling kettle with one hand, and I pressed "send."

I felt relief rushing through my morning self as I had acknowledged it.

I had put into words how bad things were and how I longed for someone to help me find a path forward. I made coffee and started filling the food bowls. The one with black and brown kittens was for Hastings, the one with pink paw prints was Miss Grey's. There were Lady birds for Inspector Japp, hens were for Lady Eileen Bundle Brent, owls for Hercule and black and white kittens for Isabelle Duveen. Countess Elena would inhale her food, so she still had her grey slow-eater that looked like a labyrinth in miniature. Finally, the metal bowl in the colour of the Swedish flag was for Shakespeare. Shakespeare did not dare to eat from porcelain.

It sounds differently when your mouth moves the dry biscuits around a porcelain surface then it does on cold metal.

Metal is what he had his food from in the refuge for almost five years, so metal was too familiar to let go of. For now, at least.

I put down each bowl in the specific order I always do for breakfast and dinner. Captain Hastings is first, then Hercule and Lady. Shakespeare's bowl is put on the large dog bed in the kitchen. I always pull the bedding back and put his bowl close to the edge. In the beginning he did not dare to eat more than a couple of mouthfuls before any movement, or a simple sound would petrify him and stop him dead in his tracks. He would stop eating and start shivering with fear, but this morning he only stopped *in between* the mouthfuls and not during. Japp and Miss Grey are served breakfast below the left kitchen window as always whilst Elena is served by herself in the dining room. Elena still vacuums and inhales her food so keeping her separate is an attempt to slow her down and to stop her from trying to raid anyone else's bowl.

Elena had food issues from a pup, perhaps linked to starvation she went through before she was dumped over the fence at the refuge. Every morning, after having served all the bowls of high-quality kibble with a dash of wet dog food, an egg, sardines, or vegetables, topped with salmon oil for the Omega3 benefits, everyone is silent. They will all eat, content and happy as part of their morning ritual. When they finish, I will open the kitchen door to let them out. However, having Shakespeare eating with the pack in the kitchen, I now had to time everything. If I opened the door too soon Shakespeare would not finish his meal. He would leave his bowl and rush out the door almost knocking the others over. To solve the problem, I started the breakfast treat club. Each dog had to sit and wait for Shakespeare to finish before they, one by one, got a treat for excellent behaviour. "Sit" is not an accurate description. Captain Hastings preferred not to sit after he had a knee prothesis fitted, and Shakespeare and Lady did not sit ever, as they simply never got the concept, but Japp, Hercule, Miss Grey, Isabel and certainly Elena would together form the most beautiful, perfectly-seated part of the group! That morning, they all had a bone-shaped dog biscuit as their treat. Even Shakespeare stretched his neck out to get one. He was always so gentle in taking food and treats from my hand. It was one of a long list of things that made me admire him so. *All gone* I said, raising my hands into the air.

Miss Grey knew what the words meant, and Elena could see the outline of my hand gesture. They all moved towards the door as one unit. It was raining outside and Hercule looked as me as to say *Please do not make me get wet.*

Go out for a wee Hercule. You can come straight back in.

He was not impressed with my answer but did reluctantly put one paw in front of the other. Just as I closed the door, I heard my phone. *Please let it be Dr D* I silently wished, and it was. Her message appeared *Hi B, it is just heart-breaking to see him. The only real behaviour drug that we use is Fluoxetine and a friend was telling me a couple of days ago how they rescued a puppy-mill dog that did not know how to be in a pack/inside and it worked a treat. It will be something on prescription from your vet. He needs some behaviour modification to help him learn as he seems completely shut down xx*

My fingers typed "Fluoxetine for dogs" into the display of my Google app and the word Prozac was gleaming at me. Prozac? As in "Prozac Nation"? The film flashed in my inner eye. I knew Prozac was a frontline drug for people with PTSD, but for dogs? The screen said, "The psychotropic medication can change your dog's brain action by manipulating its neurotransmitters in a particular way."

I texted Dr D back telling her how watching Shakespeare was like having my heart ripped out daily. We both agreed that something needed to happen, but I could not free myself from the extremely uncomfortable feeling that I was letting Shakespeare down. All were back inside after their morning rounds in the garden, scattered around, settling down. Hercule was as always following me with his eyes to make sure I was not planning to take any of his siblings for a walk and leaving him behind. Everyone thought Hercule was such a calm dog, and he was, if I were in the room, but when I left, he would pine. Even if I was just gone for minutes. If I went away for a day or two, he would stop eating, as he did the first two days when I went to Cyprus.

He would lie and stare at the door and refuse to interact with anyone. Are would of course make sure he was ok but there simply was no remedy for his longing. I stroked him over his head and in return he tried to lick my hand.

I must go out for a little while Hercule, but I will not be long I promise. Please do not growl at the others when I am away.

I stroked him again before I got my car keys out of the chaotic kitchen drawer, where I could find anything from car keys to rusty nails, chewing gum, matches, a torch, an extra light bulb for the oven, amongst many other random items. One of these days, I promised myself, I will clear out that drawer.

The vet I use for my own animals and for the Association is in the nearest village to us.

It is a dozy little village with two bakers, three cash points, one pharmacy, one optician and a supermarket, oh yes and a fantastic chocolatier. The village has a small weekly market and a large market once a month – typical French in other words. The vet-office is in the old gas station opposite the school. It was all quiet as I pulled into the parking. No school children and no sick animals of any sort. The receptionist knew me well. She and I had had the funniest of misunderstandings when I first arrived at our new home, and I went to book an appointment for Captain Hastings. To say my French was not good would be an understatement. It was terrible, but I understood more than I could speak, and during my efforts to make an appointment, the receptionist, a lady of mature years, thought I told her I knew Captain Hastings in the TV series of Hercule Poirot. The series was at the time doing a rerun on French TV and she was very vocal in her positive admiration for the lovely man.

I can only presume she was referring to the actor Hugh Frasier who plays Captain Hastings in the series). It took quite a while for me to clarify that Captain Hastings was my dog and I would be grateful for an appointment. The memory has later made me laugh many times. Luckily, my French had improved, and she seemed happy to see me.

Bonjour Madame Strandenes. Ça Va ?

Qui bien sur. Ça Va ?

I love these small pleasantries that seem exclusively French, and I really miss them when I am interacting with other nationalities.

I smiled at her and explained my errand. She gave me one of her "leave it to me" looks. She was truly a good woman to have on your side.

She crossed the floor with determination as if she were taking on a challenge of the most difficult kind.

She knocked on the vet office door and I could hear her tell the vet that I wanted to speak to him. I entered his office.

There have been times when I have woken the vet during the night for emergencies and there have been times he has come to my house, and no matter what is going on he is the calmest man in the room. Nothing stresses him and even Lady who is terrified of strangers would wag her tail at the sight of Dr Gillot. Lady even got on the examining table, despite her legs shaking. Dr Gillot knew of Shakespeare and now I showed him the video of Shakespeare hiding, trembling. I told him about my conversation with Dr D and he agreed with the conclusion, the dosage, and the plan forward.

A couple of minutes later I left with the prescription in my hand.

Good vets are worth their weight in gold!

Bonne journée. A bientôt et merci beaucoup I whispered to the receptionist who was on the phone. She waved as I closed the door behind me.

I stopped at the pharmacy to get the medication and as I sat in the car with two packets of Fluoxetine in my hand, I felt numbed. I knew it was the right decision and yet I felt like I was betraying Shakespeare. It was like I was giving up on him.

I have never been one for taking an easy route because things become difficult and, I felt that there should have been other things I should have tried, at the same time as I knew I was not being rational. I drove home filled with sadness that Shakespeare and I had not managed to avoid this, but here it was. Prozac! I hated it, no matter how right the decision was.

With Prozac came changes in Shakespeare. Not huge ones, not overnight, but after around four weeks he seemed calmer. He was still scared, and I could still not touch him if he were not on his favourite chair. His need was to survive, and my goal was for him to be able to fight his panic attacks, to breathe and to be able to sleep without being in a state of constant alert; to sleep to gain strength and wake up refreshed.

Prozac is a selective serotonin reuptake inhibitor meaning the drug blocks your body from reabsorbing serotonin, and my hope was that Prozac would balance Shakespeare's brain and body so that he did not have to live with his extreme fears for the rest of his life.

Serotonin is the chemical that carries messages between nerve cells in the brain and through the body, playing a key role in sleep pattern, moods, and wound healing.

Research has found that low serotonin levels are present in patients who struggle with anxiety and mental health issues and in PTSD patients as well. The greater the imbalance the more serious the symptoms. My only big comfort during that time was that the wounds on Shakespeare's legs got better with the Prozac and I suspected that this was linked to Substance P (and other neuropeptides) that are released and thought to be involved in neurogenic inflammation. All this I understood from my own PTSD and that made me feel a bit more at ease about giving Shakespeare his daily medication. He took the medication on top of his food, left in plain sight, and there were never any problems.

As I saw improvement in him, I also observed something that worried me.

Shakespeare no longer had the highs of joy that he uses to have. He did not have the deep downs, but he did not a have the highs either. He lived in a state of middle-of-the- road. He still wagged his tail, but he did not jump like a rabbit for joy. It made me sad, and I could not help questioning myself again and again. Was I doing the right thing? Had almost five years of solitude, the loss of Agatha, being taken out of his environment on the riverbank, damaged Shakespeare so much that he would never be able to recover? If he never did recover, my love for him would not be less but I so wanted him to experience a life without PTSD having all the control. Would that ever happen? Would it be possible?

Whilst asking questions I stuck to the plan - giving him Prozac and trying in every way to support his journey through an ocean of panic and anguish. It was the same ocean I had swam before him.

> **What's in a name** that which we call a rose By any other name would smell as sweet
> -William Shakespeare, *Romeo and Juliet*

I had long since settled for the fact that I would never truly get to know the story behind Shakespeare's name and how Agatha had come to be named Agatha Christie. However - eight months after Shakespeare came home, on a beautiful, cold, crisp December morning, I had been out walking the pack and was at the kitchen table drinking coffee. On the table were candles burning and fires in the hallway and the dining-room were sending heat through to the kitchen. The pack was sleeping, and Miss Lemon had come inside for a cuddle and some food.

I picked up my phone to check messages on my rescue page @Jane Marple. One message immediately stood out as it was from a name I had never seen before nor heard of. It was a Greek name. Christiana A. This is a copy of the message.

Dear Jane, we never had the chance to meet but I have been following you since the moment I found out that Shakespeare is with you. I am the person who first met him and managed to capture him along with his family. At first it was another happy rescuing moment for me, thinking that another dog was saved. But as days, weeks, months and eventually years passed by, I found myself feeling guilty and deeply regretting that I did capture him. Seeing Shakespeare trembling and totally shutting down every time I would visit him was haunting me.

It was the first time that I doubted that what I did was right, asking myself if the best thing we should do was letting Shakespeare free. Without being overdramatic I honestly lost sleep over this troubled soul so many nights because I couldn't see how we could get through to him. And then you came! When C. firstly mentioned your offer I had mixed feelings, I was convinced that no human could make a difference for him, thinking that over and above his anxiety he would have to endure the trip to France. On the other hand, it was a change, a change that by that time I was thinking could not be worse than the place he was at. Never in my wildest dreams did I imagine what you would achieve with him! I cannot tell you how grateful I am that you came in his life, I cannot tell you how I admire you but what I can tell you is that I have tears in my eyes every time I read your posts, tears of happiness!!

Thank you for all you have done and when you have the chance, please gently stroke his head on my behalf, something I wanted to do so many times, but it never felt right.

I have tears in my eyes, and I am not known for being sentimental. I am deeply moved for all you have done for him; I cannot even describe in words the joy I feel knowing that he is in his happy place at last.

Strangely enough I also have a history with him two years prior to capturing him. It feels that the pieces of the puzzle fall into place leading him to you.

I live in Nicosia next to the riverbank. I always have bowls of food in my parking space for stray cats and dogs (sometimes even foxes). One fine day as I parked, it was August and the heat was terrible, I saw these two dogs lying next to the empty bowls of food. I tried approaching them, but as soon as I did that the just got up and disappeared.

To my surprise the next day I found them again on the same spot, this time I knew better so I just greeted them and walked away, they did not make any move trying to escape this time. From then on, I was making sure the bowls were full of food and they would come back every couple of days. We reached a point that they accepted me filling their bowls without them moving, any attempt to touch them though would drive them away. This went on for about a year. Then they suddenly disappeared. Few months later I was notified that about a kilometre away from my house, still on the riverbank, were two dogs, and apparently the female also gave birth.

I went there, only to find out it was my Shakespeare and Agatha and 4 cute puppies. To cut a long story short it took me about 2 months and daily visits to capture the puppies, but Shakespeare and Agatha were mission impossible. I really need to mention here that Shakespeare was a very proud dog, taking care of his family. He would accept me approaching them, but if another person were with me, he would get worried but never aggressive. It was when the elderly neighbours started complaining about the dogs damaging the little vegetable gardens and one of them asked me to stop feeding them or else he would poison them, that I decided it was time to remove them from there. I coordinated with C, and we managed to trad Shakespeare and Agatha. From then on, they were moved to the sanctuary, and you more or less know the story.

What was hurting me the most is that I had met a proud, happy dog that shut down after we captured him. If only I knew! On the other hand, if we left them there it was only a matter of time before someone would hurt them.

You see they were hunting to survive and that led them to peoples' back yards, where quite often they were making damage.

BTW the whole family was named after famous authors, thus Shakespeare and Agatha.

I typed my response and ended it with: The utterly strange things is - and I do not know if you know this - all my dogs and cats are named after Agatha Christie characters.

No, I did not!!!!

In a homage to my dad and Agatha Christie I have named all my animals after AC characters. During those first days after meeting Shakespeare, I sat in the opening of his box reading about Miss Marple to him.

I was spending so much time sitting next to them trying to make them accustomed to my voice, so I was reading aloud. That is when I decided to name after authors.

I explained how I was almost floored when C told me Shakespeare's beloved Agatha was named after Agatha Christie.

If ever there was a sign!

I know, I consider myself a very realistic type of person but this whole thing is beyond me.

There it was - the history of his name, and that of Agatha's too. The questions had now been answered.

Two women who had never met, two women from two different countries had just met in cyberspace sharing their story and the love for this extraordinary dog. This dog that touched us both so deeply.

It all made perfect sense to me.

> **At Christmas** I no more desire a rose Than wish a snow in May's new-fangled mirth;
> But like of each thing that in season grows.
> -William Shakespeare, *Love's Labour's Lost*

We had settled into our winter life.

I would walk Countess Elena, Hercule, Lady Eileen Bundle Brent and sometimes Miss Grey on our ten-kilometre morning walk. In the evening, weather permitting I would walk Captain Hastings, Inspector Japp and Isabel who due to age now needed far less exercise. When I left for our walks, Shakespeare would stand with those who were staying behind, inside the kitchen door, barking and desperately wanting to come. He could however not be allowed to join us for any walks because he was simply not ready to walk back inside on our return and it was far too cold for him to go back to living outside.

The same miserable late autumn weather continued through until December. Then the cold, clear winter days arrived. The house was warm, and Shakespeare had, in his own way, settled to inside living. He would eat his breakfast and dinner in the kitchen and apart from being highly stressed when I left, he had made much progress. He dared to be in the open space of a room for minutes at a time and he had changed his favourite spot in the house - from the chair in the dining room to the corner of the white sofa in the living room. He would lay in the corner dozing off in the company of Miss Lemon who had followed Shakespeare inside.

I had bought him new sheepskins - the others were stained with blood and puss from the wounds on his legs, and the softness had been washed away. They were perfect to use under blankets in a dog basket but not to lie on directly. I would check his legs every morning and strangely enough Shakespeare would not mind at all that I treated his wounds with local antibiotics and later with honey. He would even respond when I told him to leave the wounds alone. On one occasion, I was worried he was running a temperature and when I took the temperature via his rectum, he did not protest at all. He knew I was trying to help him.

We had reached mid-December and there was a lovely sense of calm in our home now that we were all together. Elena and Lady no longer paced the floor, wanting to find Shakespeare. He was inside with us all.

We were back in lock down and movement was still restricted, meaning we never went anywhere socially. I was out on rescue, but I tried to prioritize my walks and I was so happy to be home most of the time. Home with mine.

The weather granted us beautiful crisp, freezing winter days for weeks and when it was time, I went to the barn wrapped up as a pole farer to carry in all the Christmas decorations, with eight dogs and two cats in tow. The fact that Shakespeare had decided to walk across the courtyard and into the barn without climbing on top of everything in panic, or seeking somewhere to hide, forcing his body under an item too low for him to fit, had made my day utterly joyful. It was such an enormous step in the right direction. He had even looked at me as if he were seeking approval for his courage. He had come a long way! However - after he passed the threshold into the courtyard, I could not touch him.

Once outside he was feral, but he would stay close to me as always. I had long since learnt not to approach him in the courtyard or in the orchard. I was simply happy and content that we were in the same physical space and that we shared our everyday life.

With all the bags of Christmas decorations placed in the checkered-tiled hallway, it looked like an almighty shopping spree! I wondered how Shakespeare would handle the noise and chaos.

Ordinary daily events would often send Shakespeare into a spiral of trembling and hiding, and I had to plan things like opening an ocean of bags of Christmas decorations. Which bag would make a sound? Which bag would I need to quietly carry into another room before I opened it? By that stage I was so used to having to think everything through before I acted, that I did not even think twice about the thought process.

Our home is such a perfect frame for an overload of Christmas, and I love decorating it under the slogan *"the more, the better."* There is no such thing as too much Christmas, albeit I draw the line at 1970s Christmas jumpers!

Decoration-day is always a day of hot cacao and soft sentiments as I unpack each item, each star and sparkling Santa, remembering where I bought every single item over the years.

That day was no different to the years before apart from this being the first Christmas that Shakespeare was home. The wood burner in the hallway was sending dancing light onto the bags holding the Christmas decorations, the wood in the open fireplace in the living room made small crackling sounds. In the dining room the huge blue and white Chinese vase I once bought for umbrellas, were already set up on the white circular Christmas tree mat. We do not do an ordinary Christmas tree at ours. Our tradition is now a small ordinary tree that we cut in the woods, or from our land – placed in the vase. I would hang white snowball ornaments on the branches, fairy lights and lots of miniature silver birds with white feather tails. That way we do not have to be concerned for cats climbing the tree or a blind dog knocking it over, as sensing the length of the branches could sometimes be difficult. Each year I walk Miss Grey and Miss Marple to where the vase was placed and tap a ring on the porcelain. By that, they both knew something unfamiliar had now taken its place on a floor space normally free of any items. It only took the one tap for them to know there was something there.

Are had been out to get the tree the evening before and the blank canvas was ready to be "Christmassed." I was talking to all the dogs as I was unpacking and Miss Marple and Milesi came to check out what all the fuss was about. Mrs Oliver our huge cat was asleep on one of the dining room chairs and Miss Lemon was last spotted on a window ledge in the kitchen. Miss Marple did what she always does; found a bag I had unzipped, and head first, she was in, tail and all. She always wanted to check out the contents - by feeling her way. If she found any silk paper she would purr and purr louder, as to show Christmas happiness cat-style. It is so amazing to watch this tiny cat, without eyes, finding her way around anywhere and anything. If she is with her own, she does not have a care in the world. Even Shakespeare became miraculously curious and joined Hastings with his nose in one of the bags. I knew Hastings was searching for anything edible, but I suspect Shakespeare was simply trying to figure out what was going on.

Outside the wind was howling and even if the weather were clear, there would be no walk. We had Christmas work to do! We spent the whole afternoon unpacking, with me choosing a place for each item different to the year before. I only stopped to give the dogs and cats their dinner and by nine in the evening the house was finished.

Are was back from work and we decided to open a bottle of red wine to celebrate that the house had been decorated and that Christmas was almost here.

In Norway Christmas is Jul - the midwinter fest of the Vikings, existing long before Christianity. The name has been kept to this day and on the mantlepiece above the fireplace in the dining room, placed in between evergreen ivy, big gold letter spelt J-U-L. I poured the deep red earthy Bordeaux wine into large glasses that could easily have held a goldfish. As Are was doing the last preparations to our dinner, I took my wine glass and went to sit in the corner chair in the dining room. I wanted to absorb the candles I had lit everywhere and just watch the room sparkle from the glitter. Through the window I could see the outdoor Christmas lights and the ground lights making the inside and outside seem to float into one. It was a perfect moment of peace, happiness, and gratitude. The man I love was in the kitchen making us a wonderful meal, the fireplace and both log burners were lit. I had packed away all the empty bags that had held all the decorations. I had spent a blessed day with my favourite beings - my pack - laughed watching the cats playing and the dogs interacting. I sat still, sipping and reflecting on how lucky I was.

Just as I closed my eyes for a second, I heard Shakespeare walking across the hallway. I knew the steps of all my dogs, and there was no question it was him.

He had left the safe place of his sofa-corner. I wondered if he needed to go outside but decided to sit still until I knew for sure. His nose came around the corner, followed by his body. He walked completely calmly towards me, looking straight at me. His face was soft, and he seemed unnaturally relaxed. I sat up, leaning forward, moving myself to the edge of the high back chair – he simply walked past me and jumped behind me onto the seat. I almost dropped my wine glass in the shock of it all.

Holding my breath, I thought; *What now?* With no clever answer, I turned and stroked him.

Have you come to see me? I worried about breaking the magic. Shakespeare turned his head and looked at me before he, ever-so-carefully leaned against me. In the eight months Shakespeare had been home he had never, not even once, shown initiative to physically interact with me. He had never come for a cuddle or for a stroke; in our relationship I took all the initiative, and I had got used to that.

Sitting there, in that dining room, with my dogs and cats scattered round, with the sound of Christmas songs coming from the kitchen and the house filled with the aroma of my husband's cooking, Shakespeare leaning against me, I experienced the clearest moment of pure happiness I had felt for years.

The moment that will forever be amongst the favourite moments of my life.

I held him as he kept leaning in. The whole of my being filled with gratitude for this boy that was such an intertwined part of me.

I love you too I whispered.

> **Love** is not love which alters when it alteration finds.
> -William Shakespeare, *Sonnet 116*

It was early in the morning of January 1st, after the New Year's Eve gathering the evening before, when I was woken by Inspector James D crying heartbreakingly in habitual desperation. Japp, our beautiful, silky soft, champagne-colored American Cocker Spaniel, with huge paws and circle eyes looking at you from an often-tilted head. He was now doing his *I-have-lost-Hastings* routine. *Lost* meant waking up and not seeing Hastings immediately. Japp will not follow the pattern of logic and get up and take a walk round to look for Hastings. On the contrary - Japp will just get himself into a sitting position and if he cannot see Captain Hastings, panic sets in. As Japp is born deaf, he will not hear when Hastings moves in the night to go and lay somewhere else. Forty-three kilo Captain Hastings is Inspector Japp's safety blanket. Without him, Japp's world reduces to a dangerous place even inside the safety of our kitchen.

Japp's deafness is caused by brain damage that can be the consequence of over-breeding, due to his gene pool or linked to delivery complications at birth, but whatever the reason, Japp is deaf, and our "slow child." He is completely without the ability to think logically. We have taught Japp some basic sign language; *"sit" "find your ball,"* and the all-important *"come"* by me moving my arms like I am the traffic person at the tarmac of an airport. He also knew some other words, but his communication was with Hastings and if I wanted Japp to do something I would tell Hastings, and Japp would mimic whatever Hastings did.

Japp came to us by fluke. He had originally been adopted by a family that decided they could not keep him. Japp's nonstop barking, hiding, rocking absently back and forth, knocking over the dustbin to rummage meant the resident dog did not take to him. The family wanted to return him to the rescue system. I suggested that before they did, they should come to us and have him cat tested. If he could live with cats, it would open his chances of quickly finding a new home. The family came, Japp went straight to Miss Marple who was sleeping in a cardboard box I had left outside, he licked her - and Are fell in love with him. Before the family had returned home, we had decided that his name would be Inspector Japp and he was coming home. He had been with us less than two days when I realized he was deaf - that of course explained his behavior.

The nonstop barking was fear.

He was a dog without any language other than barking - living in a lonely world of his own. He was not naughty nor wanted to disobey any simple command. When he came to ours, he did his *knock-over-the-dustbin* routine once, and as a result Hastings put a paw on Japp's back, nailed him to the floor, to tell him off. Japp never knocked over a dustbin again.

By the time I had gotten myself wrapped in my dressing gown to venture downstair I had of course given away that I was awake – creating widespread joy. Hercule joined Japp in his howling and sent everyone into one united crescendo of a choir. It made me laugh, as it always does. Oh, the joy of being the mum of eight dogs. They were all gathered at the bottom of the dark green stairs, noses pointed upwards, and necks stretched out in typical *wolf- howling-to-the-moon* pose. In the middle of the pack was Shakespeare and for the first time ever, he was howling with the choir. He looked utterly confused. *Why are we doing this, guys?* He was looking around for answers but as no one was willing to stop and explain, he continued, confused look and all.

Shakespeare had been home for two-hundred-and-twenty-seven days and every day had experienced a *"first"*. When he would let me touch him for a second when he was not in the safety of his favorite chair. When he would try to eat something, he had never tasted before, like pasta, rice, new biscuits, an apple, a banana, broccoli, sweet potato, or French cheese. The huge step of him negotiating the interior doorways, then the kitchen door. Trying to stay physically close to me in a joint open space. When he tried, he used all his physical strength to outmaneuver the PTSD that was telling him that his life was in danger.

The list continues. The first time he let me sit on the floor by his chair whilst he was leaning his head on my shoulder. The first time he stayed in his bed with Lady as I walked by, or - when he did not try to hide under the large metal bed in the kitchen but chose to jump onto the bed instead.

I was laughing. They were so cute, and they certainly are dogs with dog behavior. A pack howls to gather any lost member and the lost member was in this case me, who had been away, upstairs in our bedroom, sleeping.

It is such a privilege to be missed and to experience the effort to call me back into our pack. This pack of mine was all broken once. They are deaf, blind, and emotionally scarred and in theory this pack should not work.

The blind bumps into the deaf, the deaf have problems following what is happening, one has brain damage making him awkward in social interaction, two with severe PTSD and others with emotional scars, but - this pack does work! They take care of each other – they always make room for one more and they will always help love life back into whoever I bring home. They impress me daily with their intelligence and capacity to love, forgive and their strong ability to show empathy. Watching them, learning from them - living with them and being part of their pack is a privilege not many people get to experience – making me extraordinarily lucky!

My feet touched the warm wooden floor, putting the kettle on before wading through what seemed like an ocean of dancing dogs to open the kitchen doors. I wanted to let them out for a morning wee and a run. There were four wide, long, fully lined beautiful cinnamon colored vintage velvet curtains covering the huge double atelier kitchen doors with side windows. The curtains kept the large room warm, but they also had the blessed effect of muffling the sounds of foxes and any other wild animals, like wild boar and deer, which pass by the property at night. If the dogs detect the animals, they will of course bark to let us know we all needed to gather to fight off the enemy, and often they would not settle back down for a while, so heavy curtains were truly a blessing.

As I pulled the curtains aside, the wood curtain rings made that rattling sound - wood meeting wood - that all the dogs knew as the first morning sound, we discovered a garden covered in that whispering silent beauty only frost crystals can hold. Every leaf and grass-straw were sparkling, covered in freshly cut tiny diamonds on a backdrop of chalk matt frost. The sky that was sharp pink and light lilac seemed like a dome above, cocooning our home in the depth of the countryside.

Wow everyone. Look. Miss Grey turned her head towards me, and I reached out my hand and stroked her head, sending her tail rotating. To the west there were silver clouds, hanging on an orange water-colored sky.

The frost was making the garden look utterly magical and the contrast between the flamed sky and the matt white frost made my eyes stretch wide. It seemed too beautiful to be real. The smoke from our chimneys was dancing through the cold air in the courtyard. Swirling, descending, rising, making me think of Swan Lake.

All the dogs gathered in front of the kitchen door, wanting out.

Every morning, I must tell them to back up so I can open the inwards kitchen doors. They all knew the routine, even Shakespeare. As I pulled the door back it was like water released as they poured through the door, leaving only Miss Grey lingering with me.

Can you smell the frost, darling?

I felt in a hurry and as Miss Grey hurried after others, I turned and rushed upstairs to put some warm clothes on. In the laundry room my boots were placed just inside the door. I grabbed them both with one hand and found the nearest chair to sit on. I needed to get myself into the garden before the sun stole the frost and the crystals. Magic like that does not last. Thick pink and white handknitted knee socks, with the traditional Norwegian eight blade rose pattern made the boots fit perfectly. I tied the laces tight before returning to the laundry room to get my feather down jacket known to keep you warm in minus twenty degrees according to the shop assistant. My coffee was on the kitchen island.

With a thermos cup, dressed as if I was a pole-farer, I opened the door and walked into a wall of cold. All eight dogs were excited by me joining their morning venture. Hercule did his ritual happy dance, circling around me.

Mum, mum look at the morning. Look how wonderful it is to be alive and together!

I laughed for the third time that morning.

I know sweetheart. I know. It is wonderful. It is perfect my darling. I respond to Hercule as I touch his head in between his jumps.

He cannot stop himself from jumping. He does not touch me with his front paws but jumps round me in a circular movement bouncing off the ground as if he is weightless. I often think he must have been a kangaroo in his last life.

The grass was sparkling, the olive trees looked like they were dressed for a glossy magazine photo shoot. In the orchard the picture continued. Everything was covered in ice crystals including the twisted old branches of the plum trees.

To know that each crystal was different from the other was mind boggling. It was stunningly beautiful. I tried to soak it in, inhaling it.

The dogs were frolicking as always.

Jumping, bouncing - leaping, and tumbling - standing on their back legs only to throw themselves around midair just to start all over again. The breath from their nostrils formed patterns of frosty smoke - leaving a trail that lingered for many seconds after they had moved.

Here was Hemingway, and Ronda, and the bull fights! Shakespeare was chasing Lady or the other way around. To watch him interact and play is amongst the biggest rewards ever bestowed to me. He still did not know how to play properly but was trying to find his footing in play, as in everything else. I stood in the orchard under a frosted plum tree sipping my hot drink watching this unspoilt pure joy unfold. Such energy. Such happiness. My breath made frost trails too.

I wonder how many other humans on the planet got to drink morning coffee in their frost-crystal-covered garden, under a domed flamed sky, with their pack of eight dogs. My mind was wandering back to when I first saw Shakespeare and what the year 2020 had gifted, he and I, and our pack. The journey we had been on and were still on. How all our lives were changed by my trip to Cyprus.

I was already in love with 2021. The year was an infant, only hours old, but I had a strong sense of peace with its arrival. The beauty of the morning was hard to take in. I wished I could put it in a jar and keep it on my sideboard, beside the jar of whitewashed shells from last summer's walk on the Ile d'Aix.

2021 would bring new changes. My journey with Shakespeare and the pack would continue. My pack was completed by Shakespeare coming home. I touched happiness every day, but the journey had also been filled with heart wrenching moments and despair, making this journey even more valuable.

Standing there under the frozen plum tree I was the most centered I had ever been, thanks to these wonderful paws and especially to Shakespeare who had forced me to climb within.

I reached out and touched the branch above my head and as I did the thin layer of ice that had wrapped itself around each branch broke, and tiny pieces of ice dropped to the ground as shattered thin glass. In a sun beam moment, it would exist no more, but turn into water and soak into the ground.

For most people on this beautiful blue planet of ours, 2020 will be remembered as the year of COVID. The year we experienced confinement.

The year of closed schools - with home-schooling driving parents to despair. The year one's office was in the bedroom or simply on their lap. For the first time since World War Two there were empty food shelves. It was the year facemasks became mandatory.

For me however, 2020 meant Shakespeare. The year we met, and I got to bring him home. The year my soul became complete. The year I had let go of fears knowing I was the person I was supposed to be. 2020 was the year I became aligned, together with my pack and with Shakespeare. His journey was also my journey.

I smiled with a sudden remembrance that a palm reader once had told me - that I would be a late bloomer. She had been right.

As the sun mustered heat, moist air from the ground was evaporating and as it was warmer than the frosted air I was standing still. The fog rested over the ground for moments, making it look like the dogs were playing in an ocean of cotton. It was a thick magical blanket. Slowly the fog was rising. It reached the height of my waist, leaving the dogs behind underneath the blanket and half of me above.

I felt like dancing with joy. This was advection fog. It was crazy, unreal, in its beauty.

Rarely have I felt more alive than those minutes of that morning of the new year.

I stood still as I so often do, just to be. Experiencing something I had not even known was possible. Half of me over, half of me under a blanket of fog. The fog was everywhere, in our orchard, in the farmers' fields, covering the tractor trail.

Everywhere as far as my eyes could see.

I could hear the dogs continuing their happy interaction underneath the blanket. A bird was chirping. The sky had gone from pink to frosty blue and the silver clouds were now pure snow white. I looked up. There were rays of straight sunlight. Angel rays. I felt so un-alone and yet I was the only human present.

I could hear Shakespeare. He was barking his happy bark as if to join in my joy. It was less than a year since he had left his concrete prison. Time seemed long and short all in one. We still had such a long way to go to wherever we were going but for Shakespeare and me it was not the destination that was important, but the journey.

The fog blanket kept rising, soundless, with a sense of grace, until the whole of me was reunited with the rest of me, and the dogs.

The fog had summed up the years that had passed. How part of me had been hiding in the shadows after the accident. How I had come to France to push myself to chase my dream of trying to run again after the accident, a dream not granted but it did not matter one bit, as in chasing that new dreams, bigger dreams had surfaced. My dream, of living in the depths of the countryside, sharing my life with my husband and my animals. That dream had come through but only by meeting Shakespeare was my circle complete. The meeting on a bleak sunny February morning in Cyprus inside a cold, dim, grey concrete box had completed me.

My cup was empty. The fog had evaporated. There was a smell of deep brown soil and decomposed leaves, burning wood, chimney smoke and joyous dogs.

I called the dogs as I walked towards the kitchen. Shakespeare, Lady, and Isabel ran in front. Hercule and Captain Hastings on each side of me and Inspector Japp following in my footsteps close enough to trip me over. Miss Grey and Countess Elena still played in the orchard but soon they caught up. In the end everyone rushed past me, knowing to where, and why. It was time for breakfast for both humans and our forty-eight paws.

Inside the kitchen there was the smell of winter and still that of Christmas. Oranges prickled with cloves in red silk ribbons hung in the windows side by side with gingerbread hearts. Scented candles and wood burners.

Some of yesterday's glue wine with star anis and cinnamon still sat in the large pan on the black gas stove and on the table in her old winebox with a wide, red Christmas ribbon around was Miss Marple, rested on her white sheepskin, purring with the contentment of having us back inside.

We were all exactly where we belonged, in our home in the

depth of vine growing country, in the middle of nowhere, in France, where the fog could do magic tricks and where breakfast came when we were ready.

> When daisies pied and violets blue
> And lady-smocks all silver-white
> And cuckoo-buds of yellow hue
> **Do paint the meadows with delight**.
> - William Shakespeare, *Spring*

On the glorious spring morning of 24th February 2021, I would keep my promise to Shakespeare and open the gate to the orchard and then the gate to full liberty outside. I had decided this was the day he would come walking with us and it was up to him to decide if he was ready to come back in.

I had prepared myself for the fact that he would not come back inside but chose to stay in liberty and I had come to terms with that. I was, however, of course, going to do what I could to convince him to walk back inside.

The dogs were just as excited as they were every day, as if every walk were the first in months. For Shakespeare it would be. He stood just meters away staring at the gate. Staring. Looking at me.

Yes, darling you are coming with us. I promised you, remember? I said that when spring came, I would let you outside again. Well spring is here.

As I opened the gate, he rushed past me and through the gate with such speed, like a dog canon ball! Euphoric. He was sprinting around in the field. We all passed through the gate and the other dogs stood still for a couple of seconds watching him as he released his joy for all to see.

I was laughing and with my laughter the dogs joined him – chasing him round the field. All the dogs were simply joyful, but for Shakespeare it was elevated to such a height that he was bubbling over.

Shakespeare was still on Prozac, but I had reduced his dosage. There was no question it had helped his anxiety, but he would still hide, and tremble and I was starting to think that no medication in the world would be able to stop the anxiety attacks.

The only one who could make the pieces of his soul puzzle drop into the right slots was Shakespeare himself. Shakespeare needed to fully understand with all his being - that he was safe. That he could trust me. That he would have liberty also whilst living inside with us. Only by this would he be able to let his guard down. He would of course have to follow the set of rules we all did in our coexistence, but within that framework, he was free. This was the balance I was seeking for him, and by that free him for whatever was keeping him from being truly happy.

I walked across the meadow onto the tractor track and six dogs, Captain Hastings, Japp, Countess Elena, Hercule, Lady and Shakespeare were rushing back and forth on the track. Shakespeare set off to the nearest field searching for the sound of fields mice whilst Lady preferred to put her nose to the ground. For a moment Shakespeare watched Lady and followed her until she stopped and marked; she had found what she was searching for – field mice! Shakespeare sprang into action and with Lady right next to him as always, two sets of front paws were digging with such speed and force one would think their lives depended on it.

Shakespeare was seeking to impress Lady more than anything - I saw two field mice escape through a hole a bit further away whilst the two dogs kept digging. I was rooting for the field mice as always and was glad they escaped.

It was no coincidence that I was out with the dogs that were with me, as I had intentionally put together the pack-members in that exact combination. I wanted the dogs with me that gave the highest probability of getting Shakespeare to walk back in with me. During our walk where Shakespeare was exuberantly happy, he showed no sign of not wanting to come back home with me. He even ran in front of me to every place where we had stopped for treats the year before. He waited, looking at me as if to say: *hurry, hurry I want my treats, but I do not have all day. There is too much to explore to hang around. I have not been out since last year, remember!* I was thrilled he was waiting and that he slid so easily into the routine we had created the year before.

During the time Shakespeare had been inside with us over the winter, many people who followed my rescue page and updates on Shakespeare, had contacted me privately to suggest that I of course should not let him stay outside again. That would mean he had won! I could not help but shake my head slightly. This was not a battle.

If one of us lost, we both lost. If one of us won, we both would win.

I cannot own another soul. We live in a society where we have documents to show who one is married to, what cars you own, who your children are, and dogs are registered to their owner. To me this registration shows a commitment to support the dog, train it so that it can function within a set of principles. But owning it? I cannot own another soul - a human or a dog. My dogs and cats are their own souls and I share their space and they share mine. Some forget that dogs do not exist to please us. Their purpose in life is to be a dog and they have so many roles to fill – being someone's commodity is not one of those.

For dogs to thrive they need structure - to know what they can expect of me and I of them. My job is to provide that structure and let them live in a way that they become the best version of themselves. My purpose for myself is to expand, learn and grow to fulfil mine and their highest potential and by that be happy.

I knew that Shakespeare would have to come to his own conclusion if he wanted to live inside with us, and I was convinced without any doubt whatsoever, he one day would decide to stay inside. Until that happened, my job and the pack's job was to support his journey. Shakespeare was so broken that it was and is beyond my capabilities to explain the extent of his trauma. I could feel it and I could see it, but to truly elucidate was impossible. I knew because I knew and if he had to spend another summer and autumn outside on his journey to seek peace, so be it. I would never abandon him or try to force his journey on my terms. I had promised him that I would let him back outside and I would never break a promise I had made to him or any of my animals.

We walked the semi long route, and I could see Captain Hastings was tired as we walked home at snail's pace. Our walk took us through blue carpets of birds' eye speedwell flowers where the odd daisy had decided to greet the spring early. There was a smell of a reawakening, and before long, Easter would cause me to add bright sunny yellow Easter chickens in my kitchen with yellow candles and citrus yellow glass bowls to hold fruit and eggs.

As we came towards our land Shakespeare stopped at the same spot he had stopped at the year before, to leave us to go home by ourselves. He was not ready to come back inside. I kept walking. Lady and Elena did as always and ran back to try to get him to follow us.

It was as if I could hear Shakespeare explain *"I have so much time to make up for. I have sunrise and sunsets to see and the company of the moon to share. I will sleep under the stars, and I will let my body inhale the liberty I now have been given. So many fields to run and woods to visit. I will come back in one day, but not today. I will come back in with you all when I am ready."*

Elena looked at me as to say *Mum?* and I simply responded *Darling he will come inside with us all when he is ready, but he is not ready yet.*

She seemed to happily settle for my explanation and trotted next to me on light paws, glancing back at Shakespeare who stood in the same place. I called him twice, but he did not move. I turned my head and called back to him *See you this afternoon my darling.*

> Thou know'st 'tis common;
> all that lives must die,
> **Passing through nature
> to eternity**.
> -William Shakespeare, *Hamlet*

When I started out in the rescue world, I had no expectations apart from saving lives. I began for one reason, and one reason only: my intense love of the animals. I started my Facebook page @Jane Marple with one person pressing like and commenting – but slowly it grew organically. Over time many extraordinary people have crossed my rescue path through social media or as friends of friends. People I have never met have supported me. They have laughed and cried with me. They have adopted dogs from me and offered new lives, filled with love, to so many.

Rescue is hard. It is constant roller coaster. The highs are incredible but the lows, in those darkest hours, make you question your decisions, and you are constantly wondering if you have the strength to continue. Living in the world of rescue daily confirms how fragile life is. Nothing is for granted, and gratitude and sorrow coexist. Then you sleep for a couple of hours, get up – and do it all over again!

Some have followed my work over time. They have followed the heartache of the dogs in need and the journey towards new homes. They have celebrated with me when dogs from the most horrific, heart-breaking cases have landed on their paws with new families that will love them for the rest of their days. From hellholes to households, becoming family members and sofa pooches.

People have also been able to follow the journey of my own rescue dogs as I wrote about them on my rescue page. Many felt like they knew my pack and I loved that my dogs brought joy to other than just us.

Many people has come to feel like close personal friends after we had exchanged comments on my stories and photos over long period of time.

One such couple that had followed my rescue journey, and my pack for years, was Jenny and Ian. They came into my life through a mutual dear friend when I rescued the dog, we named Isabel Duveen, a glorious looking Bruno de Jura. She has the characteristic longest ears and the sweetest face. Isabel had been chained inside an abandoned car wreck by a depraved owner. Chained up for months, left to die a painful slow death of starvation, alone. She survived by drinking her own urine. By the time she was found and rescued she was around a third of her normal weight – just nine kilos, the weight of her skeleton, her fur, and her long ears.

I still remember the exact second I saw the first photo of her. It was a grey rainy afternoon that led to an even wetter evening. The wind had picked up making the rain whip on the windows in my home office. Susan, a rescue friend, tagged me in a post on Facebook, making my name pop up in the right-hand corner of the screen. I clicked on the link and there was a photo of a dog version of a concentration camp survivor. I reacted in reflex. It is not one of those situations where I needed time to think. *I will of course take her* I wrote, and two days later I drove the four-hundred-and-eighty-kilometre round trip to pick her up.

In the aftermath a fundraising campaign for special food and vet care was organised and that is when I met Ian and Jenny online. They donated towards Isabel's food and when they later came from England to visit our mutual friend in France, they came to our home and met Isabel Duveen, named after an Agatha Christie character, of course!

Jenny and Ian had by this joined many very special people in the universe of my rescue work. When Shakespeare came home, Ian, an amazing photographer made me a book – *The Moon and Back,* after a post I had written of my love for Shakespeare with the same title. The coffee table book is so beautiful, so thoughtful and so moving. Ian's photos came with text, and I became completely overwhelmed and cried when the photo of fragile flowers in full bloom was contrasted with a black and grey photo of a large padlock screwed onto old wood with solid screws. The juxtaposition between the beautiful flowers and the cold metal was haunting. The text read: *Freedom is everything. Just ask Shakespeare.*

Jenny and Ian so wished to meet Shakespeare, but it was not to be for Jenny.
Not long after I got the book, I learned that Jenny's cancer had taken a turn for the worst. I felt immense sadness for them and for their families - their friends and for the world. People like Jenny make the world a softer place for us all.

I was at a loss as to what to do but I finally sat down and wrote to them both:
Dear Ian and Jenny
I am curled up in my favourite chair in my favourite hour.
The twilight.

Spring has arrived in France and the fruit trees are in full bloom. From inside it looks like late spring. The courtyard is sun filled in the day but just outside the garden walls the wind bites.

Seven dogs are snoring in front of the log burner in the dining room and my huge cat Mrs Oliver is stretching her leg in the air, grooming herself as if she is making herself look pretty for an upcoming cat ball.

It is silent in the house. It is still.

The only noise breaking the silence is the deaf Cocker Inspector James D Japp snoring like a sailor on shore leave.

Shakespeare is the only one missing from around the fire.

He is again, living outside on the top of our land in total liberty.

Every morning, he comes running to greet me and the other dogs.

He eats his breakfast, and dinner al fresco, and he has never been happier. Of that, I am sure!

In many ways he reminds me of Elsa the Lion.

My bond with Shakespeare is stronger than ever. He has made me into a better version of myself and I love him even more for that.

One day Shakespeare will move back in, but it will be on the day I least expect it.

I promised him that he should have his liberty and I kept my promise. For the fact that I was able to do that I will always be grateful.

As I was walking in the flooding spring sunshine today with my eight dogs through the sharp green field, with the grass swaying in the cold March wind, I was thinking about what I should write to you.

How do I say the right words?

I very quickly concluded that I would never really know the answer to what the "right" words will be.

Since I was a child, I think I have always seen the world from a slightly different angle than others. I can "see" people's hearts or so I believed growing up. I could walk into a room, and it was like some hearts had invisible strings connecting them to each other.

I loved it when I could see strings between people. I would sit as still as I could out of everyone's way just observe the hearts that knew each other.

Later in life I learned that those strings were an easy and to me natural way of recognising a heart you know. You know it because it carries the same patterns as your own, like the pattern of the childhood kaleidoscope. The patterns match. The small facets make the same pattern, until someone turns the kaleidoscope, and the beautiful pattern is gone, and a new pattern appears.

It does not matter if the pattern changes because you know. You saw it.

I both saw it and I see it dear Ian and Jenny.

In these hours of each day when things are so difficult, I wish nothing more than to have been able to take away illness and pain. Sadly, I do not behold such a gift.

Please know that I see your heart, Jenny. There is that invisible string that will always be there. That string will never go away, and I know I will see you again. I will recognise you in that instant as that string is pulled.

Please Jenny, the light I hold for you is light. It always will be. You have touched me more than I can explain, and I am so privileged for you having chosen to cross my path.

May your onwards journey be filled with love, and calm. Filled with your wishes and wisdom. With memories and softness. With hands held and hearts shared. With strength and peace. You are both so loved.
With light, warmth, and gratitude.
Always!
Borghild xxx

A few short weeks later Jenny passed away at home with Ian and her three daughters by her side.
The morning after I learnt of her passing, I left my house in the early hours to walk with Elena, Hercule, Lady and Shakespeare. There was a sense of peace and calm.
As the sun was coming up, I reflected on life and death. How everything can be gone in an instant. How our time here is just a blink of an eye.

The grass was chlorophyllide green, and the baby blue sky had small pure white cotton clouds dotted randomly above my head. The wind was still cold but less so now every day. I headed for our ten-kilometre walking route. My phone was switched off as I felt a deep need to be present in the moment. To absorb the change of seasons. I was watching the dogs run, stopping to dig for a field mouse or five, and reflecting how Shakespeare was staying closer than usual. We had crossed the small country road and were walking on the dirt road used by the farmers and the people working in the vines. Rows of vines to my left, open newly ploughed huge fields to my right and woods in front. The green of spring was fighting against the cold air, determined to win the battle of the seasons. The winter winds would soon have to declare the battle lost, and retreat.

I will never get tired of these walks I told Shakespeare who was taking no notice of me at all. He was in a world of his own. The other dogs were playing hide and seek with a rabbit in the vines, but Shakespeare was very unusually not participating.

As I was talking to him, he trotted on the grass as an Andalusian dancing horse might. So gracious. Then, without warning he came to a sudden stop, like he had almost walked into something or someone. He went into a hunting stand, one leg pulled up under him with the hackles on his back standing up like a mohawk on a Native American chief. He was staring at something straight in front of him, but nothing was there but open landscapes and never-ending vines.
Is that you Jenny?
I have no idea why I asked the question. Maybe because I had been thinking so much about her. I had lit a candle for her the day before as I wanted Jenny's path to be brightly lit. The candle was still burning as I had left the house.
Thank you for coming to say goodbye.
As Shakespeare was standing in his frozen position a cuckoo sounded from the woods in front of me, strong and clear.

I had walked that route daily for almost ten years and I had never heard a cuckoo. Not a single time in all those years.
As the cuckoo sounded, Shakespeare put down his paw but remained completely still. I listened. The cuckoo kept calling - just returned from the winter break in Africa. Yes, they should all return about now, I thought.

I smiled and I cried.

I do not know what Shakespeare had seen nor do I know why a sense of calm was in every molecule of me. *It is only Jenny* I told Shakespeare. He turned his head and looked at me and as I called him, he followed. He was back to being completely at ease and soon the rest of the pack was next to us finding our rhythm. There we were, a pack of trotting dogs, me - and Jenny.

We walked the same route for the next days and every morning the cuckoo was there calling. It lasted for a week, the song fading a bit more every morning. After a week, the song was completely gone never to be heard again on any of our daily walks. Neither before, nor since.

I love the thought that it could have been Jenny who came to say goodbye to Shakespeare - the dog she had so wanted to meet. I love to think her wish had been granted.

> **To weep** is to make less the depth of grief.
> -William Shakespeare, *Henry VI*

Shakespeare had been home for three-hundred-and-sixty-two days.

He had now been back living outside for around eight weeks. We had settled back into our walking routine from the previous seasons. My rescue life had been hectic to put it mildly when in February I became involved in a rescue of sixteen dogs - eight adults and eight puppies born within hours of the rescue. What was demanded of me was the endurance of an athlete within an extreme sport in combination with the skills of a trapeze artist. I was chasing my tail constantly and catching up on everything was an impossibility. One of the rescued pups needed emergency microsurgery and the specialist hospital was in Bordeaux, two hours' drive from home - the pup was elsewhere, and the roundtrip took eight hours. The dogs needed foster homes, vets needed to be contacted, papers needed to be filed, bills needed to be paid, fundraising organised, snap decisions made in the best interests of the dogs. Almost in parallel, Monika and I rescued dogs out of a kill shelter in North Romania, where dogs sat in the waiting room of death in unspeakable conditions. We had a window of three weeks to save them. Monika also took dogs off the street that were facing a horrendous life of abuse and starvation and I needed to find them homes. Dogs on the streets were considered vermin in their part of the world. Alongside it all, I continued to support families that had adopted blind or shutdown dogs. For months I hardly slept, my nightmares were back, and I certainly was not as calm when I spent time with Shakespeare as I needed to be, and I could tell it affected him. It felt like I was all over the place, and I knew I was ill. My PTSD was back with a vengeance, having circled just under the surface for weeks, like a shark watching its prey. I had problems breathing. It was like someone was standing on my chest even when I was standing upright. My dyslexia was worst, and each sentence I wrote demanded me to focus beyond what felt physically possible.

I had no idea how deep it was, but I was sinking, and I had a clear feeling the bottom was still a long way down.

The floor was moving as I walked, and I knew it was a sure sign of needing to slow down, not for a day, but for months.

You have never been good at balancing your life, I kept reprimanding myself.

I felt bad for not rescuing more and I felt bad for not spending enough time with my pack. I found myself crying in the bathroom or having to pull over whilst I was out driving so that I could close my eyes for ten or twenty minutes before my journey continued towards another rescue dog, for pick up or delivery. Dogs were abused, beaten, and kicked daily - starved, and neglected in ways that I could not wrap my head around, existing on the receiving end of torture-like behaviour from humans. Dogs were dying in cages whilst giving birth, never having had any life, having done nothing else than to be used for producing puppies sold for financial gain. After a life in cage confinement - if they did not die - they were thrown away like garbage, literally. Worthless puppies were thrown on landfills or in dustbins to die a cruel, slow death. Dogs like my own pack.

I had spent sixteen hours a day available on social media in reference to the rescue I had named the Hell House rescue. What the dogs had been through is reflected in the name. There was an outpouring of reaction and support. I had answered questions, sent thank you cards to donors and driven more than four-thousand kilometres in the name of that rescue alone. All this within a period of four weeks, and still after eight weeks I was handling new situations daily, involving both foster - and permanent homes.

The rescue world is not for the faint-hearted and every rescuer will tell you the same thing: it is the people that cause the biggest and most serious heartache for any rescuer - and often it is fellow rescuers. I do believe that the majority of people in the rescue world start out with the best intention, but then jealousy, envy and misunderstood power becomes a priority. The animals take a back seat to self-boosting egocentricity.

And that is what I experienced during those early, hectic spring months of 2021.

A couple that I considered to be friends defrauded documents related to my association, leaving me shellshocked. A man who donated to the Hell House rescue had written me a threatening letter, addressed to me privately, as my association could not give him a tax-deductible receipt for his donation towards the Hell House dogs. I replied to his letter explaining in detail how small my association is, and why I at that stage could not give him a tax deduction receipt so he could claim deduction on his taxes.

I thanked him for his kind act and attached a cheque refunding his donation. Within a short time, a breeder pursued my association in social media after a lady would rather offer a home to a rescue dog from the kill-shelter through me, than buy a pedigree dog from the breeder. This made the breeder set out on a campaign of lies both about the lady, my association and me.

Social media is both blessing and curse!

Someone wrote to me that she would like to go through all my documents and posts with a red marker and correct my spelling mistakes as my association deserved better than the misspelling caused by my dyslexia. When I am exhausted my dyslexia gets incredibly bad and at that stage it was physically painful to write because I was so tired. The red-marker message had made me sob, sitting on the edge of the office chair.

I came to the point where I could not take any more.

To deal with each incident separately would be no problem but to deal with all cases on top of each other in combination with no sleep and truly heart-breaking rescue cases simply unplugged me.

It had become too much. I was breaking and I was fully aware of it.

As we entered the week of Easter 2021, my body was constantly pumped full of adrenaline signalling my life was in danger. My heart was threatening to jump out of my chest. I had nerve endings shooting signals in all directions. I truly was in extremely bad shape.

Having lived with PTSD for over a decade I knew the signs all too well and I knew I had to get off the carousel. I had pushed myself too far and now it had all caught up with me.

What made me feel worse was that I, on top of everything else, was missing Shakespeare so - my counterpart on four legs. I had not had much time to share with him over the previous six, seven weeks. I knew he missed me and the pack too. I would see him in the vineyards across from the house every time I left and returned. He was standing with that longing look, saying: *why have you left me?* I often cried as I drove off to rescue someone else who needed me more in that moment.

Just one more day to do the filing and I will be done I thought as my shaking hand carried the coffee, heading for my home office.

I needed to clear the desk to feel some kind of ease, to let the stress go, and I would close the door and not return - for a long time, I thought, to even close the door for good.

The room was all white with sharp orange curtains from the nineteen-fifties. The bed was white as were the ceiling lamps made of white plastic circles, hanging from metal frames making the light spread into circles pattern on the ceiling. The bed was filled with orange pillows with white cherry blossoms. The bedspread was a golden orange, hand made from the late eighteen hundreds. Dreamlike.

I noticed the bedspread was full of black cat hairs from Mademoiselle Milesi. She was normally my office cat who slept in an old wood wine box, as all my four cats do. The box took up the left corner of my desk. As I sat working, she would curl up, purr, and occasionally stretch her paw lazily in my direction to remind me to breathe. But that day she was out hunting somewhere.

I was restless. I could not concentrate.

I felt extremely uneasy as I glanced through documents without any interest, but somehow, on autopilot I managed to get through the stack of papers. A fabric print of a sleeping woman, Flaming June, originally painted by Sir Frederic Leighton, was on the wall behind me. I saw its reflection in the large vintage mirror behind the bed. The mirror was off balance, like me.

By late afternoon I could finally see the desk surface. I closed the drawers, responded to some messages from different vets, and finally moved away from the chair to stand at the window. From the second floor I could see the top of our land. It is a huge field outside the courtyard and orchards. The grass in the field was still luminous green. It was the surest sign of spring as later when summer arrived the grass would turn brown due to the intense heat. The summer before we had over fifty degrees in the courtyard, and even growth-willing grass gives in to those temperatures.

As my eyes swiped the field, there he was. Shakespeare!

He was standing in the middle of the field facing the house with his head held up high. He was staring towards the windows or at least that is what it seemed like.

It was as if he had come for me.

I had moved before my brain had given any commands, hurrying down the stairs and into the hallway where Shakespeare first lay in his opened crate, where he had taken his first steps into liberty, where we had shared so many moments. As I rushed through, I felt a spurt of joy that came from a place in me I had not touched over the last couple of months. He was waiting for me. It mattered. I mattered.

To him!

Normally me rushing through the house would rouse the pack but strangely enough they all just glanced at me as I hurried through. The only one paying attention and getting to her feet was Lady Eileen Bundle Brent - the girl who offered Shakespeare emotional support when he first came and for all the days since. Being a hound, she would normally howl to indicate a walk was coming up, but she was completely silent as the other were lazily resting. We snuck out the laundry room door and out the side gate undetected. The small track alongside the house goes straight to the top land where I had seen Shakespeare.

Would he still be waiting? The answer came in form of the beautiful maroon coloured body jumping in the familiar rabbit-like jumps on the track.

His tail spun like the blades of a helicopter.

Shakespeare! Shakespeare, my beautiful boy.

His wise brown eyes were looking straight at me as he barked in joy.

I reached the field and there – the scoops of energy left in my body left me. I could not walk another step. I could not move, my inner scaffolding collapsed. I sank to the ground, sitting on my knees with my upper body touching my knees like those praying in Friday prayers towards Mecca. I could not breath and leaned forward further. My head was touching the grass, warm from the sun and the smell of childhood summers filled my nostrils, filtering through. I was breathing in, trying to supress the feeling of drowning.

I sobbed. It was like those last month's pressure came to a crescendo.

Breathing out.

I knew that is all I had to do.

Breathing in.

Breathing out.

I lost track of time. It was not important. I was going nowhere.

As my sobs abated, I noticed bird song in the tree above me. In the distance I could hear a dog bark. Miss Lemon had appeared from her hiding place in the old wooden trailer and was brushing against me. She purred and was trying to get underneath me so she could climb on my lap. After she had brushed up against my body and I had failed to sit up, she turned her attention to my face, and with her sandpaper tongue she licked as if to make it all better. I lifted my head to see Lady Eileen in the grass next to me. She was so still. It is like she is saying *Take your time*.

I raised my upper body and Miss Lemon climbed on my lap.

Shakespeare was standing about a metre from me. He looked serene. He was not scared, nor did he seem worried. It hit me how different he looked, so proud. As we exchanged looks, he sat himself down. He never sat down near anyone when he was outside. He was making a clear exception to assure me.

We will all be fine. Take your time.

Lady and Shakespeare exchanged glances before they both looked back at me.

I wiped my tears as I stroked Miss Lemon with my other hand.

She purred even louder. My breathing was finding a regular rhythm.

When you are ready, get on your feet. Put one foot in front of the other and follow me. Take your time. That is all you must do. Take your time and follow me.

Shakespeare was looking at me.

I followed.

There was no rush. I realised that we were not heading anywhere in particular. I was not in front leading but behind following.

Lady and Shakespeare ran into the large field - last summer packed with sun flowers as tall as me. The field was now bare, with patterns from the farmers tractor having turned the soil that morning. The soil was deep dark chocolate brown, and the air carried that smell of freshly turned soil. I inhaled whilst lazily walking a bit further to where citrus yellow rapeseed was blooming one side of the path. It was a short drop from standing to sitting.

The two dogs were digging in the middle of the field. I could not see their faces, but their tails were moving rapidly in joy over being on the trail of field mice.

I was watching them as they helped each other to get to the nest. Shakespeare had a technique I have never seen any dog but him use. He ripped up large pieces of turf or soil with his teeth and threw it to one side. Such pieces were now flying as he was slinging his head back.

I caught myself laughing and as the sound escaped my mouth both dogs stopped for a split second and looked at me before a second glance to each other, returning to the hunting task underneath their paws.

Sitting still, I let myself seek calmness in the birdsong, the sound of a tractor ploughing another field in the distance.

The smell of the rapeseed was different closer to the ground than standing up. The smell was slightly urinous and faintly that of wattle but gutsier. It was rich, round, syrupy and sharp at the same time. It was the smell of early spring in my countryside universe.

I sat, just being, with no thoughts of yesterday or tomorrow. For now, it would all have to take care of itself as I could not. I simply sat still and watched the dogs, tried to breath until the sun was indicating it was setting. I smiled in admiration of the sun that was never in a rush – not to rise nor to set. As always, it rolled on the horizon playing with the colours of orange and yellow before it pulled out the pink and red. The most talented artist - she dimmed her bright light behind the colours of an unreal sky that was oh so real. I would never tire of watching her.

I was inhaling through my nose, breathing out though my mouth.

Shakespeare gave up the hunt first. He came rushing over the field and I could see him looking for me as if he thought I had left.

As his eyes caught the sight of me, he went onto the tractor path and stood still - his body outlined against the backdrop of the woods ahead.

Are you coming?

I smiled. My body felt heavy, my soul ached, and all I wanted to do was stay put, watch the sun, and fall asleep right there, but I responded.

Yes darling, I am coming.

Lady came across the field worried she would miss out and all three of us were back on the tractor trail heading towards the woods that had given its name to our address. I know every tree close to the path and some even off track. I know where the mushrooms will sprout after rain, where wild orchids will come back year after year. I know where the wild strawberries grow and where the deer will bring their fawns just around that time of year. I normally did not walk the pack through the woods at that time of year so as not to disturb the fawns – there are also wild boar in the woods that will be on the move as it gets dark and after. You do not want to meet them as they track through the woods searching for food, heading for new pastures, but that evening Shakespeare were leading and deciding. The woods seem mythical in the dimming light. Every branch and leaf become mystical, and my head was traveling back to my childhood's history of trolls. I noticed neither dog was chasing nor hunting. They were both walking close to me as I was breathing in the air that always smelt differently in the woods than outside in the vast open landscape where air was flowing so freely. In the woods there were still the smells of last autumn's leaf decay. The air was colder in the woods, and I closed the zip on my pink softshell jacket - the same jacket I had left with Shakespeare in his box in Cyprus, what seemed a lifetime ago.

Walking in the dark with my two dogs seemed effortless.

I did not have to look where I put my feet as my body knew. The dogs were utterly relaxed, and their calm energy somehow was passed on to me. My shoulders were loosening up and my breathing came from my stomach, not my chest. I could hear a mouse hawk somewhere above us and the faint sound of dog coming from a pack of hunting dogs in the next hamlet, but apart from that it was silence of the loud kind.

Bringing Shakespeare home had made me walk by moon light. I never used to walk after dark, even in the moonlight, but now it was my favourite walk. Something magical always happened in those quiet hours when no one was around. My feet and their paws walked on the path that took an ever-so-slack bend - soon we would see the exit. My eyes searched for the opening that would lead us either towards home along the edge of the woods, or towards the small country lane that also eventually would take us home in a loop.

Just as our last steps left the bend behind - that is when I saw something I had never seen before. A full moon in the warmest orange-red filled the whole opening of the woods as if the path would make you walk into the centre - into the heart of the blood moon. It was only me who gasped in amazement but both dogs came to a halt with me. The moon light so intense as if the opening were on fire. My right hand was touching Lady's soft head, and as the beauty of it all became overwhelming, I sat down on the damp surface! On each side stood a dog. We did not move, and it seemed like we were holding our breath as to not disturb the luminous, magical round ball that was tossing light far into the woods making all trees look like shadows, intangible. It was unreal in all its beauty - like we were given this moment as reward for just being.

I reached out to stroke Lady, and she willingly leaned against me. She nuzzled my neck, and I could feel her wiggling bum. She was happy and grateful, as was I. I knew that touching Shakespeare was fruitless as he would bolt if I tried, but it was something about that moon that made everything seem possible. My hand stretched and found his head. He did not move. He did not try to avoid my caresses, or bolt. He stood perfectly still and let me stroke his ear between my fingers the way I had when I spent time within his box in Cyprus. I could not see his facial expression, but he made no attempts to leave my side nor avoid my strokes. The moon was giving us some precious moments, where time stood still, before it lifted itself higher still illuminating the woods. Shakespeare took the first step forward – Lady followed and as we came outside the moonlight landscape carried a breath-taking beauty. Everything seemed just slightly different in the moonlight, branches more faded or twisted. Everything seemed weightless as if the landscape floated. The vines seemed crooked because the moonlight let the leaves throw shadows that did not exist during the daylight.

We were surrounded by a calmness that made everything seem possible - to go home and peacefully sleep to awake the next morning to another day.

We walked towards home along the edge of the woods, me and my two PTSD dogs.

I knew they both had felt what miserable shape I had been in. Their calm presence lowered my heartbeat and restored my breathing - repaying me for the times I had supported them. They stayed close to replenish my soul.

> It is not in the stars **to hold our destiny** but in ourselves.
> - William Shakespeare, *Julius Caesar*

We moved from spring to summer with ease, walking long distances every day.

I had slowed down my rescue work but not left it. By rethinking my rescue efforts, I tried to focus on rescue work I could do from home in form of supporting families with blind dogs and dogs with PTSD. Most of these families had not adopted through me but from different associations from all over Europe - and further afield. Each day I spent a couple of hours in front of my PC in the white bedroom office.

The cold coffee was not drinkable. My tastebuds were protesting with yet another mouthful. After hours glued to the screen, stiff-necked and cross-eyed, I got up. Any further office work could wait till another day. I walked down the white painted wooden staircase, crossed the hallway with the chilly tiled hallway, and my feet touched the wide wooden oak boards in the dining room below the large chandelier. I loved the feel of wood under my feet. Coming from a country where every house had wooden floors, I was truly at home crossing the floor, and next - a step down into the kitchen with more wide oak boards. The kitchen had originally been the barn way back when, but now it was a huge space with a kitchen island, black kitchen units and a large table brought from India that easily could seat six with room to spare. The tabletop was sanded wood, whilst the round legs were a deep earthy oiled reddish colour. Over the table hung three industrial lamps in a row. On the far end wall was an old pharmacy cabinet I had painted white.

Through the glass doors it was easy to spot the large selection of glasses in all shapes. I had a "thing" about vintage crystal glasses that I picked up at local flea markets for pocket change. The cabinet was overcrowded, making it impossible to move anything, according to Are. Occasionally, glasses fell out, or broke whilst in use, resulting in random sets of hand cut antique glasses.

The staircase to our bedroom was also on that far end wall - currently deep bottle green and in need of a fresh lick of paint. I would get to it as soon as I could decide on a new colour, I kept telling myself, in my latest avoidance technique.

I had the same morning changed the cover on the large dog bed, now a deep Bordeaux red with paisley patterning in golden colours. The spread had once been expensive for sure, but I had picked it up at a local charity shop for the price of a baguette.

On the dining table was the cat-bed, a wooden wine box, once holding twelve bottles. It is marked Vinho Rosado de Mesa. Sec. The box had travelled in time and physical distance before becoming Miss Marple's bed. It was there but there was no cat in sight.

All seven dogs were scattered. Captain Hastings lifted his head to make sure it was me. He dropped his head back down with a thump, when he had confirmed that I was not a stranger that just had the same footsteps as his mum.

I had not had time to walk the pack that morning, so I knew Shakespeare was close by, waiting for me and some of his paw siblings to turn up. Standing by the kitchen door looking out over the courtyard I called for Miss Marple a couple of times, before I turned and walked up the stairs to our dark blue bedroom. The colour was soothing. Above the bed there was a large white canvas framed in a white wide wooden frame, holding the Napoleonic bee, and the signature of Napoleon, in the same blue as the bee and the walls.

The canvas and frame was recycled from an old painting I had painted years earlier. The bee was a stencil and the signature of Napoleon, was written by my mother, who is an artist. We had laughed whilst copying Napoleon's signature, joking about the crime of having a fraudulent signature of Napoleon above our bed.

The blue colour continued into the bathroom with its huge eagle-footed *baignoire liot*, a mid-eighteen century cast iron bathtub. The bathtub was amongst my absolute favourite second hand finds after our arrival in France. I had bought it from a manor house that was being renovated into a minimalistic, hyper modern boutique home, which had made me shake my head at the deep injustice to the pre-revolution ornate building. I was convinced the bathtub had never been in use as much as it had been after it had arrived in our house.

From the bathroom a sliding door lead into our walk-in closet, where I looked for a pair of shorts for my planned walk with the dogs.

My choice of shoes gave away my plan for a walk. Blind Miss Grey knew that shoes that had heels and made a click-clack sound on the wooden staircase meant no walk, shoes without such sound meant walks. She was already sitting by the open door wagging her tail in anticipation.

I could still not see Miss Marple. It was more than unusual she did not respond or appear when called. It simply did not happen. I inhaled, held my breath as I felt a flash of panic.

I suddenly remembered that the gate on the top of our orchard was open. I had left it open the evening before as I did every night in case Shakespeare might decide to come in during the night, something he of course never did as going through the gate was his biggest fear. There was a gate leading from the courtyard to the orchard and I had secured it with chicken wire so Miss Marple should not be able to get through but for a blind cat she was beyond smart, and I knew that if there was any way to find a way through, she would. If she had managed to get from the courtyard to the orchard, she had free passage to the outside world.

I could feel the panic rising.

In the seven years since Miss Marple came home, she had got outside the property twice. The first time she had walked around five hundred meters. I had been searching frantically for several hours and in the end, Hercule found her. She sat crying between the rows of vines with her nose in the air, trying to pick up the scent of the trail home. She would never have found her way back before she would have been taken by the eagles or killed by a fox after sunset. Hercule was so pleased when he discovered her and would not stop licking her. As I picked her up and carried her home, Hercule danced around me in relief. We re-secured the property and had tried to secure every possible way out, and yet she got out a second time about three years later.

We were about to leave for lunch with friends and both Are and I thought Miss Marple was safely inside. We had stepped outside the wooden door-gate of the property, not knowing she had got out, when I heard a scream as that of an injured baby. Instinctively I knew it was Miss Marple. I dropped my bag and ran the few metres across the road towards the sound, which came from some brambles, just in time to see a huge male cat disappear. Left in the bushes was my blind baby that just had been attacked and raped by the male. She was petrified and kept screaming a scream I will never forget.

I tried to talk to her as I untangled the brambles to get to her, but she did not hear me. Her panic was such that she was not capable of hearing anything, maybe not even her own screams.

When I got to her and touched her, she bit me and was fighting for her life with teeth and claws and not until I managed to get a proper hold of her and put her inside my blouse next to my skin did, she calm. I was heartbroken for her and still have the scars from her scratches of that day. She was wet from semen, and I smelt a strong odour mixed with her own urine as she could not hold on to her body fluids in panic. I carried her back into the house. In the bathroom I bathed her back-part in lukewarm water whilst she kept fighting against a now imaginary presence. I spoke to her softly as I dried her and eventually, wrapped in a soft, clean towel, she calmed down.

For days after this incident Miss Marple would hiss in panic, moving her head without eyes back and forth, as if she were scanning the room. I also soon discovered that each time she moved her body, she panicked. I figured out she could still smell him, so the bathing was repeated until she smelt of nothing but lavender. This is when she started sleeping on top of me at night. When I went to bed in the evening it would take seconds before she would come and jump on our bed. As I slept on my stomach, she would climb on my back and curl into a feather light fluff ball. Sometimes she would use her paw to find the side of my face before she would settle down. She would stroke her paw on my chin, and I would whisper the same thing each time You *are welcome darling. Sweet dreams* and by that she would move a bit further down my back and curl up whilst purring and soon she was fast asleep.

I was now searching everywhere. Under the bushes, in the flower bed, in the barn, under every outdoor piece of furniture, of which there suddenly seemed a lot. I kept calling her with no response. Miss Marple would always either respond to me by meowing or she would walk towards me, and I would in response talk to her, telling her how beautiful she was, but that day it was dead quiet with no movement anywhere. Even the dogs did not move to search for her in the courtyard. I knew she was gone.

I hurried out the gate, leaving the dogs as Shakespeare was outside and the last thing, I wanted was for him to get super excited thinking we were going to walk. I tried to calmly talk to myself. *It will be fine. You will find her. She will be safe.* I was trying to manifest her safety.

The early summer breeze was soft but strong enough to sway the trees and make the temperature perfect on that beautiful, sunny day. The sky was azure, blue with bleached white cotton clouds looking like plump marshmallows.

The grass on the top field was still green, with a bit of movement in each straw. I was grateful for the colouring, as in that landscape I could easily spot Miss Marple's white fur, with her tortoiseshell back legs and tail. I scanned the landscape as I kept moving. My heart had picked up pace and my feet wanted to run but I could not rush. If I rushed, I might overlook her presence. I kept calling her.

Miss Marple. Miss Marple? Miss Marple!

I walked the parameters of the land before I went onto the tractor track. To the right I had vines and to the left the fields before the narrow dirt road came to a small T-junction. After, I had fields on both sides.

As I passed the field, high with barley, I saw Shakespeare. He was standing frozen, statuesque, in the field, about twenty meters away from me and uncharacteristically, he did not move towards me. Normally he would come running. I questioned why he was acting so differently but I quickly concluded that it was because I was alone without any of the dogs. I spoke to him and told him I was looking for Miss Marple and continued walking with a strange feeling that I was missing something.

Later, looking back, I now know I should have paid closer attention.

I turned a couple of times to see Shakespeare had not moved at all. He stood in the exact same spot, looking like the proudest dog, royal, in his own kingdom.

I so loved those fields that later would have bales of straw dotted around. However, the thought of any harvesting sent shivers down my spine as Miss Marple would never be able to get out of the way of a combine harvester. She would end up inside one of those barley bales if she were in the fields when the harvest started, and that would be within days.

I quickly decided on my walking route by trying to eliminate where she would not walk. I had watched her for so many hours over the years that I knew her mind and way of manoeuvring. She would of course not cross the small trickling stream at the boundaries of the fields.

She would, unlike other cats, keep in open landscape if she could, as she would try to orient herself. She would avoid the woods as the woods would disguise any scent trail where she could backtrack. Miss Marple was however not good on backtracking no matter how I turned it.

She moved so freely in our courtyard and orchard because she had mapped out every centimetre. On unknown territory she was walking blind - literally. I turned left, heading west. I glanced back and could see the house and our land but no matter how much I scanned the landscape, there was no small white patch anywhere.

I had my mobile in my pocket, and I remembered that Are soon would be back from his trip to the local supermarket. I called him, grateful I was within net coverage, something that was not always the case here in the middle of blessed nowhere. The conversation lasted under a minute. We knew the drill. Are would park up and take the bike and cover a bit further distance then me and he would criss-cross over the paths where I had already walked in case, she was heading home along any of the lanes.

The track led me towards the stream and the landscape was sloping slightly. In the distance there was a bright Christmas red tractor out working on a field and I could see people in the vines – otherwise there was no movement. My panic had for some reason subsided and I had a strong feeling I would find her. I stopped, listened, closed my eyes, and tried to picture where she was, but of course, I had no inner image coming up.

As I slowly opened my eyes hoping by some miracle I would spot her, I instead saw Are on his bike, heading towards me.

His worried look made my heart swell. This man that had been so concerned about first meeting Miss Marple because she had no eyes, had fallen so deeply in love with her. This cat without eyes was loved by her dad even more than I had pictured possible.

Are had not seen any sign of her either. He had also passed Shakespeare in the field, just like me, and from his brief explanation Shakespeare was in the same spot. Are kissed me, squeezed my hand, before we went our separate ways. He had tried to comfort me, telling me she would be found very soon, but to be honest I perceived it to be an attempt to convince himself as much, or more, than me.

The landscape changed depending on where I was standing, and I noticed details I had not seen before as I never walked down the track by the brook.

The slope was steeper than what it looked from the track on the other side of the field, the barley straw seemed even taller from that angle, the sky wider and the horizon shorter and closer. As I came to the end of the track, I sat down in the grass and called her name again, for what seemed like the thousand time that day.

Miss Marple. Please. Miss Marple.

I could feel the sun on my back, and I suddenly felt sure Miss Marple was sunbathing somewhere. It was one of her favourite past times on days like this. She would stretch out and purr, lick her paws and go to sleep letting the sun warm her. In the summer I would put sun block on her pink translucent ears. As she was sunbathing the dogs would randomly stroll over and sniff her, as to make sure she was breathing, and Hercule would lick her face, cleaning her one eye socket.

The other eye socket had been surgically closed after Miss Marple had a bleed from a broken blood vessel in the depths of the other.

I had cried at the vet office thinking she would die, but the vet had as always, been calm, sent me home with instruction to pick her up that same night and by that she had become our one eye-socket blind cat.

The only logical thing was now to try to figure out how far she could have walked. I had been in the office for four hours and the last time I saw her, that I could recall, was that morning at around eight o'clock. Sitting in the grass I looked at my watch that showed almost two o'clock. Dear God, she could have been out walking for six hours. I tried hard to recall every movement of the morning in the aim to comfort myself that I had seen her after eight, but I could not recall any meow nor any conversation with her.

Getting up, brushing off my shorts I decided to backtrack - to walk back home to ensure I had not overlooked her anywhere. It did not seem to make any sense to expand my search area.

Where are you darling?

As I came closer to the point where I had last seen Shakespeare, I started to look for him as well, but he was gone from the place in the field. He must be lying, making him invisible to the human eye, I reflected.

The light grey clay track seemed almost silver coloured in the landscape, and I could follow the track with my eyes all the way home. I would have been able to see the roof of our sandstone house if it had not been for the huge trees creating a virtual wall at the north side of our land.

I kept sweeping the landscape. Sweeping and calling. My eyes were tired from glaring towards the sharp sunlight, and I realised I was thirsty.

The birds were chirping carefree, and a hare crossed my path - I followed the hare with my eyes. Rewind! I follow the same line back to where the hare had come from, and yes, it had to be. That intensely chocolate brown animal laying on the verge of the grass, by the track up ahead had to be Shakespeare. No animal I knew had the same colour as him. What an odd place for him to lay. From what I could see he was laid between the track and the vines. I could not really see it clearly but I knew every metre of the track so I could easily conclude exactly where he was. I had never seen him lie at that spot and it was completely unnatural for Shakespeare to rest in the sun like that. Shakespeare was a creature of habit, a consequence of his mundane isolated life in Cyprus, and his PTSD. He still did not like change and for him to lay by the track, in the sun, worried me and for a couple of moments my focus was shifted from Miss Marple to Shakespeare. Was he injured? Is that why he had not moved in the field? Had I been so absent-minded that I had not noticed any injury?

I was picking up pace wanting to get closer quickly. I kept scanning the scenery, kept looking back at Shakespeare whilst calling for Miss Marple.

Then… it cannot be!

My brain was trying to synchronise the information from the images my eyes were picking up. From the distance where I could see Shakespeare clearly, with his spotted legs crossed in front of him, and that intensely regal look, I could see a white cat in the middle of the track.

My feet started running in pure instinct. I was in two minds if I should run as fast as I could or run just as fast as a steady phase would let me as to not scare anyone. Against my motherly instinct I chose the latter. I was jogging, trying to run in the middle of the track where the growing grass would soften the sound of my approaching feet.

Shakespeare watched me. He interlocked his eye with mine - he was stoic still. I tried to decipher his expression but there was nothing, there was no expression, only a softness.

I slowed down. I was only meters away in a huge landscape as Miss Marple seemed so tiny.

Miss Marple?

I looked form Shakespeare to her.

She lifted her head, with her pink translucent ears, her pink eye socket, her perfectly shaped face that has silky soft fur covering half of her face - where her eye should have been. Her nose was vibrating. This creature that has filled every corner of my heart and my being, had turned her face against me before she laid back down to do her favourite past time, sun bath. It was in that instant, I realised she had been in the field with Shakespeare when I passed him. Passed them! That is why he had stood so still. She was by his paws.

She had not responded to me as she was safe. There had been no need to respond. She was so used to being looked after by the dogs that she had not been worried nor concerned. She knew Shakespeare. During the winter months inside she had spent time with Shakespeare and he with her. They were part of each other's pack.

I could hardly believe it, even if I were standing looking straight at them; a former hunting dog from Cyprus towering over a born blind cat in France, as the lions I had seen so often in South Africa towering over their cubs. Shakespeare had stayed with her, and when she had aimlessly headed for the path trying to find a point she would recognise, he had protected her. The warm sand on the track combined with the fatigue after her excursion had made Miss Marple decide to stretch out for a nap in the sun, in the middle of the T-junction of the tractor track. There were rarely any cars here, but all the same there were tractors and a tractor in this part of the world would not stop for a cat in the road. But as most of the farmers were hunters, they would certainly stop to admire a beautiful stoic, hunting dog from Cyprus. The hunting dog that killed nothing but field mice, and who protected the weak. This miracle of a dog that never ceases to amaze me.

I slowly went over and stroked Miss Marple. She was purring louder than a jackhammer – a sound she has perfected and that makes us all smile. I picked her up.

I knew Shakespeare would not let me touch him, but I would have liked to hug him. We were outside and he would never let me close enough for me to "catch" him. I spoke to him in a soft voice, thanking him, telling him I would bring Miss Marple home and I would be back with the others, and we would walk together. In the slowest motions he got up, stretched his long running legs, yawned, and followed us a couple of metres behind, towards the house. I met Are at the gate as he returned from his rounds on the bike and Hercule was doing his dance when he saw who I was carrying.

If we had not lived for as long as we have, with everyday miracles of the animal world, we would not have believed this possible.

But it was. That and so much more.

> **Come what come may,** time and the hour runs through the roughest day.
> -William Shakespeare, *Macbeth*

There was no question that the Prozac Shakespeare had been on since the December had helped, but it was time to try life without it. Shakespeare was free, and this was absolutely the best time to stop the medication. After he had moved out, he had refused to take the tablets and I was of the clear impression that he had been helped to the extent he could be helped by drugs. There would have to come a time where everything the pack and I were trying to teach Shakespeare would be of use to him, and as he refused to take the medication, the stress of getting him to take it was causing more stress than what it was worth in the long run.

I had started to hide the tablets inside sausages I would cut up for him. This meant I would bring two small plastic bags of sausages. One bag of pieces of sausages with a red zip for all the other dogs, and one small yellow zipped bag - containing sausage pieces with Prozac for Shakespeare. I would give the dogs the sausage treat, at the same time as we stopped to have the dried biscuit. In the last days leading up to that day Shakespeare had looked at me as to say, *if you want to fool me you should at least have the same colour zips on both bags.*

His eyes would indicate he wanted a sausage from the red zip bag and not the yellow zip bag. I tried to suppress my giggle and I tried my best to fool him but failed miserably each time.

He was simply refusing to eat any sausages that came out of

the yellow zipped bag. As an attempt to get him to take his medication I then made two red zipped bags. If I needed to sausage bribe my dogs to get them to take any medication, something that was rare, I would simply give them the sausage pieces with the medication and make sure they had another sausage piece immediately afterwards as they then focused on the second piece of sausage. With Shakespeare this did however not work. He would watch me closely. I gave him a medication free sausage, followed by a medicated piece and then a medication-free piece but he would know exactly what was coming.

That morning, we had left the house early while the morning was still cool before the sun brought scouring temperatures.

There was blue sky with pure, bleached, feather-like clouds and a cacophony of birdsong.

Amazingly I could even hear the owl that lives on our land. Shakespeare had been waiting by the top gate bursting with life. It was like he wanted us to understand the adventures he was on every night, bubbling with energy and new tales to tell. Tales of the foxes, the deer, the wild boars – how he met rabbits and hares - and where he dug for field mice to his heart's content. He even had hedgehog friends.

I kept water for Shakespeare at several different places on our land, but I also made sure there was water for the hedgehogs. I had seen Shakespeare lying by one of the shallow water bowls looking at the spiky creature, like he was trying to understand it. Shakespeare was living in unfiltered liberty and this liberty had changed him so much in the right direction.

Amid all this joy and liberty, he was clear in his signals: it was time to stop the medication, and I agreed. I had reduced the dosage over time, and we only had one more week of the last tablets to go.

The sun was warming over the horizon. The morning dew was present in tiny temporary drops in the grass on the side of the track as we were heading for the woods. Elena, Lady and even Hercule were rushing in front of me, bouncing off each other and crossing the field that will also take them to the woods, whilst Shakespeare was staying on the track with me. His body was relaxed, and his head was held high. I reflected over how long it had been since I had seen his head hanging lower than his body. Liberty had changed him profoundly.

Daily I reflected over how this dog had never left me. From the first night he had hidden under the metal heap in the junk yard, he had never left and always, without fail, been within ears' reach of me calling him. When I did, he would come rushing. He knew left and right and I would call to him from afar when we were out walking - *not that way Shakespeare but this way* and point in a different direction to where he was heading. He would immediately turn and head in the direction I indicated.

I had always spoken to him in Norwegian apart from those first few days at the sanctuary where I spoke both English and Norwegian to him without really knowing why – he knew neither   language.

Shakespeare had perfect recall and had responded to his name within the first weeks of coming home. We had a bond I cannot explain.

Dialogue bounces back and forth between us; sometimes the dialogue is funny, sometimes informative, and sometimes it touches on sadness and devastation.

As we entered the woods, the light changed, from bright optimistic morning light to hushed wood light. The ground was covered in evergreen ivy and moss. The crowns on the slim trunks were swaying in the morning breeze letting sunbeams in amongst the leaves in an incoherent lazy dance. The dogs were rushing to catch the odours swirled up by the breeze and pirouetted across the soft surface we walked on. Shakespeare was not, that morning, interested in the trails of all the animals that has passed through the woods in the night. He already knew who had been there. That morning, he was waiting for me to offer him a sausage-treat so he could have the pleasure of rejecting any tablets for the last time. He had made up his mind and he was about to challenge me in a way he had never challenged me before.

This path would join our usual path through the woods, and as we got closer to the opening of the woods, we always had a treat-stop. Shakespeare was excited. It was by no means any full-on Elena excitement, but excitement of the subtle kind. The other dogs were still roaming but I knew they would notice us having arrived at the treat-stop-spot so they would join us soon enough. I was thinking it would be a good idea to try to give Shakespeare his medication before the others arrived, and a new silent dialogue began between us.

As I pulled out the red zipped see-through bag, I asked the silent question:

Do you want your sausage?

He responded by moving his eyes and tilting his head ever so slightly whilst looking straight at me.

Yes, please but one that does not have any tablets in it. We are done with medication.

But we only have one more week to go and it is only one tablet per day. Only one every morning.

I know you want me to do this, but we can stop now, and it will be ok.

You know it can be dangerous if you cut out the tablets too quickly.

I am fine. It will be fine. We are done with the tablets.

He now looked at me with an unfamiliar expression for him, a challenging look I knew from my other dogs.

I handed him a sausage without the tablet. He took it without even smelling it as he never smelt anything. I handed him a second piece and he, again, took it without smelling it. When I reached out my hand with the third piece, he did not smell it, but he did not touch it.

You do not fool me. He smiled and took two slight steps backwards, away from me.

I was trying to figure out what had given me away and the only thing I could think of was that I had held the sausage containing the tablet in my left hand as I had picked out the two other pieces with my right hand. Shakespeare kept smiling. He had the look of a dog having fun. I started to release the audible sound of amusement, admiration for him confronting me, and for him not letting him be outsmarted by me.

You win. We are done.

I broke the skin of the sausage open, with the nails of my thumbs, and released the small tablet on to the ground. My fingers felt wet as I handed Shakespeare the sausage that now was tablet free. I put it in front of his mouth expecting him to take it, but he kept staring at me without acknowledging the sausage at all. He stared at me, then he stared down at the tablet, then back at me.

I stepped on the tablet and crushed it to powder under a dark blue and pink Nike heel. Shakespeare wagged his tail and his bum, showing a spurt of happiness, and as to reward me for my tablet bravery he moved forward and took the sausage out of my hand. I could not stop laughing.

This mighty dog had just made me crush his tablet and by that he had paid me back by doing something he did not normally dare to do. He moved forward and took the tablet free sausage out of my hand and let me stroke him.

He had won. We would never see another Prozac again. Ever!

> Things growing are **not ripe until their season**.
> -William Shakespeare, *A Midsummer Night's Dream*

Since Shakespeare arrived home, he had continually used only one sense. When he ate his breakfast or dinner, he stopped chewing midway into the mouthful, to listen. He did not turn his head to look, nor did he vibrate his nostrils to filter any particles in the air warning or alerting him. Shakespeare had learned to rely only on his sense of hearing during those years of confinement, and that had become his norm.

In his box at the sanctuary, he would listen by moving his ears. Sometimes it was a tiny movement, almost undetectable to the naked eye, but nevertheless the movement was there. Shakespeare would listen to different barks as people came through the gate, as the staff moved from box to box to feed and clean, or just random barks from the other dogs. He would listen for gates opening and closing. If steps came closer, he would start trembling, and then go into convulsion-like shaking. He moved his ears to pick up different tones of different barks. As I had sat watching him, I had followed his ear movements and watched how some barks would send him trembling and some barks would pass without affecting him noticeably.

The dogs in the sanctuary in Cyprus as in every refuge I have ever visited, have the same emotions as humans finding themselves locked up. They have reactions to stress, they have grief, they show spurts of joy, and they show signs of depression. After a while, dogs also become institutionalised, but most have mechanisms based on the coping skills taught to them by their mother and siblings. Shakespeare had no coping skills. In his confinement he simply sank into a deep black hole and disappeared. His solitude had slowly been killing him, and no medication or temptation made any difference. C and the others had been at their wits' end, attempting to change the situation and fighting a lost battle. It was all to no avail.

I have always thought, since I first sat with Shakespeare in his box, that he had been taken from his mum long before he should have been.
Coping skills are passed from mother to litter and the interaction with siblings also teaches a dog how to reduce stress in challenging situations or environment. Shakespeare had absolutely no tools to handle the stress of confinement. He had shut down all his senses apart from his hearing as there was no other stimulation. There was the daily routine of food at the same hour every day. The same food every day. There were the cleaning rituals of the boxes. At the same hour, every day. There was nothing to smell nor to look at.

When I spent time with Shakespeare inside the box, I noticed that when the dogs started to bark, he would tremble and press himself closer to the wall. I closed my eyes as to try to figure out what bark affected him the most. I was also trying to decipher why the different barks affected him so differently. As I spent more time with him, I saw a clear pattern. The bark of one dog petrified him. The dog was in a pen close to the main entry gate of the sanctuary - a female that had arrived a couple of months before my visit. She would be the first to warn the others when anyone arrived, but even when there was no one arriving or moving around her barks would affect Shakespeare badly.

I could hear the bark was that of harrowing sadness but the barks of so many of the others also told of sadness and longing. The bark from the female however was set apart from the others and Shakespeare would slide downwards as if that bark would squeeze out the last bit of strength from him.

When Shakespeare later arrived in France, the knowledge from my stay with him in the sanctuary was of huge value. I knew he was a dog with a broken sensory system. I also knew that unless I could awake his senses, he would never come fully alive.

As part of our journey, I had tried to get him to smell food. All food. Chicken, beef, salmon, pork, pigeon and - duck. I allied myself with a local hunter and offered him raw meat of deer, wild boar, rabbit, hare, and pheasant.

I had of course also tried offering him treats of all tastes but there was no reaction whatsoever. No response at all, apart from him turning his head away from every offering.

He was telling me he had not ready to give up the only control he had had in his life for the years at the sanctuary - the power to refuse food and control what and when he ate.

As his first summer passed, he had eaten mousse de canard from my hand but never used his nose. He had eaten his breakfast and dinner but never smelled what was in the bowl as dogs naturally do. He would eat sausage, but it seemed like it was a mimicking of the other dogs and not for pleasure.

He had now been home for ten months and would still not use his nose.

There was a promise of beautiful weather in the blue cloud-free sky as I walked out the gate for our evening walk.
The nights were still long but the morning arrived minutes earlier by the day.
As I walked out the first gate, I reminded myself that I needed go to the barn to dig out the vintage Easter eggs - the yellow porcelain Easter rabbits and the citrus yellow vases for the daffodils. Every year the very items filled me with fond memories of the country I had left.
As I closed the gate behind me, I felt fatigued. It had been a hectic, long day. In record time I had entangled myself into the trap of returning to the rescue world where days started at six fifteen most mornings, often lasting to after bedtime.

What kept me going throughout the many adoption conversations and getting everything in place for another twenty-six dogs arriving from North Romania in a couple of days, were the walks with my pack and with Shakespeare. It was the only way to put distance between me and some of the abuse, neglect and suffering I witnessed daily.
Countess Elena was bouncing next to me like a pup, Lady Eileen Bundle Brent was howling telling the world a walk was coming up and Hercule was almost losing the plot with his over-exuberant excitement over the evening excursion. Time with mum was his favourite time of any day. The same joy, every single time as if each walk is the first in months. He always made me smile. If we all could be that excited over the small gifts in life. Behind me Captain Hastings, Inspector Japp and Isabel were barking in disappointment over being left behind. I would walk them early the next morning, but they of course did not know that, so they were absolutely entitled to their disappointment.

We passed through the first gate and out the second.
Shakespeare was awaiting our presence. His greeting ritual was now always the same. He would play-bow to Elena, greet Lady with a brush up against her and he would ignore Hercule - in pretence but out of respect.
For all Hercules' soft loving sides, he also had a nervous *"do not approach me"* side to him. Shakespeare understood that and respected Hercule and left him be. I loved Shakespeare also for that.
I was so often struck by Shakespeare's sweet, intelligent, considerate nature that was the soft opposite of his strong stubborn side. How had he maintained this softness after all he had been through? What would I have done if he had emerged from his black hole as an aggressive dog. The question always died before it came to the question mark. If Shakespeare had been an aggressive dog, he would have attacked me the day I "unglued" him from the wall in Cyprus. There was absolutely no doubt in my mind about that. He could have attacked me and seriously injured me or worse in those days back in his box. He never did, nor would he ever attack anyone unless you were a field mouse in the French countryside. If you were one of those, he would have you for a snack.

The evening walk took me on to the gravel country lane past our property. We passed the straight rows of vines and went in the familiar half circle route that would eventually take us back to the path home. The temperature was mild and recent rain made the freshly turned soil smell of earth.
The dogs they were frolicking as always in the huge farmers' fields. They playfought, throwing themselves into the air like

spring lambs. My soul was filled with nothing but gratitude and love for them.

Forgotten was the heartache of the early hours of the same day when I had cried for a dog, I was not able to find a home for. No-one wanted her and it felt like raw pain. I had been in the predicament that I could not publish what had happened to her. Nor could I show the video I had in my possession. I could not tell the world why this dog needed a home more than most dogs. If I showed the video or described her story truthfully Facebook would close my Facebook page, or at least ban me for a while. They would have claimed graphic images and violent content. They would have shut me down for descriptions of torture with sexual undertones.

She was safe where she was now, but I had woken in the night thinking of her, as I so often would do with cases that haunted me. She had been a prisoner in the hands of a deprived man. Then, rescued, and now rejected. No one fell in love with her. She was seven years old.
I knew with my whole being she would be the most wonderful family member as I had seen her with other dogs and humans after she was rescued. She was wise and reflective. She would recognise love in a nanosecond, and she would hold on to that love with all four paws. I knew she would.
I had carefully worded her profile and home-seeking post, but no one had stepped forward and the transport to France would arrive without her. Knowing she had no home made me feel nauseous. I wanted to shout. Look! *Please look at this girl*! but I could not without breaking the rules.

I had felt all day that I had let her down. The only glue for repairing my broken heart was right in front of me. It was being with my own.
They were all once dogs in need and now look at them, I thought. I stopped and inhaled the joy of the ones dancing in the field. I tried to observe every little movement in their ritual. The way they read each other. The leaps, the jumps, and the bond.

I came to a slow halt, stretched out my arms with my face turned towards the evening sun. Like da Vinci's Vitruvian man I stood with my arms stretched, legs apart and palms turned upwards.
Inhale.
Exhale.

The familiar calmness I felt in no other place on earth, but amongst the vines near my home with my dogs, was slowly spreading. I inhaled and I made a wish. For the universe to find the girl a home. A home better than I ever dared to hope for. I could feel the evening breeze. As I stood still breathing a certainty came over me. The female dog would have a home. It had been manifested. I did not know how I knew, but I knew.

Slowly I opened my eyes and I saw Shakespeare standing still watching me. The three other dogs were still playing but Shakespeare was still. He was staring at me, *What are you doing?*
I am breathing darling. Breathing and wishing for a dog to have a future like I so wished for you I responded to his silent question. In slow motion I put my arms down by my sides. Shakespeare was not letting go of my eyes and as so many

times before we were intertwined. A dog and his human. A bond, the love, the mutual respect and understanding.

My hand reached for a treat in my pouch. Shakespeare was not interested but Elena who came flying across the field was. I laughed and the other dogs came rushing. They all gathered round, and Shakespeare changed his mind about wanting a treat.

We started our walk towards home.

By the time we got back to where we entered our land, I was surprised to find Shakespeare still with us. He would normally leave us around fifty metres further up the road but that evening he was trotting alongside us all. My heart skipped a beat and with that my pulse started picking up pace in anticipation. Would he come back in? Would it happen like this? Would he just trot back into the courtyard?

In answer to my silent question Shakespeare stopped. His beautiful body looked better than it ever had. His fur was shimmering. The wounds on his legs that he had struggled with so much were better. His eyes that would change between amber and hazel brown, were crystal clear. His paws had got bigger and wider after all the digging and his docked tail with the small fur tassel on the end had no more cysts. The white spotted socks on his front legs were whiter and more defined. Shakespeare was stunningly beautiful as he stood in the lazy evening sun with the backdrop of rows of vines. As he stopped, so did I. I was curious as to what made him come to a halt.

He stood perfectly still for no apparent reason, exactly like he had done whilst he was watching me earlier. I watched him in silence, holding my breath as if I intuitively knew something

was about to happen. He lifted his head slightly. Not much but just enough so that the head was higher than his body.
He turned his head so that the evening breeze was blowing towards him. He widened his nostrils. His nose started to vibrate. Slowly, slowly, he stretched his head higher. I could feel his awakening just as much as my eyes could see the physical change in him. He stretched his head into the air as far as his spine would permit. His neck was elongated making him more beautiful than ever.

His nose kept vibrating: he was moving his head millimetres to the left as to catch the wind - to filter the odours of wood, decomposed rotten leaves from last autumn, soil, field mice, foxes, rabbits, hare, deer, and the wild boar tracking by our land.
The odour of the woods and seasons past. The odour of a new life and a new beginning. The smell of spring, of daisies between the newly leafed vines. The smell of the evening sun. A scent of liberty. Total unchallenged liberty.
We both stood still as if there was no one else in the universe. Just a human and a dog sharing an awakening so longed for by both.

Tears were rolling down my cheeks. Tears of joy. Tears of gratitude for Shakespeare letting me share his moment. The moment he realised he could smell.
It was an epiphany for the dog I love so much. Shakespeare had regained his most important sense. I tilted my head backwards to detect what he could smell. I reflected on what it would mean to him. How he now could filter each of the scents and process them. I thought about the astonishing fact that if

my olfactory receptors were the size of a stamp, then dog's olfactory receptors would be the size of a handkerchief.
Mind boggling!
The evening sun had been hanging by an unseen thread. It let go. As the last rays were bidding good night, Shakespeare looked at me before he slowly turned and walked up towards where he normally would have left us. He was in no hurry to find his bed for the night, sleeping under the stars. He was not coming back inside. Not that evening either. His body language was different and as I watched him move towards his night nest, I saw him lift his head, again filtering the air through his nose.

What had made him walk all the way down to the entry of our land? I still cannot answer why he walked me all the way home but in some strange way it felt like he did what he had done to share the moment with me.
As I entered the orchard the plum trees that were in full bloom looked so beautiful covered in white flowers. Ghost-like.

I stopped and smelt the blossom as the moon was coming up. I wished I could click my heels, wiggle my nose, and experience the evening walk all over again just as it has been -
Shakespeare finding his sense of smell and the universe finding the female a home.
I knew that this would be an evening I would remember for a lifetime. The night Shakespeare came one step closer to becoming the dog he was always meant to be.

Good night, Shakespeare, sweet dreams. I will see you tomorrow and our journey will continue I whispered into the evening air. *Thank you so much for letting me be your human and for sharing your awakening with me. I love you.*

> Summer's lease hath all too short a date. Is, as in mockery, set. **The spring, the summer**. By their increase, now knows not which is which.
> -William Shakespeare, *A Midsummer Night's Dream*

My promise to Shakespeare and to myself, was to give Shakespeare the opportunity to find his balance and keeping that promise came easy to me.

I was walking with him as much as four hours every day, and of course that made me have to rearrange my schedule constantly. Something as simple as leaving the house to go to dinner at friends, where we normally were invited for eight o'clock in the evening, meant I had to start walking at four in the afternoon, and during hot summers days that was simply not possible.
Instead, I would complete my ten-kilometre round at dawn, on the track taking me past the farmers' fields, through the cool woods, then crossing through the vines, before returning in a loop to the woods near to our house.

When the walk was finished, I would go straight into the kitchen to prepare breakfast for all, including the cats. Then, I fed the dogs inside and went to the vines to feed Shakespeare and Miss Lemon. I would sit with them both whilst they ate, and that could sometimes take thirty minutes as Shakespeare would not always come for his meals straight away but stand at twenty or thirty metres distance confirming that all was safe before ever so slowly crossing to his bowl. If he got startled by something - a car passing in the distance, a child squealing in

delight at a jump into a swimming pool in the hamlet, or an unknown dog barking, it could take another thirty minutes to get him to come back to finish his meal. I could not do anything to get him to come back more quickly. Simply, I had to sit and wait until he decided he would return.
Then, I would repeat it all for his dinner.

For both meals I needed to sit calmly in the same place, show that nothing startled me and projecting onto him that he was safe.

As I had moved the bowl closer to the gate, I started adding different choices to his food. Shakespeare had showed, whilst living inside in the winter, that he feared food he did not know. He took it as sign that someone was trying to trick him, and he refused to touch his food bowl if there was not just his dry biscuits and the wet dog food he knew well. I started by giving him mousse de canard on top of the food, as I knew he loved that. Then I ventured on to different vegetables and before long, he would woof down the food. But he put his paws down at spinach. Spinach was a step too far. I respected that albeit it would be good for him to have the vitamins it contained. By him now finally accepting other food choices he was telling me his guard was slowly coming down, and at least he did no longer take unfamiliar food as a threat.
I stayed during Shakespeare's meal to build a bond with him beyond us walking together. If I just left his meals outside, I was telling him human interaction was a danger. I was trying to show him the polar opposite: human interaction was good.

During all of the summer of 2021 I kept moving his food bowl closer and closer to the gate.

In the beginning I moved it about twenty centimetres, until I saw he trusted me enough to move it a metre at the time. His food -bowl-body-language also changed. Earlier he would come sneaking between the vines as if he were a thief in the night - his head low, his body close to the ground, and his tension clear. By August, his head was up, and he was walking with ease. These changes were due to Miss Lemon, the cat who would share meals with him every day without fail. Miss Lemon could also be skittish but what Shakespeare did not know was that Miss Lemon trusted me entirely and even if something spooked her, she would not leave me whilst we were outside. I used Miss Lemon's confidence in me for all it was worth - I would sit myself on the grass only two or three metres from Shakespeare, food bowl turned sideways so that I could have eye contact with him as he approached for his meals, with Miss Lemon cuddling on my lap. Shakespeare could hear her purr.

When Miss Lemon purred, Shakespeare would be relaxed as he came towards his food bowl and me. Just before Shakespeare reached his bowl, I would put Miss Lemon's food down. Miss Lemon would take no notice of Shakespeare as he approached, and the fact that she was so relaxed eating her meals had an ongoing calming effect on Shakespeare. Who would ever have thought that a rescued hunting dog from Cyprus would be helped by a rescue cat in France?
By what felt like a small miracle I could now get Shakespeare to come inside the first gate, into the orchard for his breakfast and dinner, but only just inside.

He would let the pack and I stand behind the wooden gate and be with him whilst he ate.

He was back to being hypervigilant but at least he would cross the threshold and come inside to the orchard even if it were just for the moment of eating in the dappled shade of the plum trees. The pack was always generous towards him, not disturbing him as he came tip-toeing into the orchard. They stood patiently next to me in a row, watching him come and go.

I decided to try something new. As soon as he and Miss Lemon were finished eating, I would open the gate and let Elena out. Elena, the mighty white dog with bones of kindness and empathy that Shakespeare loved, would bounce, and run towards him with a wagging tail and Shakespeare would mirror her behaviour. My aim was to release Elena before Shakespeare reached the gate to leave the orchard. It was all about timing.

It was on a Tuesday afternoon in the last week of August. We had been watching Shakespeare have his dinner after our second walk. Shakespeare was observant but by no means overanxious and he even had time to exchange looks with each one of us - something he normally did not do.

It was like Shakespeare had all the time in the world. He and Miss Lemon had come to the orchard for their dinner, and I was standing inside the second gate, with Japp, Hastings and Hercule on one side of me. Miss Grey, Elena, Lady, and Isabel stood on the other. I was holding Miss Marple, who had decided to turn on her back in my arms and expose her belly for me to caress. She was purring away with that continuous rolling R, described so well in the French word for purr, ronroner. I was smiling at Miss Marple who, despite being without eyes, had a presence and enjoyment of life in her little body that was enviable.

I was filled with happiness and gratitude for these animals of mine. As I opened the gate to let Elena out, I witnessed how Shakespeare waited just those few seconds extra for Elena. Shakespeare greeted her with one of his play-bows and the games were on. They were rushing round the orchard, jumping, both up on the hindlegs, and then, there in front of me, Shakespeare took a brief break to yawn. I could hardly believe it, Shakespeare had yawned. I wanted to do a happy dance.

A yawn in a dog in a situation like this has two functions; to signal that the onwards play fight is just that, a play fight. But dogs also yawn as a natural way of calming themselves down if they are anxious.

It was the first time since Shakespeare had arrived home four-hundred-and sixty-eight days earlier, that he had shown any sign of having the ability to yawn or do any of the other actions a dog will do to self soothe, like lip-smacking, drinking water or stretching to release tension in the body. Shakespeare was at that moment stressed because he was inside the orchard, but he now tried to convince himself he would be ok. Shakespeare's yawn was more prolonged and intense than a sleep yawn would be, and it is easy to see the difference when you know the dog; this was a self-soothing yawn. What a victory for Shakespeare who had managed to come to a level where he dared to help himself to reduce stress. I could not have been prouder if I tried!

> That time of year thou mayst in me behold
> When yellow leaves, or none, or few, do hang
> **Upon those boughs which shake against the cold.**
> -William Shakespeare, *Sonnet 73*

We were in November.

The days were shorter and the night colder and it was time to get Shakespeare back inside. I had a picnic plan involving Captain Hastings, Japp and of course Shakespeare. I had packed my soft round wicker basket. Today it was filled with lemon cake baked with lemon from the trees in the pots each side of the kitchen door, and a thermos of sweet tea. For the dogs there was meatballs and dried puppy biscuits.

Behind us was a wonderful summer. There had been days when it had been demanding but my bond to Shakespeare was stronger than ever. Each of the dogs had also strengthened their bond with our Cypriot boy. That summer I had walked a distance equivalent to Paris to Istanbul and back - or the equivalent of well over the distance from my home in France to the North Pole in air miles. I had bought new walking shoes twice since I let Shakespeare out in February. But on our picnic day today, we were not walking far.

I had been walking Hercule, Elena, Lady, Isabel, Miss Grey, and Shakespeare early in the morning, and those five dogs were now scattered and sleeping. Miss Grey was snoring on the outdoor sofa in our summer living room under the open barn, whilst Japp and Hastings lay in the shade by the courtyard gate. Hercule, Lady and Isabel shared the vintage bed in the kitchen, the cover just changed from green to soft spun-sugar pink. Elena was stretched on her back with all four paws in zen position. I had my basket popped under my arm. I was sure Japp and Hastings would bark as I came walking towards them, as it was evident I was leaving with them as I did not tell them to go to their beds. They were slightly confused by me carrying a basket, something that normally would mean me leaving the property in my car without any dogs. There was not a sound as they bounced hopefully either side of me.

Shakespeare was just outside the gate waiting as always. He greeted Hastings with a bow and a bark filled with hope of another walk, and he glanced sideways at me.
I walked to the far end of our land outside our property before I threw down the quilt and sat myself down halfway under the huge walnut tree. From where I sat, I could see our top gate and the wall around the orchard. I would be able to hear the other dogs if they started to bark or howl.
Shakespeare looked bewildered as I sat down on the lavender quilt that had small white flowers woven into the thick old fashioned cotton fabric. The grass had regained some green after the rain that followed the scorching hot summer that had left the field a dull, dead beige. There was a wind from the north, with frost-white clouds moving on an ice blue backdrop. It smelt like autumn with the decomposing leaves and the hazelnuts on the ground getting wet, drying, getting wet, then drying again.

The wind made it one of those chilly days with the pledge that the wood burners would soon be burning round the clock. The cranes had already flown further south, and the hunting season had begun. That year as the year before, I was concerned and worried that Shakespeare would get injured or killed by the hunters. But Shakespeare had clearly shown he feared the gunshots when we heard them whilst out walking. If nothing else that meant it was unlikely he would hang around the hunting dogs as they "washed" through the woods.

I put my hand in the basket and took each item out: my lemon cake in a see-through box, the tea in a thermos cup with a gold lid, a large Pyrex glass container with a happy Granny Smith green lid, filled with meat balls. Last the large zip bag with the dry biscuits enough for three dogs. Hastings and Japp were actively curious whilst Shakespeare, wondering why on earth we did not walk, kept himself at a few metres distance.

I started to spread the biscuits on the grass - not too wide apart, in a half circle from the quilt.
Hastings did of course start nibbling straight away and by the time I had emptied the bag and was back on my picnic quilt, all three dogs were grazing calmly. I had lemon cake and tea whilst watching them slowly sniff and search for the biscuits. Shakespeare did not take a blind bit of notice of me even when he was within arm's reach.

Hastings looked over a couple of times to check if my lemon cake could be another option on his picnic menu, but he decided he better keep grazing as to not surrender his dry biscuit to Inspector Japp or Shakespeare. I could see how Shakespeare slowly relaxed. The muscles on the side of his body were letting go of tension, he was using his nose to find the biscuits and his ears were not in an alert position, simply hanging flopping down the side of his face. His facial expression was soft and carefree.

I sat motionless with only my eyes moving and the warm thermos cup warming my hands, absorbing the calmness of the dogs. My energy level was as calm as it could be, and the dogs were in the same space. This had been the goal of my picnic. To share the calmest energy possible with Shakespeare. That is why it was specifically Captain Hastings and Inspector Japp who were with me. Hastings has a natural calmness and Japp simply mirrored that.

As pack leader I tried always to be calm when we were together. Only humans follow unstable leaders it is said, and I believe this to be true. I could show vulnerability with my pack without any problems as they still knew I would lead them, but I needed Shakespeare to feel the utter calm that I could project. I had planned this day during the last week, and before the day arrived made sure to set aside time to meditate every day. If I could not get Shakespeare inside on his own accord, I needed to drug him as I had the year before but this time I would be prepared, and it would all be calm.

Hastings was the first to come and lay down closely to me, followed by Inspector Japp, who looked so tiny next to his large companion. My hope was now that Shakespeare would copy the behaviour of the two other dogs. After having weighed for and against for a couple of minutes, he carefully put his left front paw on the duvet. I had picked this exact duvet because it was large. It could easily hold three dogs and their mistress with space to spare. Shakespeare, with all four paws now on the duvet, stood still, lifted his nose, and perked up his ears, and whilst scanning the landscape in high alert his brain was finally telling him there were no danger lurking. He was safe, and with that knowledge he laid down on the far end of the quilt, opposite where I sat. I opened the Pyrex box. The snap of the lid made Hastings pay attention at the same time as it made Shakespeare concerned, but he stayed.

I handed each a meat ball, stretching my arm as far as I could reach to get to Shakespeare, but it demanded some effort on his part as well. He stretched and ever so gently took the meat ball out of my hand. I kept sharing. The dogs waited their turn with low energy and no signs of jumping the queue. Shakespeare was happy and Hastings knew it would be a fair divide, so he did not stress. Japp was completely calm.

All three dogs kept licking their lips and Hastings' heavy bushy tail kept swiping the cotton surface in a sideways movement. When all meatballs were gone - the ones with sleeping tablets for Shakespeare, and the ones without for the others - we simply sat still. Hastings nestled up again the side of my leg, and with a deep sigh of contentment went to sleep with Japp curled up touching him with his left front paw, so he would be warned if Hastings moved. I closed my eyes, breathing regularly, keeping my ears open for any movements from Shakespeare. There were none. He was completely relaxed, breathing regularly with us, with his head resting on his paws. His fur was shining in deep copper, the white knee socks stretched out. He was greyer round the eyes and his muzzle than when he arrived - but no wonder! The shock to his system to fly from Cyprus to Belgium, then thirteen hours' drive home, living in a home for the first time in his life, walking on grass for the first time in five years.

Living in liberty, with all the choices he could have taken, he chose to stay.

The changes from solitude to pack. The demands of him and on him. Working through deep grief for having lost Agatha, the only other soul he had ever trusted, and the only one he had ever loved, The idea of being deeply loved by a human was a concept completely alien to him and something with which he had truly struggled. Yet, there he was, by his own free will, in my company. Breathing in the same rhythm as us.

He had changed so much, but generally I could still not stroke him whilst we were outside.

My wants were of no importance. I had not rescued him to fulfil any need in me but to give him his life back and I had long since learnt to cherish the fact that we could share the same space, breathe the same air. That in itself gave me a contentment unknown to me before. It was hard to explain, but perhaps that is what a selfless act feels like.

It was enough - sharing a vintage, square, summer cotton quilt on a cold autumn day. As I glanced over at him, I wanted for nothing. As always, his beauty and presence took my breath away.

Shakespeare was lazily washing his legs with circular movements of his pink tongue. He was laying relaxed, against the backdrop of dry leaves in tones of green, ochre yellow and shades of cigar brown. Laying in front of the walnut tree that would be surrounded by bluebells in spring, with the air moving enough to carry the scent of the countryside from one wood to another, with the sun losing its heat but yet not its light.

In that exact moment I was filled with every emotion and every experience I had ever lived throughout my life. In that moment on that quilt with those three animals my life came into one. It all fell into place; love, exhilaration, excitement, joy, relief, nostalgia, anxiety, anger, grief, pain, fear, shame, and horror - every emotion and experience that had led me to that exact moment. I felt touched by gratitude in its clearest form. Shakespeare had been the force that had made me climb within. He and I mirrored each other and by me trying to help him I had gained an in depth understanding of myself that I had never had before. By meeting Shakespeare, I had to face my own fears and my own broken brain and all that came with it.

I was also, at that moment, for the first time, immensely proud of my body. It had never given up on me. The body that was still here to walk with my pack every day, metal enforced spine and all. Gratitude for Shakespeare's heart that had kept beating against all odds whilst his soul had died. We had recognised the other, and by this we had let someone else into the coves and secret paths of our broken brains.

Immense gratitude for my pack. This pack of blind, deaf, broken dogs that supported each other, and me, and always had space for another. We ebbed and flowed with each other - like the most natural phenomena in the vast universe.

As I opened my eyes, Shakespeare lifted his head and looked straight at me with such softness. I had to gasp for air, realising I had, in that moment, an awareness of having accomplished what we all seek: a deep sense of peace within.

> **I count myself in nothing else**
> so happy as in a soul
> remembering my good friends.
> -William Shakespeare, *Richard II*

We were so used to living with a petrified dog - that we had adjusted our lives around him, inside and out.

During the time Shakespeare had lived outside I had served around fourteen-hundred al fresco meals for him and Miss Lemon. I had given Shakespeare countless bones and served licking mats with probiotic yogurt. Every day as clockwork, Shakespeare and Miss Lemon had been fed together. We had adjusted our lives to help him find his footing and now when he was back inside, we did the same thing.

Even the most mundane chores would be done in a way so as not to scare Shakespeare. We would only walk around a table on one side and not pass him. We would not use noisy kitchen appliances in the kitchen but move the task to the large laundry room that had vintage Sylvester and Tweety cartoons, framed in happy colours hanging over the countertop. The kitchen-aid, I used for baking now lived here. We would not hoover if Shakespeare were inside but coax him outside before the noisy machine went on.
We would make sure not to slam doors and secure them if they were open. We took out the large dustbin that made a terrible noise when it was rolled over the gravel, after Shakespeare was in his safe chair at night. Everything we did to help him had become second nature, I kept trying to find ways forward. I constantly went back over my own PTSD reaction patterns to

different scenarios, and I always came up with the same response as to how to help Shakespeare.
Time, love, understanding, repetition!
Time, love, understanding, repetition!

Many people thought of us, and especially me as crazy. *He is only a dog*, people kept repeating and some even suggested he should be put to sleep, killed - shot. Neither Are nor I paid any attention but over the years we have removed ourselves from people who do not understand.

With Shakespeare safely back inside after almost ten months, we seamlessly adjusted our lives around new routines. There was a change in Shakespeare's behaviour. His favourite hiding place now was under the buffet sideboard in the dining room. This old heavy wooden buffet with a white full-length marble slab on top was over two metres long. I bought it at a second hand shop many years earlier and it had taken three men to lift it. I had, optimistic as always, brought it home and painted the wood white, leaving the ornate gold metal parts around the four doors. To finish off the transformation I had put jute tassels with porcelain blue and white beads on the cabinet keys.
The buffet was set against a dark grey wall with two silver lamps on the marble surface, together with a blue and white antique French porcelain rose holder. Due to lack of interior funds, I had had to come up with the idea to find something inexpensive to hang on the wall above the buffet, and one day I found a piece of large wood for next to nothing at a local lumber yard. I had painted the wood white and glued an assortment of porcelain plates to it. The plates in blue and white told the porcelain story of my life; one from my great-

grandmother, a plate from my paternal grandmother, one from my maternal grandmother and a couple of small plates I bought at my first flea market in France. Yet again, I was mostly back lying on the floor, flat out on my stomach, spending time with Shakespeare.

Shakespeare's favourite chair, covered in blue and white cotton fabric was in the corner of the dining room to the right of the buffet, but he would only use it if I were alone in the house with him and the other dogs, and not even always then. The year before, Shakespeare had hidden in the bed under the billiard table, he had hidden anywhere and everywhere in the garden, and the outdoor living space and he had hidden under the countertops in the kitchen, but that second winter inside would be different. Shakespeare would find sanctuary under the buffet in the dining room and would sometimes spend whole days there. He would come out for breakfast and dinner but after a trip into the garden he would be back under the sideboard. The oak floor in the dining room was far more comfortable than the cold tiles in the hallway I thought. I was trying to count my blessings.

I would read and listen to podcasts and poems through my earplugs. I would do online rescue work from the floor position and eat my lunch from down there.
The dogs would go to sleep scattered around and Hercule would try to be under my skin as always. All the dogs understood why we were there, and they showed a patience that seemed natural and effortless. None of the dogs ever complained or made anything difficult. When I did walk part of the pack, alternating as to who came, Shakespeare would come out from under his hiding place and stand behind the

glass in the kitchen door and bark in sadness over not being chosen, but I knew that if I let him out, he would not come back inside. He was by no means ready to face his darkest fear - the gate - and it was far too cold for him to stay outside during the night.

Shakespeare's recall was amazing but that did not help him to overcome his fear. When we were out walking, I could call him, as he was running in front, and as he turned to look at me, I pointed to the left or right and he would understand immediately where we were going. He understood my Norwegian instructions in record time, even if they were in a language he had never heard before we met. He was such an extremely clever, intelligent boy. He, without question, loved me to the maximum of his capabilities, and he would follow me to the end of the Earth - yet he could not walk back inside, through the gate, for neither himself nor me. It is classic avoidance behaviour that anyone suffering from PTSD will recognise but I was not sure it was the gate itself Shakespeare feared or something else. The gate could simply symbolic. When Shakespeare saw the gate, he did not use the rational part of his brain, but the primal instinctive part of his brain was activated, the fright-flight-freeze motion was outside his control, and I knew this all too well.
After my accident people often asked me if I feared driving a car. I always gave the same answer.
No, I am not scared of driving my car, but I make a terrible passenger.
What I never told anyone was that I however had become scared of bikes after my accident. There was no bike involved in my accidents and yet the sight of a bike, a bike sign or a

bike path would send my body into flight mode. My pulse would rise, and I would sweat, feel dizzy and nauseous.

It had been on an afternoon in June, over a decade before my accident. It was midsummers day. I sat in my car in heavy traffic in Bergen, waiting for the traffic light to change.
It was a day filled with that clear summer light that is so rare when you live in the high North, closer to the polar circle. There were people on the sidewalk dressed in soft pastel-coloured tones. One young girl had a summer dress that was flowing as she was moving, with a graceful body of a ballet dancer. I let her cross the street in front of me and she smiled and waved her hand as a thank you. It was a day where it was easy to be kind. The sunshine made everyone seemed carefree, sprinkled with anticipation of the midsummer night celebration that was upcoming that evening. The sunroof of my car was open, and I could feel the sun on the top of my long blond hair. On the local radio station "Morning Mood" by Grieg was playing and it felt like nothing bad could ever happen. The traffic light changed and BANG! In an instant the world changed!

A man on a bike had passed the cars in high-speed thinking he would beat them all over the intersection. I could tell he had dark curly hair softly rounded off the edge of his helmet. A large black Mercedes with a middle-aged male driver had obviously not paid attention to the traffic lights and was crossing after the light from his direction had turned red - and then the sound of twisting metal.

The cyclist hit the side of the car and went into free spin like a flying trapeze artist with no bar to reach for. He went revolving over the car, twisting his body, continuing in an unnatural manoeuvre, at the same time as his bike was airborne, weightless, with both wheels still spinning.

Time stood still. Everything and everyone stopped. The colours somehow seemed to change, like there was a sudden eclipse, as the man continued his journey towards the inevitable -cobblestones. No one moved, until a lady opened her car door and leaped out, and as that was the cue to break the frozen moment, several others jumped out of their cars too. Way back in the traffic light queue someone was honking their horn thinking the traffic had stopped for no good reason. The ambulance was there within minutes and slowly we could leave. It had all in all taken less than twenty minutes.

Suddenly, on the second night after my accident, as a flash from nowhere the memory was there as vivid as if I were in my car on that mid-summer's day. I could smell the summer air, feel the warm summer sun on my head, hear the music and see the man flying.

I did not understand what was happening but for the next couple of years - I would be that cyclist, separated from my bike and flying, waiting to hit the cobblestone to die.

Was it because I could not remember my own accident fully? Was it because I had observed as a bystander every detail of the man on the bike, so my brain simply swapped the two? I do not know the answer, but this experience had made me realise that the memories I did not remember - were sometimes just as important as those I do, and they can become swapped or entangled.

Whenever Shakespeare had reactions that did not make sense to me, I simply thought; *this is his bike moment.*

The brain - and memories - sometimes play tricks that are not logical, and I know this first hand. That knowledge helped me understand Shakespeare and it gave me strength to never ever, not once, think I would give up on him. I knew that I could help Shakespeare towards managing his fear, but I could not do it for him. I was trying to give him both a map and compass, like the one I had created for myself by learning how to breathe again.

Shakespeare hiding under the sideboard was all part of him trying to filter the world, to decide if the world could ever be a safe place. He was making himself an observer from floor level, taking in every sound, smell, and movement. My job was to show him that, yes, his new universe was a safe place to be, gates included.

The longer I laid on the floor, the more we supported him, the more he understood that I would never force him, the bigger the chance was that he would one day be able to function in the same universe as us. We spent our days and evenings on the floor of the dining room - I stretched out my hand and held Shakespeare paw as I was sprawled out, or sometimes curled up as I fell asleep to the sounds from the wood burner and Japp's snoring.

Shakespeare would rest his paw in my hand for hours, never withdrawing it or signalling he was uncomfortable. By his paw resting in my hand, we were physically connected.
As late autumn turned to winter in 2021, I got used to seeing the cold blue winter sky with delicate, wispy, cirrus clouds traveling over, from my position on the floor between the large

white floor mirror with a ground view of the heavy feet of ten dining-room chairs.

By the beginning of December Shakespeare started to spend more time in his high-backed chair than under the sideboard. I would now move to sit up against his chair - the buffer between him and the world, as he was curled up on his sheepskin. I would read and he would fall asleep, leaving his head on my shoulder whilst he sank into a deep state of dreamless slumber. This was a change in his sleeping pattern. From constantly dreaming, making small distress noises, and having feet that never rested, he now slept in a motionless deep way without any twitches to his eyelids. He rewarded my determination and constant presence by breathing warm regular breaths towards the side of my neck, and soon, very soon, he would sleep on his side with all four paws stretched out to the side, telling me he was beginning to dare feel vulnerable.

> A victory is twice itself when the achiever brings home **full numbers**.
> - William Shakespeare, *Much Ado About Nothing*

When change and progress is utterly slow it is sometimes hard to appreciate it as progress at all.

As Shakespeare was back inside in the months leading up to Christmas 2021, I had my notes from the previous Christmas to use as base for comparison (if you live with a shutdown dog, keeping a small diary with progress can be lifesaving for your motivation). The notes and photos from the previous Christmas made it so easy for me to see how far we had come.

Shakespeare was still an utterly broken dog and would by this stage still have been considered a difficult rescue case, but Shakespeare would, by the second Christmas eat with the others in the kitchen without panicking with every sound. He now had his own upside-down wood wine box for his food stand, just like the rest of the pack. Shakespeare would pass me and brush up against me daily, and on the odd occasion he would let me stroke him even if he were not underneath the buffet or on his chair.

When I got out the same bags of Christmas decorations as the year before, he would even be curious as to what was inside the large blue IKEA bags and stayed as I opened each one. It was such amazing progress that I did not have to remove any of the bags into another room for fear of the rustling plastic sending Shakespeare into a panic attack with convulsion-like shakes. We even had a "theft" incident.

I was sitting on the floor in the hallway with lots of different sparkling items around me. Silver and gold ball decoration for the Christmas tree, red felt hearts in many different sizes - some plain red coloured and some with tartan or white material on one side. Are's favourite Christmas ornament had just been unwrapped from the bubble wrap: a sad looking father Christmas that was on the floor next to me. Every year, Are remembered how happy we were the day we bought him, in a festive interior shop packed with red, gold, white and silver, with a mistletoe over the door! I got a big kiss as we left. Are had felt sorry for the saddest Father Christmas, so we brought him home, in time for a late dinner in our candle filled kitchen. That is what Christmas is all about for us, memories of years gone by and making new memories for the years to come. Shakespeare was now part of our Christmas memories from the year before and I wanted to make new memories with him. Sitting on a cushion on the floor I was aiming to unpack all the Christmas decorations, in the presence of eight dogs and three cats. Some would see this as a pre-Christmas challenge, but I saw it as precious bonding time. I soaked up how Shakespeare stretched his neck to smell each item, moving from one item to another quickly, then slowing down to sniff and smell a heart, or a gold ball, many times.

I was trying to imagine what he could smell. Could he smell happiness, the star anise, the cinnamon sticks, and joy of Christmas' gone? Could he smell himself from the Christmas before? Could he smell the person who had made the handmade decorations? Could he smell if it had been a child or an adult? The answer was more than likely yes to all the questions I ran through my head, as I watched him moving between the decorations and memories.

I was reflecting on my utter fascination of a dog's sensory system and their capability to smell and filter smell particles. If you were to train a dog to look for a dirty sock it could identify one dirty sock in a sock-mountain of two million socks. Absolutely mind boggling!

Captain Hastings, Elena, Japp and Hercule were smelling their way around too, and true to tradition Miss Marple was inside a bag playing with something. Isabel had given up and lie on the white bench, just through the living-room door. The flames in the wood-burner were casting a warm orange light over us all whilst the wood in the large open fire in the living room was spitting, making me grateful for the old black fireguard. Lady was asleep leaning up against my back making sounds of comfort and contentment. To me it was perfect pre-Christmas magic on an ordinary Monday.

I sat still, inactive, watching Shakespeare sniffing until he came to a large red felt heart that was on the floor. He sniffed again, stood perfectly still for a serious investigative smell, and then he decided: this heart belongs to me. Ever so carefully, as if the heart were breakable, he picked it up between his teeth, turned away from me and took the heart to his bed out of the way of the ocean of Christmas decoration bags.
Shakespeare put the heart down leaving it under his chin, and then he put his head on top of it as if to say, *this heart belongs to me*. It was such a beautiful picture, it made me teary.

Shakespeare had never taken anything. He had never touched any of our ample toy supply, that only Miss Grey and Elena played with.

He had never stolen food nor been on the kitchen counters in sharp contrasts to Countess Elena who had made counter-surfing into an artform, egged on by the other dogs who shared her bounty. Shakespeare had never stolen a shoe or a remote control in juxtaposition to the rest of the pack that all had gone through phases of theft or destruction. Shakespeare had simply never ever done anything of what all dogs will do to test their humans, and there he was, having fallen in love with a red felt heart that he wanted to keep.

You can have all the red felt hearts in the world Shakespeare I said whilst looking at this beautiful dog, shiny and deep copper brown in the orange light, curled up in his basket with a red felt heart unevenly sewn by a child's hand at a small school in Cognac, ten years prior. The sight of him with the red heart sowed a small hope in me. Maybe 2022 would be the year he would come to live with us full time.

Maybe, I said to Lady as I turned to stroke her whilst she was repositioning herself.

Maybe!

> All things are **ready** if
> our minds be so.
> -William Shakespeare,
> *Henry V*

I knew that I could not keep Shakespeare confined any longer. It was not good for his mental or physical health that he was not walking with us. I kept weighing back and forth what to do.

Over Christmas my friend Anniken had travelled from Norway to spend time with us all. During one of our many walks she mentioned that there was a new dog lead, which was sold in long lengths. It was a round clothes-line-like lead that would not get entangled. It was invented for hunting dogs when they needed liberty in the woods, but it gave the owner the chance to stand on the lead and bring the dog back. I thought this could be the solution. That could make it possible for me to coach Shakespeare back inside when he came out with us. Anniken returned to Norway and soon a neon yellow, easily seen, twenty-metre lead arrived.

I started to fit Shakespeare with a harness daily, having purposefully chosen a walk-in harness: I could get the harness under him even when I laid flat out on the floor with him under the buffet, and it did not involve anything going over his head, something that often will trigger negative reaction in scared dogs. On good days Shakespeare would sit in his chair as I put one leg in the harness, then the other, securing the harness with a simple click. He would let it happen without any protest but making no efforts to participate. There was no trembling, no shaking and that made me pleased and optimistic.

I would fit the harness in the morning before breakfast and take it off before dinner in the evening.

For some weeks Shakespeare was wearing a neon yellow harness that suited him in colour and made him look like an ordinary dog. He also had a blue fabric collar, that I had bought for him before he came home. The collar had a metal tag with our contact details - not that anyone would ever get close enough to read the information, I often thought. All the dogs also wore a collar to protect them against ticks and fleas. As soon as I felt confident that Shakespeare was comfortable with the harness, he would come for a walk.
Simultaneously I kept checking the ten-day weather forecast. *Darling, when you feel comfortable with the harness and the weather is good you will come walking with us. I promise.*
I stroked him and caressed his ears like I had done when we first met, and I tried to always have the same calm soft monotone voice, giving him a treat each time I put his harness on. Sometimes he would take the treat but other times he would just turn his face away as to say *I can do this without a bribe!*

I had always kissed him on his forehead - it was a habit I had with all my dogs, and one day, I had put his harness on, he rejected his treat and I made to walk away. He glanced up at me saying *Have you not forgotten something?* It took me a second to realise what this movement of his eyes and minute tilting of his head meant: he was asking for his kiss! I had to compose myself before I bent down and kissed him on his forehead whispering *Thank you for reminding me how far we have come.*

Shakespeare had endured me loving him. With few exceptions he took no evident comfort in my physical strokes, my cuddles, and kisses. He had let me love him, and never protested, but for me who had an expressive pack with huge appreciation for physical contact, Shakespeare was like a no-man's land. Flat. Motionless.

With the few exceptions of flashes, some very few precious incidents, or glimpse of awkward appreciation, he never sought out physical love - yet there he was, having just reminded me I had forgotten to kiss him! For anyone who had been present in the room it would have been unnoticeable but for me it was enormous. Overwhelmingly enormous - it showed me that all my efforts to reach him were working. He accepted my love and I realised he would even miss me if I were not there. I cried without a sound, in gratitude for the reminder of the rewards of love.

Mid- January the forecast promised early spring-like weather and I decided to take Shakespeare out for a walk during the upcoming week. He seemed comfortable enough in his harness and the lead was ready. It weighed next to nothing, and that was the important thing as Shakespeare would not be spooked by weight and sound. My only concern was that the lead was round and small in diameter, and if I stepped on it on soft ground, it could simply just glide under my heel.
To ease my mind, I had tested the lead on Captain Hastings during some of our walks leading up to the big day, and I felt comfortable that I had developed a technique to ensure I could step on it and get hold of it if I needed, and so get Shakespeare back inside the gate.

On the morning of 19th January 2022, the sun was slowly stretching over the horizon as if it had all the time in the world. It could of course not know that I had laid in bed listening to Are snoring, from four o'clock, in anticipation of Shakespeare's walk. Miss Marple had sensed I was awake and had climbed up towards my neck to be closer to me. She stretched out her right front paw and started to stroke my chin putting more effort into her purring. I smiled in the dark, trying to go back to sleep but at five I gentle lifted Miss Marple aside, put my feet on the floor, shivering.

The evening before I had left my clothes hanging ready over the bathtub, making it easy to silently dress and slip down the stairs to make coffee.
The dogs were scattered round, and no one bothered to even lift their head as I descended. It was all so utterly calm, and no one would know there were eight dogs and four cats in the house.

I had left Shakespeare's harness on the floor by his chair the evening before and as the water was working itself to a boil, I entered the dining room to find Shakespeare under the sideboard. The harness was still on the floor where I had left it the night before, something that would not have been the case if it were any of the other dog's harness. In our house a harness equalled walks and it had taken some time to make the dogs understand that Shakespeare's harness was an exception.

The harness was luminous neon yellow, matching the new lead by coincidence. Contra to popular belief dogs can see some colours. They can see yellow, blue, and brown but the rest are as hues of grey, black, and white, hence I had chosen the bright yellow harness for Shakespeare to make it stand out from the other dog harnesses that were black and red to the human eye. Shakespeare's harness could, a while after I bought it, be left anywhere without it causing exuberant excitement and certainly that morning no one was bothered. It was still – only I knew it was a big day.

I lay myself flat on the floor and as we had eye contact, I whispered the news.
Good morning beautiful you. Today is your big day.
I stretched my neck and put my head under the buffet. I kissed his head without him moving, but I detected his shivering. He was not cold, but he was worried because I was breaking my morning routine. This is what had made him go into hiding.
Today is the day you are coming walking darling.

I stretched out and got hold of his harness. I positioned myself and carefully lifted him up on one side, putting one leg in the harness whilst pulling the harness so the clip was hanging loosely over his back. It was like getting a sleep-drunk child ready for school.
I repeated the motion on the other side, and just as the kettle wanted to whistle, I clicked the harness closed in the confined space under the buffet. I crossed the floor, in time to grab the kettle before it would become as loud as a football referee. With Shakespeare under the sideboard, I had my morning coffee sitting by him on the floor, trying to contain my excitement for the adventure ahead.

Slowly the other dogs got curious. Why was I up? If I was going somewhere, why had I not left? One by one they stepped out of their beds, to join Shakespeare and me.

I was trying to prepare myself for all possible outcomes. Shakespeare might not come back inside with me. I would spend all day trying if I had to, but I might fail despite the lead. If he did not come back in with me, I had a Plan B. I would get the lead off him when I served him dinner outside in the evening, as he could not be outside by himself dragging a lead no matter how weightless and tangle-proof it was. I tried to tell myself it would not come to that.

The night before Are and I had agreed he would feed breakfast to those dogs that were left inside. I would take Lady, Hercule, Elena and Shakespeare and we would start walking the ten-kilometre route Shakespeare knew so well. When finished, I would try to come back inside, and if that did not work, I would walk the same route again, all day, if I had to. I had packed dry biscuit breakfast for the dogs that were coming with me. I wanted them to have breakfast out of my hand whilst we were outside so Shakespeare would relax.

I split the pack by closing the double doors between the kitchen and the dining room. On the kitchen side were those not coming - in the dining room were the dogs that would walk with Shakespeare and I, on this day of days. Elena, Hercule and Lady immediately twigged.

It was walking time.

To Shakespeare, wearing a harness and lead meant nothing whilst it sent others into a spin of energy.

I lay on the floor and clipped the round lead onto the metallic hook on the harness without any hiccoughs. This sent the other dogs into overdrive and as I said Shakespeare's name several times I got up and moved towards the main door.

I could see Shakespeare's eyes as his head poked out from under the buffet like a tortoise poking its head out from its protective shell. Then, it clicked! He came out with his bum wiggling and in an instant, he was up on all four legs. He was excited and started to bark. I laughed.
Yes, I know. Its walking time.

Shakespeare looked dapper in his harness and the new lead following like an anorexic snake wiggling across the floor, slithering onto the gravel.

As Shakespeare moved forward towards the gate, with the lead behind, I watched him turn his head, open his mouth, give the snake one chew and it was gone. Left on his harness was around five short centimetres of the lead, and the shining silvery buckle. My heart sank! He was so excited and now proud of having rid himself of whatever enemy that followed him. He had conquered a snake and was about to go for walk, all before the day had even properly started. Shakespeare was without a lead before we had even reached the first gate. I had to take a snap decision. There was no way I could not take him with me for the walk. I could not crush the joy he was expressing.

Slightly reluctant and with my head spinning I opened the first gate, and he was the first dog through, like an arrow from a bow.
Hercule was dancing around me, with Elena running back and forth between the second gate and me. Lady was barking as if we had not walked for months, and suddenly Shakespeare joined in.

I could hear the other dogs barking in the kitchen and I knew Are's sleep had been abruptly cut short by the stereo barking.

I opened the gate from the orchard and the dogs were like confetti scattered by the wind, all in different directions, before swirling, reuniting, joyful with tails wagging. The energy was that of elated joy and intense appreciation for their paws running in liberty, hardly touching the ground.
Shakespeare turned his head and looked straight at me.
Thank you!
You are so welcome I smiled.

I stood watching Shakespeare trying to search for field mice, run over the naked farmer's field, play with Elena, and bark, all at the same time. He was euphoric.
Lady stood still, looking up at me as if she were rolling her eyes. I giggled.
He is happy Lady. Very happy. At that she ran to join him in his contagious explosion of joy.

The branches on the trees were still bare with the sun low as we walked. Unpolluted air spun in the landscape that had stayed the same for centuries. Soaring above us was a Peregrine falcon. This large falcon with its blue-grey back, barred white underpart and black head, was gliding on the uplifting air, dropping in the air pockets, then returning to follow our trail with its binocular vision. Welcoming Shakespeare back.

We walked past the donkey farm where the donkeys were braying in a hee-haw choir. The dogs paid no attention as they were used to the sound carried by the wind over the flat landscape. There were people working in the vines, cutting them back, preparing them for the shoots in spring, but again the dogs paid absolutely no attention. Shakespeare and Lady stayed behind digging for mice but soon they caught up when they had given up the hunt and sought another trail.

By the time we had walked full circle and were heading through the woods, I was hoping with all my being that Shakespeare would walk all the way home, inside both gates. That he would come back into the warm kitchen, go to his chair, and curl up, or cross the floors to the corner of the white sofa where his empty sheepskin awaited. I reached for some treats in my pocket as I unzipped my blue jacket, not knowing if I was hot from walking or from my rising stress level as we got closer to home. With just metres left before reaching the gate I knew before he physically stopped, he would not come back inside with me. I watched his legs slowing down, as he reflected on what to do. He put his nose in the air, to filter, to decide if there was scent, he had not yet found the source of.

His body was relaxed, and he seemed at ease with his decision. I knew I had to respect it, but I was worried: we could still be hitting the coldest weather of the winter in the weeks coming up and his short fur and lean body were not designed to be outside during the coldest nights. He was also no longer a young dog.

I called the other dogs and kept walking. I did not look back hoping that my lack of interest would trigger him to follow me. I knew better but my internal dialogue was not, in that moment, linked to past experiences, it was high wired to my everlasting hope for happy endings.

My attempt to show no interest did nothing and as I walked through the top gate, I could not see Shakespeare as I glanced back.

Inside Are had lit both the wood burners and the open fire. We had insulated this beloved old building as if it were placed at the polar circle, and as I stepped over the threshold it felt like a warm blanket. There was the smell of freshly baked buns, and I knew Are had been in the freezer to get me my favourite. Norwegian fluffy large yeast buns with coarse sugar and cinnamon.
Is he not with you? He poured me fresh coffee and pointed towards a set breakfast table.
Aaaa thank you so much. No, he decided to stay outside. I heard my own disappointment. *I'll go back out again after breakfast.*
I looked at the table set with the blue and white porcelain plates of my childhood.

The warmth of the house, the wooden floor, a flash back to the summer I was nine, having breakfast on the steps of the summer cabin by the sea with seagulls circling above waiting for me to share my cinnamon bun - I was tearing up, swallowing hard to keep the tears away. Shakespeare had been home six-hundred-and-ten days and suddenly I felt deflated.
I could not keep drugging him to get him inside.
Do you have a backup plan if he decides to stay outside permanently? Remember we once spoke about building him a shelter outside?
On the table were the warm buns in a pleated basket, sharing space with dark bread – a jar of my homemade raspberry jam, tasting tangy and sweet at the same time, and of course local

butter in the vintage butter dish. There was a sense of calm and peace in our familiar kitchen, as always.
Yes, I remember I said as I reached for a bun. *The problem is he would never use anything we build for him. He would think it was a trap and it would drive him away.* We remembered times when his fear response had determined his moves and he had not dared to cross the land.
It would be the same with any shelter. I must keep faith in the fact that he will, one day come inside of his own accord. We must! I wiped a tear rolling down my cheek.
Hercule who had picked up in the change in my energy came over to show support and comfort by putting his head on my thigh.

Are helped me split the pack for my next walk as leaving without some help was always slightly chaotic. Noone wanted to be left behind and my placid pack went from just that - to overly elated and ebullient. Hastings, who once easily would have run for hours hunting rabbits or grouse was now almost thirteen years old and going blind. He still loved his walks as the runs without lead gave him a sense of liberty even with failing eyesight. Isabel was in her black and red K9 harness, and I had a lead round my waist with Isabel pulling me towards the gate.

Shakespeare was there, waiting only a couple of meters away from the gate, barking in joy and wiggling his bum. He greeted Hastings and even took time to greet Isabel on the end of her lead, whilst bucking and expressing such joy. There was absolutely nothing in Shakespeare's behaviour in that moment to give away how broken he was, and I recognised that.

My looks had never given away the incredibly bad shape I had been in for years.
PTSD robs you of the inside you once knew, but often leaves the outside looking unchanged, making people think all is well. A curse and a blessing in one!

We walked and returned with Shakespeare leaving us around fifty metres away from the gate. By sunset I had walked around thirty-five kilometres, changing the pack several times. The sun had gone down after a spectacular sunset, and it was dark by the time I returned from the last walk of the day. The temperature had dropped, and the wind had picked up but thankfully it was a starlit night.

I knew Shakespeare's belly was full as I had handed him dry biscuits throughout the day. I knew he was exhausted. Dogs cover at least double the distance of a human whilst off lead, but I suspected Shakespeare had done far more meaning he might have covered as much as hundred kilometres. He would find a warm place to nestle up, in the wide hedge surrounding our top land and he would go to sleep, resting for tomorrow's walk.

Night, night Shakespeare. Until tomorrow. Please find somewhere warm to settle for the night.

I could not see his face in the dark, but his posture seemed unsure as he watched Elena, Lady, Hercule and I walk the last metres home. The other dogs were too tired to put any effort into bringing him back inside with us. I was exhausted too and knew I had walked as far as I could to get him to bond and come back inside with us.

As we walked into the entrance hall to the awaiting dogs and Mademoiselle Milesi laying draped on the mantle above the warm log burner, I caught Lady's eyes. She looked utterly sad. I sat down a cuddled her, held her and whispered, *one of these days my darling he will surprise us all.*

> **If you can look into the seeds of time** and say which grain will grow and which will not, speak then to me.
> - William Shakespeare, *Macbeth*

I woke with Miss Marple caressing my cheek. *Good morning beautiful.*
She purred in response. I stretched and could feel how my body was stiff form yesterday's long walks. *What time is it?* Miss Marple purred again. Through the window bright sunlight was dancing on the floor. The house was quiet. No barks, no paws crossing the floor - no Hercule pining to get to where I was. Intuitively I knew it was not early; I had slept far later than I had done in years.

My polka dot coffee bowl was on my nightstand and cold to the touch. Are had left it there before he went to work and that must have been hours earlier. Wrapped in my dressing gown I went downstairs to exchange cold coffee for hot. The dogs were scattered round but no one paid much attention to my presence apart from some drumming tails on the wooden floor. They were like me, exhausted from the day before and interested in nothing but resting up.

I could tell Are had fed them before he had left. Their bowls were in the large oyster basket on the kitchen island. *How I love that man*, I thought as the kettle whistled.
It felt so exclusive not to have to think about anyone but myself as I sat down by the table sipping coffee, with a dry cinnamon bun from the day before. I reflected on yesterday whilst trying to plan for today. There really was no other solution but to get dressed and start all over.

I could drug Shakespeare and force him inside but for what? There was no point and even on days when I truly questioned myself, I was sure that Shakespeare would one day walk back in. Walk through the gates. It was twenty-four months since I had met him in Cyprus, and he was no longer leaning alone against a concrete wall. His PTSD was less active, he was more relaxed and some of the bone-deep fear he had when he first arrived had subsided. Sleeping freely outside for as long as he had had changed him. If he needed to stay out longer, so be it. If we were to hit extremely cold nights, I would reconsider what to do but, on that day, the decision was simple. We would continue walking.

The changes in Shakespeare were huge but that would be hard for others to fully understand, as he still, at that point, would have been considered a difficult rescue case. I knew how he had fought to get to where he was. The last hurdle - to walk through the gate and come inside to live of his own free will, would happen. Until it did I could do little else but to make sure Shakespeare understood he was a part of us, that he belonged as part of our pack.

I got dressed, put on my walking shoes causing no excitement as I walked through the kitchen and upstairs to my office. From here I could see the land outside the gate. I needed to respond to emails and some messages before I left for another day of walking.

I love the view from the window in the bedroom that serves as my office. It was from that room dogs I helped found new homes. On the old desk that my grandfather had built was my computer. Drawers were filled with new beginnings for dogs and their families. Standing in front of the window I tried to sum up what needed doing before I could walk. My head was not really working.

It was hard to change focus from Shakespeare to adoption of other dogs. I stood still, glancing, my eyes following the path from the courtyard, through the first gate that was closed to the second gate that I had left open for Shakespeare the night before - just in case. I did not ever want him to pass or arrive at the gate and it being shut, with him on the outside.

The gate was left open to let him know he was loved, and we wanted him home. Just as I turned my body to go and sit by the desk, I caught a movement in my peripheral vision. I turned my head back, and there - in the opening of the top gate stood Shakespeare.

The sun was behind him; making him look taller and greater than his physical size. I had experienced this once before; like he was looking up at the window, knowing I was there. I swallowed a growing lump in my throat. My heart started racing and then – then suddenly - I knew! I opened the window and called his name.

Shakespeare. I am here.

My feet were following my racing brain.

It is today!

Hercule had opened the kitchen door as he so often did and Lady, Hercule, Captain Hastings, Elena, Miss Grey, Inspector Japp, Isabel and Miss Marple were all in the courtyard. Hastings was sniffing round the small well-house; Elena was laying on her large cappuccino coloured cushion in the open summer room with Miss Grey flat out on the old iron bed.

I called Shakespeare's name again as I walked as fast as possible without running. I did not want to scare him and

excite the other dogs. All turned their attention to me within a second. Elena jumped off her cushion as did Miss Grey.
I was joined by seven dogs heading for the gate and there strolling through the orchard – after having walked through the first gate - was Shakespeare. He looked utterly relaxed, promenading as if he had all the time in the world. My senses were playing tricks on me as I felt he was glowing. Relaxed, with the body language of a dog that had nothing to worry about, he touched noses with each dog through the opening between the planks of the bottom gate. Lady's tail was whipping, Elena was spinning in excitement, whilst trying to catch my eye.
He is here mum. Look! He is here.

Hastings had a small bark and if Hastings could bark so could Miss Grey. Japp was also dancing round, whilst Isabel was trying to figure out what the happiness was all about.
I turned the wooden knob on the lock and slowly opened the gate. Shakespeare looked straight at me. His expression had lost something – the intense fear I was all too familiar with was gone. His eyes interlocked with mine.
I am ready to come home!
I know I said. *I know.*
The other dogs simply stepped to each side, dividing, to make it possible for him to walk into the courtyard without anyone in his way. His head was high, his body relaxed, showing the muscles of his torso as he moved elegantly through the gate. He did not stop but simply continued walking, in through the open kitchen door, where he jumped on the big dog's bed, lying down as if he had been there always.
Lady looked at me.
I told you darling. He just needed time.

The moment was simply so big my body felt too small to hold it.
The other dogs took a couple of minutes to settle, but because Shakespeare was so at ease they soon went into their different beds - apart from Lady who jumped on the bed next to Shakespeare.

I sat myself down by the table, trying to breathe calmly. I had waited for that exact moment for over twenty months and when it finally happened it was like it was meant to happen on that exact day. Why that day? I have no idea, but it was a perfect day!
The pack slept and Shakespeare was stretched out with Lady's head resting on his back, the way they had slept in the crate when Shakespeare first arrived. I did not move - watching, absorbing, breathing. I was taking on board what I had just experienced - that Shakespeare had decided that he belonged. That his life was with us, inside our home. That he would embrace what we offered and be a part of us. No one had coached him, no one had enticed him or convinced him. He had decided by himself.

My life changed the day I met Shakespeare in his box in Cyprus, and it had changed many times during our journey. The biggest change was the day he came home for good. Later, before I went to our bedroom to rest, to meditate, I stroked Shakespeare.
I am so grateful to you. For everything.
He looked back at me as if he could see my soul.
I went on to stroke Lady and whispered, *today was the day, darling.*

> **The worst is Death**, and Death
> will have his day.
> -William Shakespeare, *King Richard II*

The weeks after Shakespeare came back inside, we walked every day. Shakespeare now knew the difference between soft shoes and shoes that made a sound. He knew what a lead in my hand meant and he knew that we would still stop at the exact same spots to have treats. He would be the first out the gate and the first back through the gate upon our return. I loved the new calm in our existence amongst the vines.

The peace and slow living was however to be abruptly broken. On the 24th of February 2022 - Russia had invaded Ukraine. I had always thought I would be the first generation that would spend my lifetime in a peaceful Europe. I was wrong.

Everything happened so quickly. A Russian woman living in Paris, who had adopted a dog from me, contacted me and asked if I could help some friends of hers that wanted to help dogs after they had arrived in Poland, from Ukraine. *Yes. Of course*, and by that, I was thrown into rescue work I had never imagined. Together with four other people I had never met, I became part of a team rescuing dogs displaced by war. In the strangest twist of fate, the image that I had seen whilst in the hallway with Shakespeare that day under the billiard table, had in some inexplicable way prepared me for what I was to witness. Dead dogs, butchered, suffering beyond what I have words to describe. Dogs eating each other in attempts to survive as bombs pulverized villages and towns that were left deserted but for abandoned animals.

Dogs crazy with fear of the bombs raining from the sky, were hiding, trying to seek shelter where shelter no longer existed.

In every dog I saw my own. I lived on adrenaline whilst the dogs came out. My extensive local and international network helped with everything I asked for. We were fighting, in our own small way, the Russian war machine. The Polish press wrote about our rescue efforts and somehow the name of my association was released. I had messages and calls from people in Ukraine, who in desperation called me as they called everyone they could find through social media. There was nothing I could do but to be a fellow human.

One girl I spoke to had three dogs and all she dreamt of was to get them to safety in Poland. She never mentioned herself. I spoke to her several times, during two intense weeks at the same time as the news told me her town was about to fall into Russian hands. Then it all went silent, and I never heard from her again. She has never, not to this day, ever picked up any of the many messages I have left for her.

I took twenty-four dogs from the warzone to France, working round the clock to get money to send dog food back in. I was back to balancing on a knife edge. My PTSD was knocking me off my feet and I knew I was rapidly moving towards making myself ill again. I was not sleeping, my nightmares about flying were back and now the images were accompanied by bombs.

The dogs I took out of Ukraine were traumatised. Many of them suffered from PTSD and sat in their crates staring at the wall. They had been in a shelter in the region first hit and had seen other dogs in the same shelter killed as the bombs hit. The owner of the shelter had fled with as many dogs as she could, through the freezing night. In the videos from the escape the dogs are crated in the back of an old van, with many dogs in each crate. All the dogs were silently staring into the night. It is a miracle anyone got out of there alive.

To let the dogs decompress, I kept them in a kennel in a small wood, fifty kilometres from home. Every day I drove there and back, some days twice a day. Every day Shakespeare and the other dogs would be crying behind the kitchen door as they saw me closing the gate. It was heart-breaking as every day I felt I was abandoning my own.

As weeks turned into months I was trying to hang on by the tips of my fingers until all the traumatized dogs I had taken to France were adopted. When they were all homed with wonderful families, I pulled back from rescue-work to stay home with my own, to regain my balance, knowing better than most that my pack was my remedy.

Research shows that living with a dog lowers blood pressure, slows heart rate and breathing, and relaxes muscle tension.

Living with a dog reduces cortisol which is a hormone linked to memory of trauma. Having a dog also lowers the constant adrenaline production in PTSD patients. Studies show that having a dog raises levels of oxytocin also known as the "love hormone." It takes ten minutes of stroking a dog before there is a measurable effect.

I had the world's best "medication" for my PTSD at the tip of those same fingertips that had enabled me to hang onto that shelf, on that cliff with the deep drop. I wanted to be with Hastings who was getting old, with Lady and Isabel close behind age wise. They deserved to have time with me after all the support they had given me over the years. I wanted to be with Shakespeare and the pack was my balance. To walk and to write my book about Shakespeare and our journey. I had a need to quiet my mind and to stop flying. To watch sunrise and sunset with my boy who now was bouncing in joy and was the first dog back to the gates after every walk!

I made a break by writing a post on my rescue page that I was slowing down. I did not tell anyone how bad I was, not even Are. By September 2022 life had yet again found its own rhythm and the nightmares had slowly subsided but I was not fully recovered. We had a scorching hot summer behind us, with before-dawn and clear-night walks. Now I touched Shakespeare for small strokes when we were outside the gate. We cocooned ourselves in our own universe between the vines, and I wanted it to last forever.

Then, one night I heard Lady breathing strangely. Lady had a collapsed trachea, and her breathing could often sound like that of a child with false croup and I had long experience in treating her irregular breathing fits, but this was different.

I was sure it was her heart and by one o'clock in the morning, as she laid on our bed heaving for air and coughing, I asked Are to call the emergency vet and let him know we would bring her. As she slowly walked behind me down the stairs from our bedroom, the pack became uneasy. They were all sniffing her, letting me know for sure that something was wrong. If you live with a pack and you are ever in doubt if one of the dogs are ill, just watch the others. They will tell you.

I had never met this vet before. I knew it was my vet's birthday so he was not on call, or I would of course have called him. He knew the dogs and he knew me.

This vet was an elderly gentleman with kind eyes, and he gave Lady a thorough examination with ultrasound of her heart. He turned to us and told us there was a faint heart murmur but nothing to worry about and that the irregular breathing was due to her trachea.

Both Are and I were so relieved as we drove home on the quiet roads, but I had a niggling feeling in the back of my chest, behind my heart and as the days progressed, I kept saying to Are *I don't know why but I am sure it is her heart* and a week later when I took her to my regular vet to ease my mind, he told me I *am so sorry to have to tell you, but it most certainly is her heart. She can go into cardiac arrest in fifteen minutes, or she can live some weeks more, but this is sadly the beginning of the end.* I felt like being sick. The morning had suddenly lost all colour. The vet gave me medication to ease her breathing but there was nothing more he could do.

Lady was dying!

> **My bounty is as boundless as the sea, My love as deep**; the more I give to thee, The more I have, for both are infinite.
> - William Shakespeare, *Romeo and Juliet*

With the vet surgery behind us, heading home, I pulled over to the side and sobbed. I held Lady and fell apart. I put my nose in her fur, remembering the first day I ever saw her in her cardboard box in the refuge. The box was shaking so much that it moved across the floor as she was tried to make her world as small as possible. The first time I visited her at the shelter, she had dragged her belly along the ground next to me as she did not dare to stand up in fear that I would beat her back down. This girl that squinted with her eyes when she was happy had chosen us to love her after she had bolted a couple of weeks after I brought her home. I walked searching for her day and night - I later came to realise she had stayed in a nest she had made in the hedges, watching us come and go. On the fifth day whilst we were out searching, she dug herself back onto the property making a large hole in the ground under the top gate - laying herself down to sunbathe outside the kitchen door. My girl with the statuesque paws and the beautiful eyes. My girl who would have given her life in an instant to defend me against anyone or anything, my girl who had been Shakespeare's saviour – was dying!

As I walked over the courtyard Are appeared in the kitchen door. He took one look at me and started to cry. *She is dying* I said with a broken voice. We held each other. The dogs were all quiet, and after Lady had jumped on the big kitchen bed with surprising lightness and elegance, I went to cancel every appointment I had in my diary. I was going nowhere.

The first week Lady slept with us during the night, but I could hear how the other dogs were tossing and crossing the floor. I could hear how Shakespeare would not settle. I could feel his energy bouncing off the walls. Isabel, who was also very close to Lady could not settle either.

I had moved Lady up with us, but she belonged with the other dogs, and it was selfish of me to keep her with us in the bedroom.

I moved her back onto the big bed in the kitchen where Shakespeare and often Isabel would curl around her to keep her warm. I gave Lady a new coat, soft and feather light. She started losing weight and she did not want to eat. I knew that the only one who could get her to eat, if anyone could, was not me but Shakespeare. With that in mind I started taking Lady and Shakespeare out together, just the three of us. I would stroll on the dusty tractor track with Lady walking ever so slowly, sniffing the grass before she would turn her head, look at me to tell me she wanted to turn around. Shakespeare would not take his eyes off her nor leave her for a second. When we were back on the open large field outside our gate, I would sprinkle dry biscuits and dried duck treats on the grass and Lady and Shakespeare would graze together. It was the only time Lady would eat effortlessly.

Our quiet days were the same as our first days with Shakespeare. It was now Lady we circled around. We were breathing as one collective body, holding on to our grief. Miss Grey took herself off to the orchard, away from the pack. She was grief stricken and did not respond to my strokes or soft voice of comfort. She needed time, so I let her be.

Isabel would sniff Lady constantly, keeping track of her decline. Many times, a day Isabel would look at me as if to say *Mum please make her stay*. Hercule reacted as he always did when he was sad or scared - by gluing himself to me, crying if I left the room. Captain Hasting was stoic whilst Inspector Japp was hiding under the stairs.

We were all trying to find our way.

As hours and days passed, I was increasingly concerned for Shakespeare. I picked up signs that his PTSD was flaring, and he was not sleeping. I could hear him, restless, anxious, as he was waking over Lady every night. He was making sure Lady felt safe and by that he was destabilising himself. It was beyond heart-breaking. I got up early every morning and I never left the house. I stayed amidst the pack trying to be the glue that would hold us together.

No one moved. No one asked to be walked.

I made breakfast for them all every day. Lady was served on the bed, but she was not interested.

After, I would lift Lady from her large bed to a dark blue dog bed next to me, by the kitchen table.

I had folded a quilt in four, making a soft bottom in the bed and put it inside the cover in grey and white stripes. On top of the quilt was a sheepskin and then two chenille blankets. Lady looked like she was floating on a cloud of soft. I sat writing by the kitchen table and Lady would sleep through the day, just waking to glance up at me to make sure I was there before she dropped back to sleep. Each dog had their own bed close to Lady and everyone would stay calm but present. I found it hard to concentrate often moving onto the floor next to them all, stroking Lady and whispering to her.

Two weeks after she first became ill, as I lifted her, I had the vivid image of one of the many chicks fallen out of a nest that I had tried to save as a child, a skeleton of a chick covered in almost see-through plume. I had picked it up and carried it home and made a nest for it out of cotton wool. It died within hours, and I buried him in a shoe box in the garden. Later I made a cross of twigs to mark his grave and bribed my brother with sweets to sing with me to mark his passing.

As the sun came out, I lifted Lady into the garden so she could sunbathe. She loved the sun and I made sure she soaked up each beam. Some days I sat holding her and other days I would place her in a bed on the large white bench outside, covered in blankets. She made her purr-like sound to signal she was comfortable and that she was grateful for being outside. I kept an intensely close eye on her in every way as I wanted to make sure she was not suffering and there was no indication she was in pain.

Later, she lost control of her bladder and started to wet her bed. She would look at me as to say *I am so sorry*. In response I stroked her, kissed her head.
Darling, it does not matter one bit, before I changed her bedding.

I always had a double set of clean bedding ready in a basket by the bed. Lady had always been such a proud dog that I was not about to put her in diapers. It would take away her pride and any use of diapers would be to make life easier for myself whilst my focus was on her dignity. Dignity for humans and animals is equally important to me.

Dignity is often the last thing we have left. I had a washing machine that could wash twenty-four hours a day - and it also did for a while. Every day, midday, I would send Are, who was at work, a photo of her with the message, *she is still here*, followed by a red heart and three kisses. Then the day came when the message read: *it is time*!

It had been a beautiful early autumn day. I was up early as had become the rhythm of my day. I wanted to spend as many minutes with Lady as possible. Lady was weak and did not lift her head when I came down the stairs, but she followed me with her eyes, faintly wagging her tail under her blanket as I spoke to her. I knew that would be the day and fought to hold back my tears, surprised I had any left by that stage. Shakespeare was on the big bed with her, looking at me with that same silent plea for me to help him as he had done in the rain that day. There was nothing I could do. Lady had lived for weeks, against all odds, with the heart condition she had. Neither she nor we, wanted her to leave. We kept loving life back into her, but her body was so exhausted that for the first time, she did not attempt to stand up.

I stroked Shakespeare and kissed him, before I wrapped Lady's blanket around her. I could feel her ribs through the coat and blanket as I carried her out for her to see her last sunrise. Sitting on the large white bench, made up of two old metal beds, with all the dogs around me, I could feel her shallow breathing. It was breathing without sound. I had an overwhelming urge to close her mouth with my hand, put my mouth over her nose and breathe oxygen into her lungs. I knew that no action I took would help her.

Breathing oxygen into her system would not do anything for her. She was letting go of life. I might be able to keep her for some minutes more, but I could also stress her in my aim to fulfil my own need to keep her alive. I put my nose into her fur, smelling her as I had done so many times before. Inhaling that smell only she had, that had comforted me so many times over the years when I had not been well. This girl that I had fallen so intensely in love with, who had got me back on my feet after my second spinal surgery: she was about to leave. We were all silently watching the sunrise with Captain Hastings lying undemanding by my feet, as close as he could come, the others in the familiar half circle around. We watched the sky change from pink to orange with a shimmer of lilac as the sun rose over the garden wall for Lady one last time.

I held her close and as the sun was up and the first rays of sunlight gave some warmth, she turned her head and licked my cheek. Licking the stream of tears.
You will be ok. The others will look after you she whispered.

I held her all morning, through the mid-day hours and in the afternoon the vet came. Are was home and we all gathered in the kitchen. The dogs that normally would be excited about a visitor showed no interest at all. The energy in the room had one focus. Lady. To help Lady whilst she was passing. We were all quiet, all focused.

I climbed back onto the large bed and sat myself in the corner before I lifted Lady onto my lap. The kitchen was filled with candles. Just to the left of me there was a small, white table with a large bouquet of deep red dahlias in a large blue and white vase.

I stared at the flowers trying to focus on hanging on for what was about to happen. The light had gone from bright to dull.

Everything felt unreal and fragile. I had wrapped Lady in her favourite soft blanket. My girl was feather-light as if she were preparing to soar weightlessly. She looked up at me before her eyes glided shut. She was too weak to keep her eyes open. I looked at the vet and gave him a small almost unnoticeable nudge of my head. As always Dr Gillot was calm and focused, and with steady hands, the injection was set. Within seconds she was gone. Her body went from relaxed to limp. Her heart had stopped. We had lost something so precious. We had lost our Lady Eileen Bundle Brent.

The vet got up, gathered his belongings whilst I was trying to hold on to her as if that would make her come back. As Dr Gilot was about to leave her turned to me; *I am so sorry*. I nodded; *me too*. As Are followed him out through the small door in the garden wall I sobbed, sobbed as if my heart had been shattered. The dogs started howling as they do when they try to gather the pack, trying to bring her back. But she was gone.

I lifted her with me. Her bed was prepared with incontinence mats in the bottom on top of a blanket as the body can let go of bodily fluids not long after death.
I put one of the smaller mats between her tail and her bottom for extra protection and then I covered her with her blanket before I stepped back to let each one say their goodbye. Silently, without any sudden movements I witnessed something I had never seen before, as each dog went to the bed and spent a couple of minutes with her body, before leaving to

make room for the next. None of the dogs sniffed her. There was no need - they had been there when her soul ascended. Left was just the shell of her body. They were all simply spending some last minutes with her, sitting by her bed as guards of honour. Blind Miss Grey went up, sat herself by the bed and had a second, before I watched the air leaving her. She was deflating in front of our eyes. This stocky tank of a dog suddenly looked so small and extremely vulnerable. The grief was tangible. I could touch it.

Shakespeare was not in the kitchen. He was hiding under the sideboard, but when I called him, he came. We lifted Lady's bed and body into the courtyard and let them be. Shakespeare stood by her bed with a sloped body and a drooping head. He looked so broken. Yet again the girl he had loved so, had left. First Agatha and now Lady. I was holding on to Are as we stood inside the kitchen door watching the body of our girl, laying peacefully in her bed, whilst Shakespeare was absorbing that she was gone. Slowly he walked away and went onto the large cushions where he and Lady had sunbathed together so often. He looked powerful and regal as he watched over her body. His energy, though, was fragile. A gush of wind would disintegrate him.

Two hours later, Are drove Lady to the vet office for cremation.

In the weeks that followed, we wobbled. We tried to support each other, to show love, patience and understanding. We slid and stumbled, and our house of cards was several times blown over by surges of grief. We showed kindness and generosity towards each other.

We regrouped many times and at a snail's pace, we found our footing, unstable, but heading towards balance. We walked several times a day, missing Lady on every walk – but she was there with us all, forever, flying across the farmers field, and when we picked up her ashes, we decided we would scatter her on that very field when the time was right.

One morning, some weeks after, I watched Shakespeare and the others run across that field where Lady and Shakespeare so often lingered to dig for field mice. I had not seen Shakespeare dig since Lady had left but, on that morning, he came across what must have been a nest beneath his feet. I stood watching, his body giving away the joy of the hunt. With a second's interruption, he lifted his head to look at Lady, to share the joy, like they had always done. Helplessly I watched his physical recoil as he realised, she was not there, that she would never come back.

That day Shakespeare did not come back inside with us. He left us and walked off looking like an old dog with a broken heart. I went calling for him several times, but I could not see him anywhere. The next morning, I went out early and when I called him, I saw him coming out of the hedge, from Lady's old nest. I gave him breakfast from my hand.

I know Shakespeare. I know exactly how sad you are, but she told us we would be ok. I lifted my hand and stroked him carefully over his head, and he let me. Later, we walked. Not with his exuberant joy but like a pack in mourning. We stopped at our fixed spot to have treats, in the opening of the woods, where we had seen the blood-moon, he, Lady, and me. Slowly Shakespeare turned his head and looked up at me. His eye was dull, sparkless.

I need to do this. I will be back, but first I need to do this.

I know I said. *I know.*

Before he walked on, he let me stroke him again, over his head, like my touch made sure we stayed reconnected and did not float adrift in our time of loss and grief. As we returned home, he returned to Lady's soul and her nest.

Shakespeare stayed out for two nights. Then, he simply walked back in, through both gates that I had left open for him, his eyes less glazed, with a calmer energy.

And then, as to give us all hopes for the future, Shakespeare showed me something that will make me forever think anything possible.

It was a grey drizzly afternoon, cold, with soaking grass that had been reawakened after a couple of weeks of rain.

It was a day similar to the day Shakespeare had stood in the ice-cold rain in front of me on the road, except that the rain had stopped, and he was walking almost next to me. We had walked our first walk; him, Elena and Hercule and I. The light was starting to dim as Shakespeare and I left for our second walk with Captain Hastings, Inspector Japp, Miss Grey and Isabel. We were heading for the shortest walk through the woods.
Those woods that had been the backdrop of Are's and my wedding photo, where I had learned the different odours of my French homeland, where the deer and her fawn seek shelter, where the wild boar and the fox slept. The woods where I had walked, loved, and laughed with all my dogs and my cats when they used to come with me before they got too old.

Under my feet were rotting leaves in ochre, yellow, matt aubergine, cigar brown, brick red, black and the odd poplar green. Soon, they would all have turned to soil. My nostrils were filled with the smell of mushroom spores with a hint of wild marigold hanging as a delayed summer memory. Above me were branches stretching leafless towards the grey sky disclosing how many trees were entangled here.

I pulled my jacket a bit closer zipping the collar all the way up, watching Shakespeare. His body had changed shape in the nine-hundred-and-fourteen days he had been home. He was muscular, strong. His short fur looked dark, rich dessert chocolate brown in the wood light. He was shimmering, cantering at a steady pace on light paws. He lifted his head, filtering the air, vibrating his nose. Turning his head to the left, he, in slow motion, got onto his hind legs, filtering the air above him more rapidly. He stretched, trying to reach towards the treetops. I stood mesmerised. I live with hunting dogs, dogs that have been trained to hunt before they came to me, but I had never seen anything like it. Shakespeare was detecting something none of the other dogs did. He landed himself in a controlled manner down on all four paws again before he shot through the brambles of bare wild roses, raspberries, and blackberries. I stood still and waited. If Shakespeare had found something we would all soon know as he would start marking, by barking. Sure, enough within a minute to two, deep barks echoed through the woods.

Even his barks were different now.

The first time I had heard Shakespeare bark he sounded like a tiny female dog with a thin high-pitched voice.

Now, out of the woods echoed deep, bass barks from a dog in control. I hurried towards the track to where it split and headed towards the barks.

With Shakespeare's colouring it was only possible to spot him because of the sound he was making. He was on his hind legs up against a dark grey tree trunk.
I lifted my eyes, leaning my head backwards and there, in top of the tree was a beautiful iridescent large blue and green bird, with a white collar and long barred tail feathers: a pheasant.

Shakespeare had detected this bird up in the tree from some distance. This dog that had arrived home to France without the ability to use his nose, this dog who I had followed through every stage of his evolution, from no smell to some, chasing hares and rabbits.
I had watched all the changes up close - to be crowned with him detecting a pheasant in the top of a tree some twenty-five meters away. I started to laugh in pure joy, wanting to do a happy dance in the woods in the company of five of my dogs. It was hard to grasp what I had just witnessed and as Shakespeare continued to bark the other dogs gathered to check what all the commotion was about.

Shakespeare was trying to find some way of climbing the tree, Hastings joined in the barking. As I stood watching them, I could hear Lady joining in from beyond.

Shakespeare looked around, assessed the terrain, and ran off, crossing the small ditch where the tree was standing. I could see what he was thinking.

There was another tree leaning towards the tree with the pheasant and Shakespeare wanted to check if he could climb the other tree to reach the pheasant.
That clever boy.

Standing there, joyful, in the cold woods filled with the smell of rain and autumn, in the grey light the moment felt Milky Way vast. Our journey that had started in a cold grey box, in a sanctuary on a plateau in Cyprus had taken us on challenges none could foresee.
Covid closed airports worldwide, panic attacks, trembling and convulsions. We had faced fears that were embedded in us both by the trauma we had experienced. We had been on a journey to rewire our brains. By having survived we had become survivors with a strength only the reflection of ourselves understood.

One of the many jewels in my crown is to move and explore with my pack and Shakespeare, watching him grow every day, bearing witness to his journey as he has slowly rewired his brain with the aim of a full life.

We will continue to walk in this universe of ours that all of us know so well. Here, where wild orchids and calandria grows, where seasons quietly roll into each other. Here the horizon is never ending, and we can all breathe and where the moon tricks the vines into throwing non-existent shadows. Here, where we love and support each other and where Lady still runs in the fields.

Here - Shakespeare is finally, truly home!

> If thou were the lion, **the fox** would beguile thee.
> -William Shakespeare, *Timon of Athens*

Epilogue

During the days and months Shakespeare lived outside I often wondered – did he ever befriend the wild life? I have always thought the answer was yes. Shakespeare's gentle nature would present him as a non-threat to other animals albeit he is more than capable of defending himself should he need to. His body had become muscular and strong, he is intelligent and a faster runner, so I was never concerned for his safety in regard to wildlife, even with the wild boars that transcend the track around our home. It was more a curiosity: does he know and interact with any of the wild animals around?

Then, in January the year after he came inside, I was to find the answer to my question. We were on our second walk of the day in a frosted matt white landscape. Shakespeare was as always trotting in front of me but as now was his habit he turned his head to check in with me – to make sure I was walking in his direction. I had Isabel on a lead clipped around my waist and Hercule off lead next to me when I spotted a dog even further up the road, way in front of Shakespeare. The dog was an unusual red and silver coloured with white socks and as Shakespeare walked toward it, the other dog went from standing to lying calmly down to wait for Shakespeare to approach. I was thinking the off-lead-dog must belong to someone cutting back the vines to prepare for spring shoots, but as my eyes glanced through endless rows of vines, I saw no one nor were there any cars around. As so often it seemed to be just me and my dogs - and now this other dog unfamiliar to me. Shakespeare was slowly swirling his short tail telling me he was at least familiar with the laying dog.

As Shakespeare got closer to his friend, I was looking at the trail Shakespeare left on the white ground where a millimetre layer of feather light snow had fallen.

My eyes wandered to the woods behind the unknown dog, the picture-perfect landscape with ice blue skies and then - back to Shakespeare and the other dog as he slowly, stretching, got on all four paws. Shakespeare was less that a metre away when it became evident - it was not a dog. It was a fox!

The fox had silver rims on the contour of his ears, and a white marking on the head matching the white chest, greeted Shakespeare with another play bow not unlike the ones my dogs do. Shakespeare responded with moving his body sideways leaving him parallel to the fox instead of in front of him. Their noses met several times as in a familiar sniff. Shakespeare picked up his tail rotation sending his whole bum into a wag. The fox bounced off its feet to initiate play yet again.

I was mesmerized - how extraordinary!

I was witnessing a wild fox meeting up with Shakespeare who with all his body language showed true happiness in discovering his friend. Foxes will normally not venture into open landscape from dawn to dusk but keep themselves close to the tree line or vegetation that gives them a quick escape route, but this fox had left his safe area to touch noses with Shakespeare in broad daylight.

Until this point none of the other dogs had discovered the fox as the wind was carrying his scent away from us but his bouncing invitation for Shakespeare to play, made Hercule catch sight of him. I gave Hercule a firm *Stay*! just as he was about to launch into a run. Hercule obeyed as he always did, but my voice and Hercule's sudden movement made the fox fully aware of us. He now shifted his focus from Shakespeare to me and the dogs - and for some long seconds we looked at each other with mutual curiosity – before the fox took another long sniff at Shakespeare's nose. He then turned and on light paws, with his majestic bottle-brush tail horizontal elongating his body, trotted towards the woods without any great hurry. I watched as Shakespeare stood still looking and sniffing in the air as his friend left and just before the fox entered the woods, he turned his head to exchange one long last look with Shakespeare. Shakespeare did not attempt to follow the fox but turned and came walking calmly toward us with what seemed like a sense of peace.

He is my friend. I have known him for a long time Shakespeare said whilst keeping my eyes locked with his. *I know darling* I responded. *I know*

I love you with so much of my heart that none is left to protest.
-William Shakespeare *Much Ado About Nothing*

PTSD – Post Traumatic Stress Disorder.

In the human brain there is an alarm system that is there to warn us, and by that keep us alive if we are in immediate danger - like if you were to meet a lion! Oversimplified, the fear of the lion and that it might kill you, will trigger split-second changes in your brain and body, in a combination of nerve and hormonal signals, causing reactions that are outside your conscious control. The brain's reaction will instinctively cause you to choose from the three following options: *fight, flight, or freeze.*

Your blood pressure will go up, your lungs will be filled with oxygen and your heartrate goes "through the roof." Even your digestive system will come to a halt so the body can be "all hands-on deck" to handle the acute "lion" situation. Your body will produce epinephrine also known as adrenaline. Epinephrine is produced by the adrenal glands. Epinephrine is what helps the neurons within the brain to communicate, but adrenaline also has a job outside the brain, and then adrenaline is considered a hormone.

Adrenaline enables you to run faster and give you strength beyond your normal capacity.

In any dangerous situation there are separate parts of your brain that each has their own job to do: the *amygdala* that is the brains alarm system creates a full fear response, the *prefrontal cortex*, the brain's brake system works to tell you when danger is over.

With PTSD the alarm system, the *amygdala*, does not switch off or becomes over-sensitive, and keeps signalling that your life is in ongoing danger despite the danger being over.

PTSD physically changes part of the pattern in your brain.

The part of your brain that is responsible for thinking, your *prefrontal cortex*, and for memory, *the hippocampus*, can be altered so that they no longer function as intended. It can become difficult to filter safe events from dangerous events. The malfunction of the amygdala, the prefrontal cortex and the hippocampus in combination creates a perfect storm. This storm is PTSD.

On neuroimages it is possible for the naked eye to see the distinct biological changes in a brain of a person who suffers from PTSD.

PTSD can be caused by shock or is a consequence of a traumatic event/events and does not necessarily come with any physical injury.

The symptoms of PTSD make a long list: intrusive thoughts, nightmares, avoidance behaviour, memory loss, negative thought pattern, self-isolation, anger and/or irritability, reduces interest in life, hypervigilance, concentration problems, insomnia, vivid flashbacks, difficulty regulating positive emotions and risky behaviour.

The brain of a dog is different to that of a human, but the principle of PTSD in a dog is the same as it is for humans.

So are the symptoms.

The dogs and fellow rescuers in the book.

Lupin – went home to live the most amazing, wonderful life. She loves running after her ball and no one would ever know she has no eyes. She lives in a pack of now four other dogs - her two Spanish siblings and after her arrival Amanda and Tim has adopted two other dogs from Miss Marple. All Lupin's pups are thriving in UK.

Billy – the large black dog that lived in the kennel next to Shakespeare in the shelter, was adopted not long after I met Shakespeare. His mum Maryann had lost her beloved dog and was looking to give her love to someone who truly needed it. I have been lucky enough to follow Maryann and Billy, now going under the name King Billy! Billy is showered with love every minute of his life making up for all the years no one wanted him – he also now has a black, gorgeous sister adopted from the SPDC Sanctuary. The two dogs look like they have always belonged.

The GSD – the German Shepard that had lived on a balcony was adopted by a family in England and the photos of him with the small children in the family is simply beautiful and heart swelling.

Sir Henry – Sir Henry was adopted by Odette and Gary in England. He was utterly loved but sadly his head injury made him deteriorate and not long after his first birthday he was let go. In the days after his departure both his mum and I were visited by a robin – and I will never see a robin ever again without thinking of Sir Henry.

Andy – went home to a home filled with other Springer Spaniels and C is still in touch with the home.

Baxter – had eye surgery and complex surgery on his leg whilst with Monika. It took months before he could travel. Monika is the most amazing rescue lady who loved and nursed him until he could go home to his family in England. Baxter now live with his siter Heidi, a rescue GSD breeding dog. They were both later joined by another blind Miss Marple dog, Titus.

The Cypriot rescued pups – all five pups were adopted going on to living magical lives. Two of the pups have since been rehomed, moving on to living the lives all dogs should live. The little girl that survived in the fur bucket has grown into a stunning girl.

They all look like greyhound crosses and are Cypriot sight hound mixes for sure. I have been lucky enough to have news of the pups who now are long since adults. Especially getting photos of the girl made me extremely happy. The outcome for these dying pups are heart-warming and beyond.

The Hell House dogs – all adults were rehomed but sadly one of them, Diasy, was too emotionally damaged to continue her journey. The other adults have gone on to live extraordinary lives and the one dog I was most concerned about, Luka, has gone on to surprise me the most. Misty, another of the females that had puppies' hours after the rescue has turned into a loving girl, now living with another Miss Marple rescue. Of the eight pups, six live full lives whilst two have, for two years been in kennels. These two pups were taken on by a different association and are still, sadly, in a kennel with little to no efforts to find them a home by the association they are under.

The 7-year-old female – I wished a home for as I stood as the Vitruvian man. The girl got to go home and some weeks later and Monika sent me a photo of her with her mum on the beach. I was right, she is holding on to love with all 4 paws.

SPDC – Saving Pound Dogs Cyprus, where Shakespeare came from, is a rescue association that in the years from they started in 2014 and until 2023 have saved around 2500 dogs. Incredible! The tireless work is humbling - how C manage to keep it all together with all the abuse and neglect she sees every day I will never know. I am in awe of all the women of SPDC!

Whilst writing this book Elena of SPDC lost her battle with cancer and left us all. Elena's wish for Shakespeare, to find his human, did come through. I am so very grateful that Elena did get to follow Shakespeare's journey all the way, until he walked into the kitchen, and he was home. I think of her often with a heart filled with love and gratitude, and wherever she is I am sure she visits and knows we are more than ok.

Monika-Andrea Kovacs is a one women rescuer in North Romania who, with support from her husband and children rescue under the most horrendous conditions. In her universe dogs are considered to be rodents – like rats – they are very often treated like vermin. Monika is one of the most knowledgeable dog-people I know.

She is supported by a charity in UK, Zoe's Home Animal Rescue Romania, that also help her with adoptions of dogs and this way around 1400 have found new homes. Monika has also sterilised around 1000 street dogs before they have been released back onto the streets. I have such a deep respect and love for Monika and if such a thing as rescue-Nobel-prize existed I would have nominated her in a heartbeat.

Acknowledgment

I would like to express my deep gratitude to all the people who contributed to the realization of this book.

A huge thank you to my dear friend Wendy Troe, who took on the roles of editor, proofreader and mentor with unparalleled kindness.

Wendy is also the voice in the audiobook version of this book.

Wendy, who, self-proclaimed, is not particularly a fan of dogs, recently sent me canine photos while she was on vacation. If this book can help soften the hearts of the most reluctant, then my mission is accomplished.

I warmly thank Louise Petit for her impeccable translation, which allowed this book to reach a French audience. It is an honour to share this story with the inhabitants of this country that I love so much.

I also owe a huge thank you to my stepbrother Thomas for the book cover, lay-out and all your assistance.

I am infinitely grateful to the mayor of our village, Michel Filleul, for his understanding and kindness. Thanks to him, Shakespeare was able to live in complete freedom, despite local regulations. Without this freedom, he would never have been able to flourish as he did and does.

Thank you to everyone who supported me in this adventure, and especially to my husband Are, who loves us all unconditionally in our atypical home.

I also carry a deep gratitude towards my pack - and towards Shakespeare.

This book is for all the families who open their hearts and homes to dogs in need.

Together, we can - and do make a difference.

Thank you!

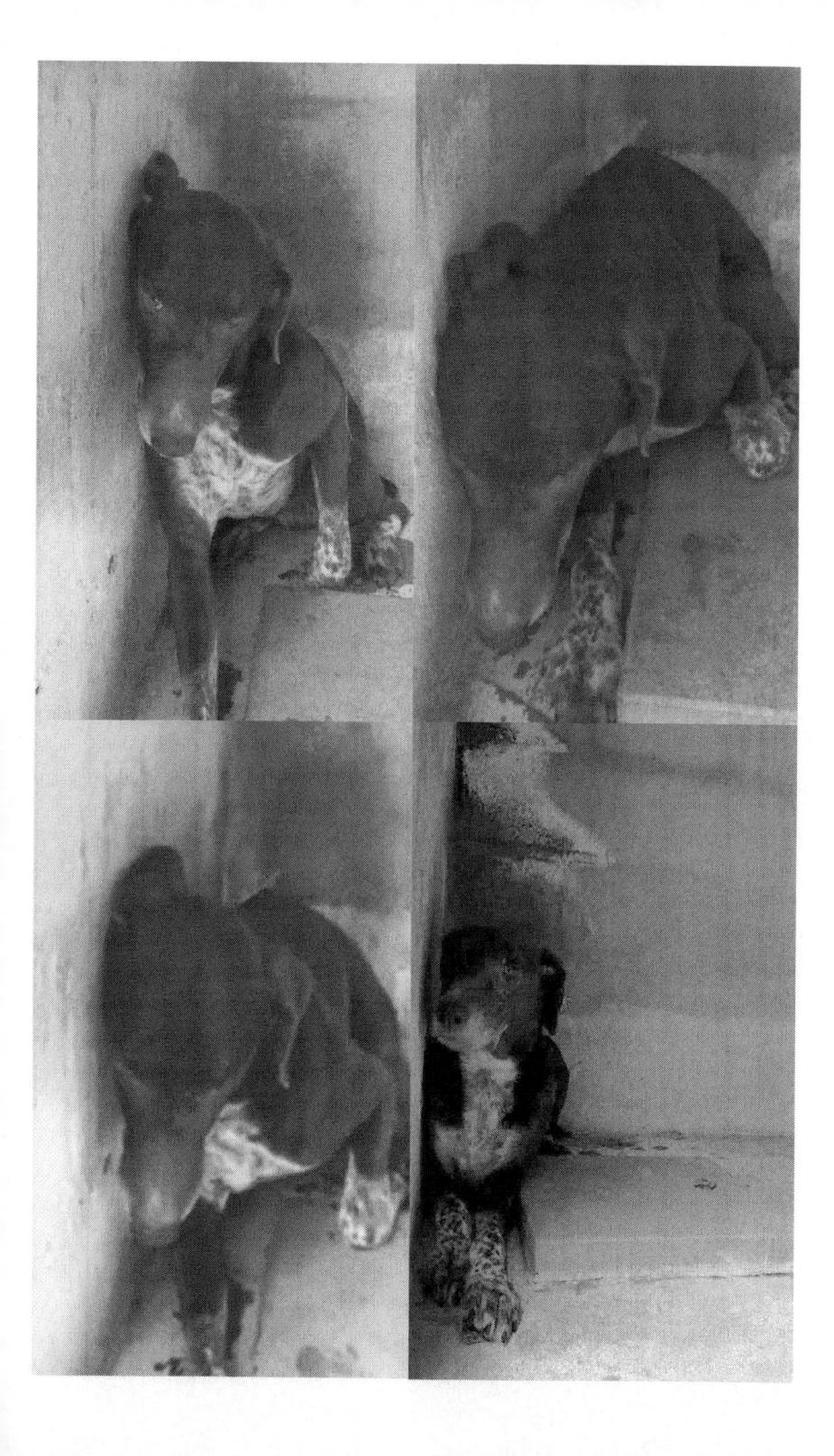

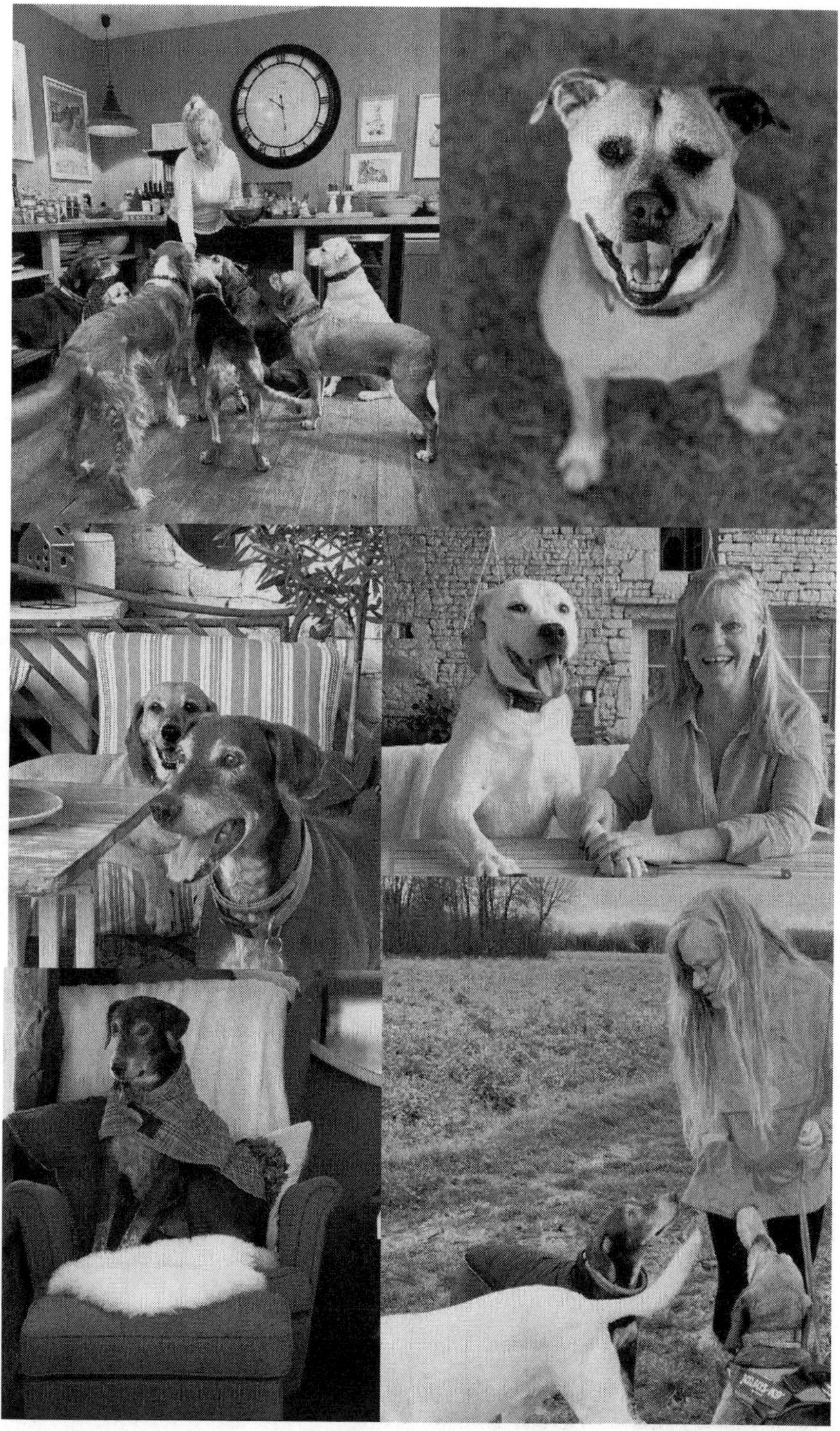

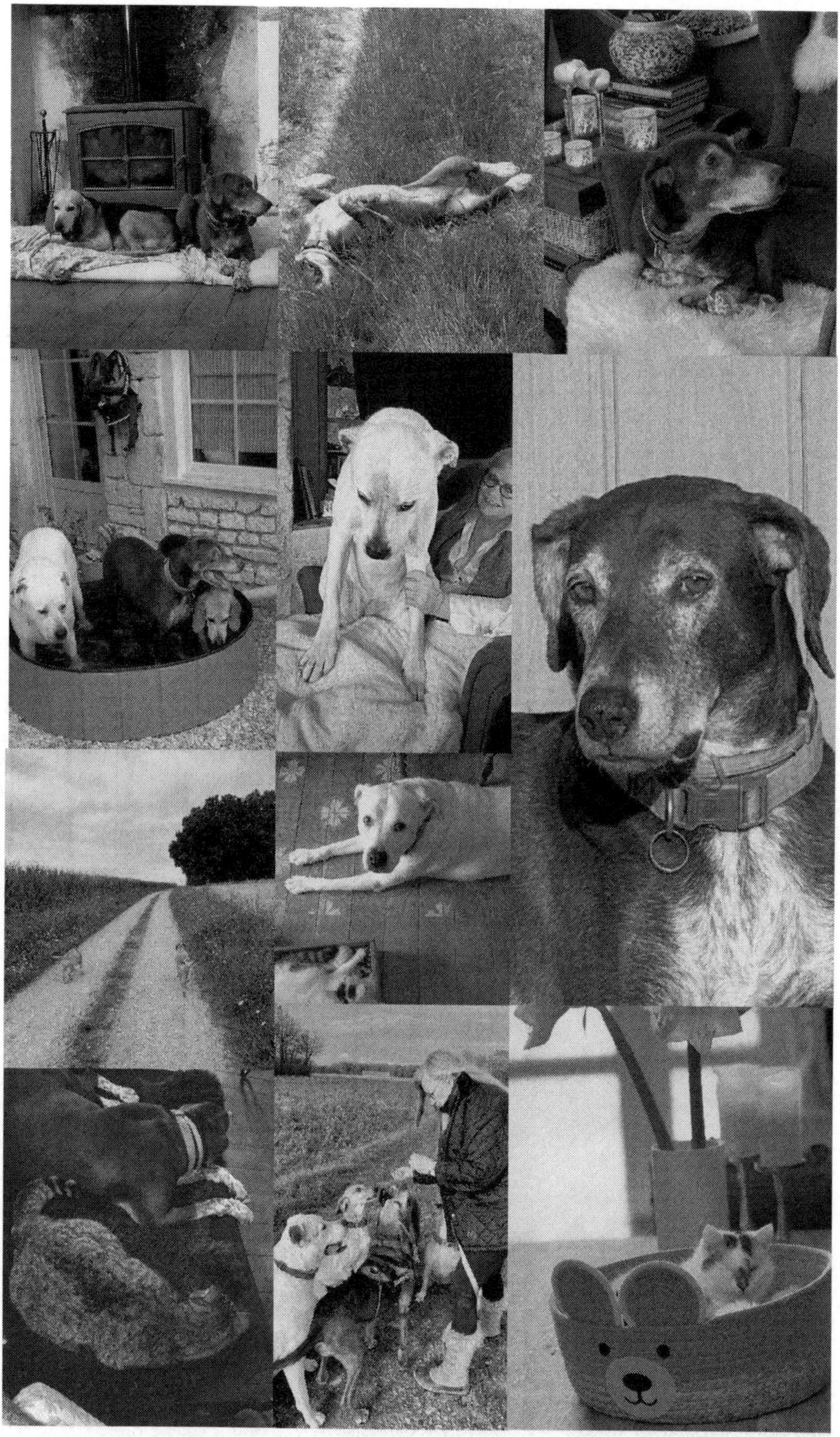

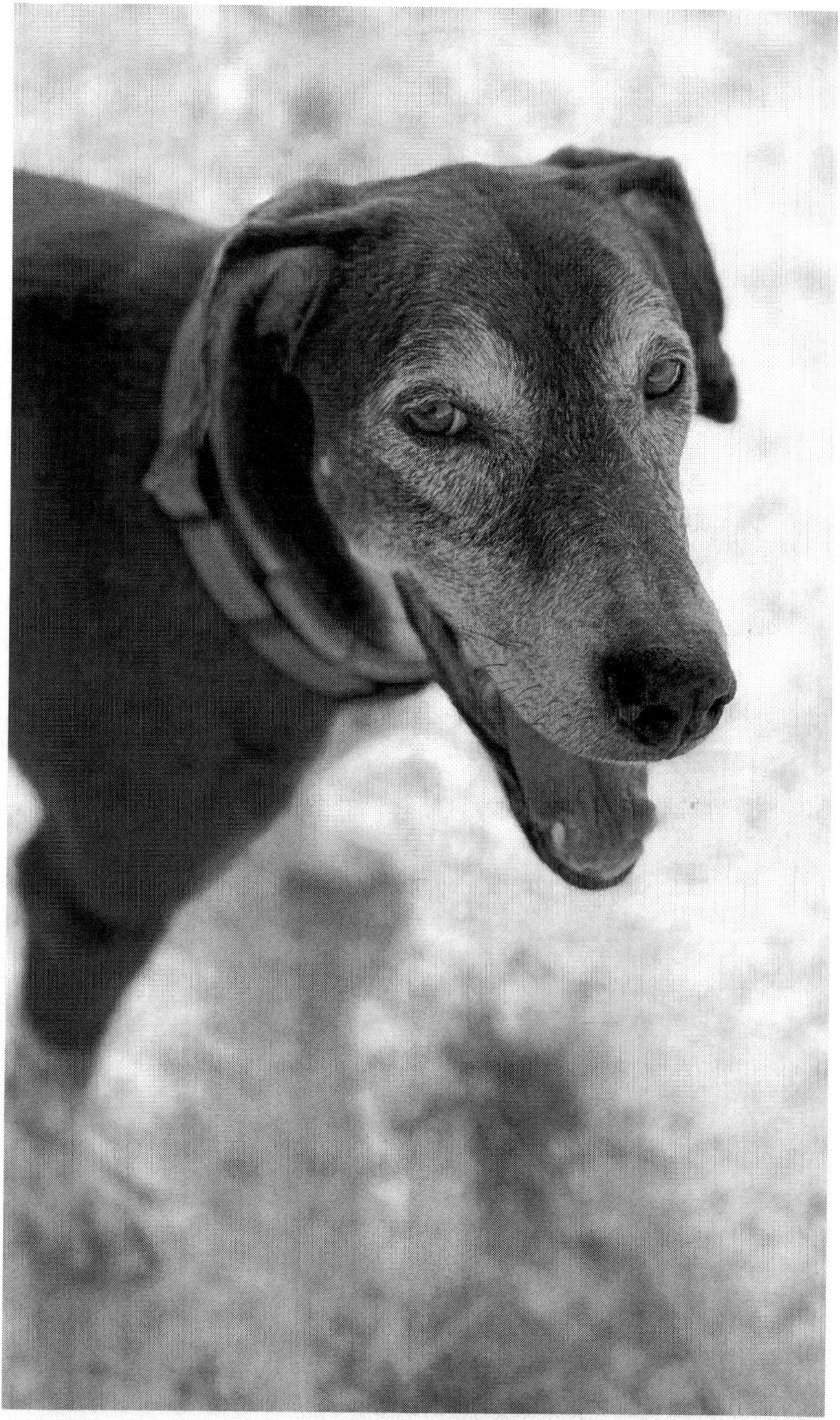

Printed in Great Britain
by Amazon